BOTH SIDES NOW

BOTH
SIDES
NOW

One Man's Journey Through Womanhood

DHILLON KHOSLA

JEREMY P. TARCHER/PENGUIN

a member of Penguin Group (USA) Inc.

JEREMY P. TARCHER/PENGUIN
Published by the Penguin Group
Penguin Group (USA) Inc., 375 Hudson Street, New York, New York 10014, USA • Penguin
Group (Canada), 90 Eglinton Avenue East, Suite 700, Toronto, Ontario M4P 2Y3, Canada
(a division of Pearson Penguin Canada Inc.) • Penguin Books Ltd, 80 Strand, London WC2R 0RL,
England • Penguin Ireland, 25 St Stephen's Green, Dublin 2, Ireland (a division of Penguin
Books Ltd) • Penguin Group (Australia), 250 Camberwell Road, Camberwell, Victoria 3124,
Australia (a division of Pearson Australia Group Pty Ltd) • Penguin Books India Pvt Ltd,
11 Community Centre, Panchsheel Park, New Delhi–110 017, India • Penguin Group (NZ),
Cnr Airborne and Rosedale Roads, Albany, Auckland 1310, New Zealand (a division of
Pearson New Zealand Ltd) • Penguin Books (South Africa) (Pty) Ltd, 24 Sturdee Avenue,
Rosebank, Johannesburg 2196, South Africa

Penguin Books Ltd, Registered Offices: 80 Strand, London WC2R 0RL, England

Most Tarcher/Penguin books are available at special quantity discounts for bulk purchase for sales
promotions, premiums, fund-raising, and educational needs. Special books or book excerpts also can be
created to fit specific needs. For details, write Penguin Group (USA) Inc. Special Markets, 375 Hudson
Street, New York, NY 10014.

Insert photographs 1–12 are from the author's private collection.
Photographs 13–15 are by Heather Henderson; photograph 16 is by Stephanie White;
photograph 17 © Lea Garfield.

Library of Congress Cataloging-in-Publication Data

Khosla, Dhillon.
Both sides now: one man's journey through womanhood/Dhillon Khosla.
p. cm.
ISBN 1-58542-472-2
1. Khosla, Dhillon.   2. Female-to-male transsexuals—United States—Biography.   I. Title.
HQ77.8.K46A3   2006   2005056852
306.76'092—dc22

[B]

Printed in the United States of America
1   3   5   7   9   10   8   6   4   2

BOOK DESIGN BY MEIGHAN CAVANAUGH

Names and identifying characteristics have been changed to protect the privacy of the individuals involved.

While the author has made every effort to provide accurate telephone numbers and Internet addresses at
the time of publication, neither the publisher nor the author assumes any responsibility for errors, or for
changes that occur after publication. Further, the publisher does not have any control over and does not
assume any responsibility for author or third-party websites or their content.

This book is dedicated to the life and memory of David Reimer, who, following a circumcision accident, was raised as a girl based on the theory that we are all born with "gender-neutral" minds that can be shaped in either direction. David's tragic story, documented in the bestseller *As Nature Made Him*, serves as testimony to the fact that each side of the nature/nurture debate is equally capable of oppression:

"When I switched back, I had two problems on my hands, not just one, because of them trying to brainwash me into accepting myself as a girl."

DAVID REIMER, 1965–2004
(excerpt from *As Nature Made Him*,
by John Colapinto; Perennial/HarperCollins)

ACKNOWLEDGMENTS

Shortly after this book deal was finalized, I found myself driving around town and writing the acknowledgment section in my mind. And as I did so, picturing each person who had walked a mile of this journey with me, I realized that my story and any success I have from now on, will never be just mine alone.

And so now I finally have the chance to tell you this, in writing:

To my colleagues at the Ninth Circuit Court of Appeals—in docketing, records, procurement, and the staff attorney's office—your kind words and warm gestures during my exposing walk through no-man's-land helped carry me through to the other side. To the judges—thank you for focusing more on the content of my mind than the body in which it is housed (perhaps simply due to the enormous caseload before you). To Cathy Catterson, clerk of the court—for consistently setting a tone of grace, compassion, and respect. And, finally, to Molly Dwyer—thank you so much for allowing me the freedom to be exactly who I am. Beneath that dry and irreverent wit lies a heart as deep and wide as the ocean (don't worry—I won't tell anyone).

My biological family: my father, for raising me with the understanding that there is "no religion higher than truth"; my mother, for treating my dreams like realistic goals; and my brother, Kanut, for teaching me that simple kindness is often more valuable than the prolific writings of a tortured soul.

To my family of friends: Susan Townsend, for so beautifully embodying the state of unconditional love; Heather Riley, for inviting me into your own family; Karen Burton, for having the courage to always speak the truth; Michelle Schmitt, for providing food, drink, and smokes during the necessary indulgence breaks; and Jeanne Classetti, for being one of the rare spiritual "alphas" out there.

To James Green and the many others who generously shared information and/or took great medical risks to blaze the trail for others to follow.

To my spiritual teachers (or three "wise women"): Nancy Powell, for guiding me back to my heart; Sandra Maitri, for illuminating the obstacles along the way; and Voge Smith, for helping to release them.

To those who helped bring this book to fruition: Elizabeth Burnett, for invaluable feedback during the (very) early stages; Lisa Wysocky, for so expertly paring the manuscript down in record time; Anthony Flacco, for providing generous support and friendship; my agent, Sharlene Martin, for fighting for this story with the kind of belief and determination usually only seen between parent and child; and my brilliant and beautiful editor, Terri Hennessy, for making it so easy to place my entire life in her hands.

To the surgeons, doctors, and medical staff, who not only honored their oaths as doctors but as human beings: Dr. Michael Brownstein, for sculpting the chest I dreamed I would grow into as a child; Dr. Edward Blumenstock and Dr. Karen Kashkin—and their amazing receptionists Beth and Jennifer—for coming to the assistance of a stranger without hesitation; Dr. Donald Laub Sr., for treating me like a son; Dr. Marilyn Ancel, for caring for me through so many complications; Dr. Mark St. Lezin— we fought like brothers, and when I needed you most, you came through like one; Nurse Mary Huyver, my biblical angel, who kept me suspended above the darkness; and Dr. Yvon Ménard, for having the strength to begin these surgeries during a time of much criticism.

To the great Dr. Pierre Brassard: no other surgeon in the world is able to match your results, and yet you remain one of the most humble and sensitive souls I have ever met. I owe you my life—literally.

And finally to the women in my life who saw the boy in me before he was apparent to the rest of the world. You've taught me that the truth is not always apparent to the naked eye. Sometimes we have to close our eyes to see it.

dhillon k.
March 2006

CONTENTS

Everyone carries a shadow, and the less it is embodied in the individual's conscious life, the blacker and denser it is. One does not become enlightened by imagining figures of light, but by making the darkness conscious. The latter procedure, however, is disagreeable and therefore not popular.

C. G. JUNG

Part One

EXCAVATING

THE BOY

One

JULY 1997

I am trying to open a door; the handle turns, but the door won't budge. It's as if there is someone on the other side holding it shut. I keep pushing and pushing—using all of my strength and weight. During the struggle, I overcome the resistance on the other side long enough to get the door open a few inches. When I peer through the opening to see what is on the other side, my own face is staring back at me.

had that dream when I was nineteen years old and I remember laughing when I woke up, wondering how dense God must have thought I was to send a dream with such a transparent metaphor.

Years later, I brought up this dream during a conversation with a friend. I was trying to explain to him why I felt compelled to keep trying new forms of therapy and meditation. I said that I believe we all have a door, beyond which lies some unknown part of our being that has been lost or forgotten somewhere along the way. It is this vague itch or underlying anxiety that comes when we stop distracting ourselves long enough to feel it. My friend let out this visible shudder and quickly said, "Yeah, no—I don't want to get near my door."

But it wasn't just some lofty principle or bravery that motivated my searching; it was a simple desire to have the pleasure of peace. I wanted to grow old and sit quietly in the garden, feeling the sunshine around me without unknown demons hovering in the air, threatening to swoop down at any moment.

It took a few more years, but at age twenty-eight, the door was finally thrown wide open.

IT WAS THE MIDDLE OF JULY 1997. I WAS DRIVING TO LOS Angeles from my home in the San Francisco Bay Area to participate in a one-week program sponsored by a music school. I was twenty-eight years old, and one of many women who had recently graduated from law school and passed the bar exam. By day I worked as a staff attorney for federal judges, analyzing criminal appeals and researching law behind the scenes. But in order to restore some balance into my legal life, I had begun working on music in my spare time. So, by night I took voice lessons, studied songwriting, performed at open-mike nights, and composed songs on my guitar and keyboard. And in between my music and the law, I dated women—some of them within the lesbian community, and some of them not.

I had been working on putting together a demo in a local studio for about a year, and as much as I was looking forward to finally having a full week to work on music without the interruption of law, my mind was occupied with something entirely different.

A few months earlier, an ex-girlfriend brought over a copy of an article that had appeared in The New Yorker *in 1994. She had been given the article in a psychology class, after a female-to-male transsexual had appeared as a guest lecturer. In the article, the author interviewed several men who had gone through surgeries and hormone treatments to transition from female to male. And as I read the things these men had said, I immediately saw why my ex had asked me to read the piece. Flashes of recognition went off in my mind, arranging themselves like the pieces of a puzzle.*

I read as one man described his fierce resistance to being treated as a girl and I thought of my own childhood when I had insisted that I was a boy, adamantly refusing dolls and dresses and hanging out only with other boys during recess.

I read as another man—who had made the transition from female—said that he never fit in the lesbian community because he was too male in some way—not "butch"—just male, and I remembered how lost I always felt at lesbian gatherings because there was no one with whom I felt that "sameness." I then thought about the girlfriends in my life who had always identified themselves as straight and wondered why I was the one exception—the only "woman" to whom they were attracted.

And then, in the final interview, I read as a man talked about all the wasted time he had spent in places where he didn't fit. He ended by saying he didn't know why this condition chose him, but he was finally the person he had always dreamed he would be.

The word "dream" hit me the hardest of all. I had spent so much of my childhood dreaming of developing a firm, male chest. I remember running around shirtless at my birthday parties and fantasizing that I was a pop/rock star like Billy Joel or Rod Stewart—always men. And in the past few years, when those fantasies and dreams had resurfaced, I couldn't think of anything to do except pray that God would make me a man in my next life.

Between the interviews, my ex-girlfriend had highlighted statements from doctors where they opined as to the cause of transsexualism. One doctor pointed out that in experiments with animals—from rats to apes—they injected testosterone during a critical time of brain development in a female fetus. In every case, while the animal still came out with a female body, it behaved exactly the same as would have any male animal of its species. In other words, contrary to its physical body, it believed it was entirely male.

But it wasn't until I gave the article to my current girlfriend, Selena, that I really felt its full impact. I remember her putting it down after she had finished reading it and saying, "Baby, this is you."

To hear it out loud, to have someone finally hold up a mirror that reflected back the truth of who I am, touched some deep place within me. I remember feeling this tremendous sense of release—like "Now you see; you finally see."

The relief, however, was short-lived. Next came the tough question: Now that I knew the truth, what was I going to do about it?

As I traveled the long road to Los Angeles, the rhythmic sound of my tires thumping against the pavement lulled me into a semimeditative state.

I let my mind relax, and I began to see an image of myself in a faraway cabin, shirtless and getting out of bed to face the mirror. I imagined touching my face and feeling the emerging stubble and widening of my jaw. As I held these pictures in my mind, something interesting happened. I noticed that the colors of the landscape outside looked richer, and I felt a solidity enter my body. It was as if I had taken on a more substantial texture and, in turn, I was more connected to my surroundings. I let myself bask in this feeling for a few moments and keep it as my company, but then tucked it away as a treat for later. I thought, I am just finishing this album and I still have a few more years at this particular job, but maybe when I am done with all of this, I will think about doing it for real. I said this to myself even though I was scheduled to have a full mastectomy in November.

Three years earlier, at age twenty-five, I had undergone a breast reduction. I was quite top-heavy, almost a double "D," so wanting the reduction was not that remarkable. I, however, kept asking them to make me closer to an "A" cup than a "B" cup, which, to my surgeons, was somewhat unusual. Not really knowing the depth of my own issues behind the decision, I simply convinced myself—and them— that it would fit well with my narrow hips. The night before the operation, I had a nightmare that I woke up with a "B" cup, and I was very distraught.

After the surgery, when I unraveled the bandages and looked in the mirror, I began sobbing. I was, indeed, a "B" cup. And while I was significantly smaller than before, the reflection I saw in the mirror still didn't conform to what I had imagined in my head. I immediately wanted to go back into surgery and take more off, but as quickly as that thought arose, I pushed it back down. It would be absurd to undergo another surgery just to take off a little more tissue.

But I never let my next thought really enter my mind: I wanted the breasts completely off, so my chest would look like the male torso I had dreamed about as a child. I had no context for such a thought, just as I did not yet know that there were people who altered themselves surgically from female to male. So I pushed away my discomfort and tried to appreciate the fact that I was at least able to finally wear those double-breasted Italian men's suits I had fantasized about without their taking on an overly feminine shape.

As time wore on, though, the discomfort kept resurfacing. When men hugged me, I felt anger at the contrast of my soft breasts against their firm chest. I felt trapped in my body and I resented the men's freedom. When I was home alone, I wanted to walk around without my shirt on, or wear my shirts unbuttoned in that casual, masculine way, but the movement of my body and the image in the mirror told me that I couldn't do either.

When I read that New Yorker *article and saw there was both a reason and a cure for what I had been feeling, my desire for a male chest immediately broke through the surface. In an instant, the two years that had passed since I had unraveled those bandages and sobbed in disappointment, disappeared.*

Two weeks later, I called one of the clinics mentioned in the article and it gave me a referral to a chest surgeon in my area. The surgeon gave me a referral to a therapist for an evaluation and, assuming that went smoothly, we could do surgery in November. I had my first appointment to see the therapist when I returned to San Francisco after my music program week in L.A.

Halfway toward Los Angeles I found myself hungry and began to scan the horizon for any signs of life. After passing several remote areas, I spotted what looked like a diner off the next exit, and I eased my way over.

I parked the car in front of the restaurant and headed toward the entrance. As I walked inside, I caught a brief glimpse of my reflection in the glass door. I shrugged off the image and heard the muted thud of the door close behind me.

The diner was mostly empty and I made my way to a back booth patterned with sunlight. When I sat down, I felt out of sorts. It wasn't that I was in unfamiliar surroundings. There was so much stirring inside me from the past two months that I felt as if I were suspended between two worlds, or more accurately, between two identities. One part of me was acting as if nothing had changed or was going to change, and the other part was already living in the fantasy of possibility.

As the sun splayed across my table and a waitress came over asking, "What can I get for you, honey?" I couldn't help but imagine myself sitting here as a man, a complete man. I pictured myself with baseball cap, T-shirt over my pecs, and five o'clock shadow. And once again, I felt this substance inside me. It was as if that image gave me a concrete identity or an anchored way of being in the world. I immediately imagined spending days on the road, driving through towns, and casually conversing with people from every walk of life.

Shortly after I read the article, I found there was a monthly meeting for female-to-male transsexuals (FTMs) in San Francisco. My girlfriend, Selena, wanted to come with me to my first meeting, but I insisted on going alone.

I arrived early. There were two men in the room talking, and as I sat down I wondered if there had been an earlier meeting that was just finishing up. One of the men was in his forties, with a beard and a receding hairline. The other guy was much younger. He was tan and good-looking, with brown hair and blue eyes. And there was something strangely familiar about him; the way he moved and spoke had a casual masculinity I could relate to.

Other people began to arrive, and several looked like the run-of-the-mill butch women I had seen in lesbian bars. I looked back to the two men and wondered if they were in fact FTMs and had already gone through the transition, but it was hard for me to imagine. There was not a trace of female in their faces or their bod-ies. Their chests were flat and their hips were square. The room continued to fill as I noticed people arriving who looked more like I had pictured FTMs would look—some had facial hair but female-shaped faces beneath it; others had androgynous faces but pear-shaped bodies. The moderator began the meeting and asked the assembled to introduce themselves.

As we went around the room, people said their names, and how they identified themselves or how far they had gone in their surgical process. One man a few seats over said he just had "top surgery" and shimmied his chest. He also mentioned he'd been on hormones for more than a year. Both his vocal pitch and his mannerisms were extremely effeminate, and he made some allusion to his sexual interest in men. When they reached the guy across from me—the man who had struck me as familiar—he spoke in an extremely deep voice and said his name was Jack. He added that he had been on hormones for just six months. I was amazed. He was the kind of guy who would fit in with the most masculine men without question. And by comparing him to the other man who had just spoken, it struck me that we each might have had a template that is brought out by hormones in the same way that genetic males do when they go through puberty. Some end up with deep voices and male gestures while others wind up with high-pitched voices and effeminate gestures.

Several people began asking questions, and I noticed myself judging some of the butch women. It was the same judgments I had made many times before, but here— in this context—I had a new understanding of those judgments.

When I looked at Jack, I saw a relaxed, casual, inherent masculinity. But when I looked at the butch women, I noticed a hard, pushed behavior. It seemed as if these women were doing a bad imitation of the stereotypical macho man—as though they were trying to use their attitude and behavior to compensate for something that was missing.

The people I most related to had always been guys who had a big heart, a fierce protective strength, and a deeply romantic side: the East Coast Italian Guido who would fight for his loved ones, then just as easily cry at the sight of his newborn child; the musician who poured his heart into a song and expressed his feelings without shame.

And yet it seemed that so many butch-type lesbians I knew were the antithesis of this. They often personnified the worst kind of men without balancing it out with the best of men: many liked to engage in macho, sexist talk about women, but when it came down to pursuing one they liked, they were too passive or afraid of rejection. Then there were the ones who scoffed at vulnerable emotions and made fun of tender or romantic gestures, while they were the first to fall totally apart when their own relationships ended.

On a visual level, I couldn't relate to the large number of butch women who made no effort to work out, and who ended up overweight and poorly dressed in cheap blazers and mismatched shirts. To me they were no different from the fat, balding guys in cheap suits.

But of course, I couldn't tell anyone these judgments as they would simply label me as suffering from "internalized homophobia"—basically a fancy way of saying that in judging these lesbians, I was showing a hatred toward myself. And how could I argue with that? I was, after all, one of them—wasn't I?

I arrived in Pomona, a small town outside Los Angeles, just as it was getting dark. I had reserved a week in a motel that had apartment-style rooms with kitchenettes. I put down my bags and guitar in the little living room and found the kitchen completely bare—not even a coffee cup in sight. So I got back in my car and drove to one of those all-night stores that have household supplies and some basic canned goods. I filled my cart and headed for the checkout. There was a woman in front of me whose baby was sitting in the shopping cart facing me.

The baby had been staring at me for several minutes when the woman said in a surprised voice, "He usually only stares that intensely at men."

I felt a thick lump forming in my throat. I wanted to say, "Yes, that's why he's staring at me." But, of course, the words were left unsaid.

The sadness from the grocery store stayed with me the rest of the night, even after I had finished cooking pasta and sauce and planted myself in front of a television that had many more channels than my own.

At the end of my first FTM meeting, I asked Jack if we could hook up sometime so I could ask him some questions. One night, he came over for pizza and told me his own journey began when a woman at his firehouse gave him the same New Yorker article that I had been given. The next morning he woke up and immediately wanted the mastectomy—he, too, had previously gone through a breast reduction that had left him unsatisfied—and as his chest surgery approached, he began taking male hormones.

At one point, he asked me if I wanted him to refer to me as "he" as he was aware that people were at different stages of transformation. And an interesting thing happened. I started to say yes but stopped. Looking at his face, an undeniably male face, I found myself wavering. So far, I had been undecided about male hormones. And so, to justify my position, I said to Jack, "When I look in the mirror, I can sometimes see a pretty boy."

He responded with, "When I look in the mirror, I see a man." His tone was neither malicious nor confrontational, just matter-of-fact. But his response hit home: it made me realize that he didn't have to do any manipulations in his mind when he saw his reflection, while I was trying to convince myself into seeing what I felt inside. I'm not sure I can explain it, but I know that the part of me that thought I could simply carry my true identity inside in my own mind fell apart while looking at his face. Because what I had been trying to create with words and explanations, he got without ever having to open his mouth.

The next day, I drove to the campus and picked up my class schedule. It included various music theory classes as well as the gospel class that was scheduled to perform several songs at the end of the week. As I was walking to my first class, I noticed that almost all the students were teenagers; it seemed that many were hoping to use this summer program to help them gain entrance to the Berklee College of Music after high school. Although I had registered under my own name, *Asha* (an East Indian name meaning "hope" from my father's side of the family), I decided to try out a new name, *Dhillon.* I had always liked the sound of the name *Dylan* and so I simply took the spelling of *Dhillon* to keep an Indian flavor (*Dhillon* is a common last name in India). I was also hoping that this name would somehow allow me to be more of the boy I wanted to be. I mistakenly thought if I heard people address me with this male name, it would be enough. In the end, of course, it wasn't.

I had my audition, and know I played a part of a song I had written, but all I remember was their referring to me as "Miss." For some reason, the use of that term hit me right in the gut, as clearly as if someone had punched me. I walked out, stinging from the pain, and unable to understand why these female references had suddenly become so unbearable. I had heard them all of my life, yet it now seemed as if finding this truth about myself had pulled off a protective layer. I kept telling myself it was the foreign environment—if I were home, surrounded by people who knew me, I would be okay.

I missed Selena and wanted to call her, but talked myself out of it. From the moment we started to get involved, I had known she was not someone with whom I was entirely compatible, yet her complete understanding of my gender issue was making me turn to her more and more. In a world where no one, including the mirror, could fully see my truth, she was my salvation. She accepted me as any other boyfriend she had been with and soothed me when I was in pain.

The day continued with a barrage of female references. Even when the students chatted warmly with me and used my new name, I could tell they simply saw me as a cute, hip, dyke-female musician, but not as a man. Never a man.

I went back to my hotel exhausted and depressed. I sat down, afraid to leave for fear of having to confront another ma'am or miss. The more I sat there, the more hopeless it all seemed. I thought I would forever be on the outside, begging others to call me "he," and angry with them when they forgot. My gender was becoming more and more consuming.

As I had done often throughout my life, I turned to music to comfort me. I began to strum some chords on my guitar and found the following words making their way through:

> Didn't I see you, not believing this is real,
> Didn't I hear you saying, this is just part of the deal.
> But if I break this shell, would you change your mind?
> If I drop my voice, would you finally understand?
> Would you see the man?

My eyes were spilling over with tears and my voice was choked as I put down the guitar. I felt completely drained, so I undressed, slid under the covers in my boxers and a T-shirt, and went to sleep.

The next day was even worse. Every "she" or "miss" left me battered and bruised. It was as if someone had climbed inside and cranked up the volume on the pain switch to the highest possible setting. I went back to the hotel and shut the door behind me. Fighting off tears, I called my voice mail at home. I thought, "Maybe I just need to hear a familiar voice. Maybe I just needed some contact."

On my machine there was a message from an old roommate. She ended the message by calling me "Missy." And that was it, the final straw.

I broke down in the middle of my living room, doubled over in pain as gut-wrenching sobs came from deep inside my belly. All I could manage to choke out was, "Please, God, please help me," over and over. I felt like a helpless, wounded animal. Everyone seemed out to hurt me.

I lay there for what felt like hours, until the room was pitch-black. Finally, I got up to turn on the light, then sat back down on the floor, taking the phone with me. I called information and found the number for the FTM (female-to-male) info support office. A man answered, and I asked if I could ask him some questions about taking male hormones. I don't remember everything I asked, but it was a lot. I must have spoken to him for well over an hour. Every question I had came fast and furiously.

I asked about possible health risks from testosterone and found there weren't any long-term effects, except some anecdotal evidence which suggested that keeping the ovaries for a long time after starting hormones was not a good idea. There was some belief it might lead to ovarian cysts or perhaps even cancer. Also, I found out about different kinds of testosterone and which was less likely to cause acne. I asked about "lower surgery," and the guy on the phone revealed that he hadn't had any mainly because of the cost, but he had designed his own prosthetic device to keep in his pants. He told me he was a gay man, and said he had to have a long talk with someone before they got involved, but it seemed the potential reaction of others was not a great source of concern for him. He seemed completely content. He added that he used to be angry and violent, and that he had suffered from stress-related health problems like colitis, but all of that went away when he went through the transition.

When I ran out of questions, he gave me his home number and said I could call him any time. After I hung up, I let out a huge breath. I had been talking so quickly and asking so much that I felt as if I'd forgotten to breathe. I sat there for a few minutes, still in the dark, and started to feel a slow, growing excitement.

Now I was brimming with news. I picked up the phone again and this time called Selena. When she answered, I launched into all of the things the man had told me, and how I could find a good hormone doctor and change my gender.

When I finished talking, she was quiet for a minute and then said, "Baby, it sounds like you have made up your mind."

I let out a deep breath and said, "Yes, I think I have." I felt this calm, palpable stillness after that, and I remember feeling incredibly close to her as I hung up the phone.

———

I WOKE UP THE NEXT MORNING WITH AN OVERWHELMING sense of joy and excitement. As I drove toward the music-school campus, that sweet intimacy with my surroundings that I had felt while driving to L.A. returned, but this time by a hundredfold. Everywhere I looked, it actually seemed as if it had rained—and yet it hadn't. The color of the grass seemed greener and richer than the previous day, the air sweeter and lighter. There was a clarity and crispness to the picture of the world, as if a haze had lifted.

When I arrived, I felt as if I were really there for the first time. In vocal class, I watched two seventeen-year-old boys sing, and tears came to my eyes. For the first time, I didn't feel envy about their budding masculinity. Instead, I felt a connection, because soon I would join them.

And so went the day. I was playful and open and social with everyone. Even the "she" references rolled off me, because I could take comfort in the knowledge that there was a remedy—that this would someday be over. The previous day I had seen everyone as cruel. Today I saw them as kind, well-meaning people who just couldn't see what was not visible. It wasn't their fault—and it wasn't mine. But I was the one who could do something about it.

When I got back to my hotel, I turned on the TV and looked at all of the men, wondering which one I would look like. There were certain men who always gave me a sense of déjà vu, and I now wondered if some part of me knew that I would have similar features. All I know is that it felt very freeing to be able to look at commercials for men's underwear or razors without envy, or the despair that I would never have them in this lifetime. I felt a restlessness and anticipation surging through my body. I wanted to have that five o'clock shadow now!

I put on my running shoes and headed out for jog. I found a baseball field by a nearby school and ran to the middle of it. It was very dark, but there was a dense blanket of stars. And although I was miles away from home and standing in the middle of a pitch-black field, I felt anchored as I looked up at the stars.

I started laughing as I thought about how I had spent the last few years in a meditation school, believing that if I just meditated enough and got more in touch with my spirit, my body would become irrelevant and I wouldn't need to change anything. Now, standing on this side of the decision, that notion seemed utterly absurd. I realized I had been fighting for the wrong side; I had been using all my strength to go against my true being rather than to serve it. And I saw all of this because the freedom I felt now held wisdom, and a certainty I had never known before.

Two

AUGUST 1997

I dream I am sitting in an ancient stone amphitheater. The theater faces the ocean and there are people moving silently around me, carrying glass jars. Every once in a while, one of them offers up their jar to me. I can't quite make out what is inside until one of them holds his up high, toward the light. When I look in, it turns into a visual demonstration—almost as if I am looking into a crystal ball. I see the blue in the ocean creeping onto shore, slowly overtaking the land. . . .

After returning from Los Angeles, it seemed every night was a descent into a dream world, where the landscape was littered with symbolism. And while the meaning of each dream often escaped my understanding, I was left with a sense that somewhere deep below the surface someone—or something—was busy at work.

I FOLLOWED UP ON THE REFERRALS I RECEIVED FROM THE FTM office and set up an October appointment with an endocrinologist for a prehormone physical. I figured I could start taking testosterone after the chest surgery, as long as the therapist who was evaluating me for the surgery would also clear me for the hormones.

Apparently there was a set of ethical guidelines for the treatment of transsexuals that set out how many therapist letters you need before surgery or hormone treatment. Some surgeons followed the guidelines strictly; others made some adjustments. Since none of this was covered by my medical insurance (almost all health plans explicitly exclude anything related to "transsexualism"), it meant paying hundreds of dollars extra just to get a stamp of approval.

I found myself resenting the psychological requirements. Part of it was distrust; after years of therapy and meditation, not one single person had noticed this truth, and now that I had finally found it, I was supposed to go to them again? The other part was fear: after having had this part of myself taken away from me once before, I was afraid it would happen again—that some "well-intentioned" professional who couldn't possibly understand what was going on inside my body would stop me. And I didn't think I could survive it a second time.

It happened sometime during second-grade gym class. I was hanging out on one side of the gym with the boys when the teacher came over. She took me by the arm and led me to the other side of the gym. I didn't understand what was happening. When I turned back to look at my friends, they were pointing at me and laughing, saying, "Look, they're putting him *with the girls."*

After class, I went running home to my mother. I was crying hysterically as I told her what had happened, my sentences broken apart by my sobs.

It was a typically chilly San Francisco morning when I arrived for my therapy session at a Victorian-style building at the ungodly hour of 7:00 A.M. I opened the door and followed a carpeted hallway back to a small waiting area. Within minutes, a gray-haired, maternal-appearing, woman entered the room and asked if I wanted to have some coffee before we started. I remember thinking at one hundred dollars a session I should definitely have a cup. We then headed to her office, which looked like a cozy living room where you might have tea in the afternoon. I sat, and with barely a prompt, began to tell my story. I started by relating some very early childhood memories and then described how things changed when I came to America.

Shortly after I turned eight, we moved from Europe to the United States. And with that move came the loss of whatever male recognition I had experienced from my peers in Europe.

I was lost and disoriented in this new culture where no one saw me as a boy. I was shocked to discover that I, as a "girl," wasn't supposed to play kickball with the boys—a rule I promptly broke. This action would later be interpreted as a feminist move but it would be a false credit, because I didn't want to do these activities as a girl. I was just being myself—a boy among boys.

One day I was talking to a girl who was swooning over Sean Cassidy. I couldn't relate to her behavior. Just to tease her, I said, "Hey, what would you do if Sean Cassidy wrote you a letter?" She sighed dramatically and said, "I'd die." I quickly retorted, "But then you couldn't read it," to which she responded, "Well, I'd faint then."

Yet I did have fantasies and crushes of my own, which were no less dramatic or romantic. But in my fantasies I was the man and I was the one in pursuit. I had a serious crush on one of my teachers who used to wear loads of perfume and blouses with plunging necklines that revealed breasts that were barely covered by lacy bras. I remember feeling this hot flush whenever I saw her cleavage, and I remember having fantasies about her in which I was a handsome adult man in a white suit, and I was on bended knee, singing Billy Joel's "Just the Way You Are."

Somewhere along the line, however, I learned to keep my fantasies quiet. Whatever seed had been sown in Europe, where the adults treated me differently from my childhood peers, bloomed fully in America where my peers had joined forces with the grown-ups. Every natural impulse I had seemed contrary to how the world at large expected me to feel and act.

So while I naturally ran to play kickball with the boys, tearing off my shirt, and sliding around in the mud, the girls invited me to slumber parties where we read Judy Blume books and talked about boys and periods. When I approached one boy who was struggling in class and told him I would do his homework for a dollar a page, he agreed. I looked at it as a guy-to-guy deal. But later in the year, when we handed out valentines in class, he gave me one.

But it wasn't the fact that I got valentines from boys that upset me so much; it was the significance of the act. In other words, I wasn't offended by having an affectionate gesture sent my way by a boy; I was upset because it meant I was no longer seen as one of them. While we were making the valentines, I had been put with the girls, while the boys sat across the room in their own section.

But unlike the boys in Europe, who had been on my side when the adults tried to separate us, these boys did nothing. And the girls continued to embrace me as one of their own.

With no one left to see me for who I was, I myself began to forget. I don't know the precise moment when this happened. I only know that sometime after I arrived in America, I stopped living from the inside looking out and started living from the outside looking in.

Throughout my monologue, my therapist had been furiously taking notes and periodically exclaimed, "You're a poet."

All of this spurred me into further self-disclosure as I eagerly spilled out more of myself. I felt like a little kid who had been left alone in a dark cave, and all of a sudden flashlights and voices were coming my way as I yelled excitedly, "Here I am—over here, see?"

When I talked about my discovery of the *New Yorker* article and recent trip to Los Angeles, saying how I felt solid and anchored when I thought about becoming a man, the therapist interjected, "you found your sense of identity."

I remember letting out this sigh of relief and saying, "I wonder if I hadn't dug in so hard and gone through so many forms of therapy and meditation, whether I would have kept this buried until I was much older."

"It's hard to say," she replied, "but probably any situation where you could be vulnerable—such as a really supportive relationship—would have helped to allow it all to resurface."

WHEN I ARRIVED AT WORK AFTER MY THERAPY SESSION, Selena was already in her office, so I stopped by to fill her in. I told her that the therapist was going to gather some more information, but saw no reason why I wouldn't be able to go ahead with my plans for the chest surgery and hormones. Selena saw the excitement in my face and began to get excited, too.

"You know, I feel like there's this man you've told me about," she said. "And while I've gotten glimpses here and there, I'll now finally get to meet him."

About a year and half after I began working at the courthouse, Selena transferred to my division and moved into the office next door. After meetings, she would sometimes stop by and talk about a case she was working on. Whenever she asked questions, I could sense her Latin American background coming through. Although her English was flawless, her words came out in a rapid staccato rhythm that reminded me of the times I had traveled to Spanish-speaking countries or watched Spanish soaps. Some people found her style intimidating or combative, so she made a concerted effort to tone herself down. I, however, enjoyed her manner because I also had a very direct, sometimes combative, way of asking questions.

Eventually our discussions veered toward our personal lives and I would tell her about the women I was seeing as she told me about the guys she dated. She had one lesbian friend, but had never had any attraction toward her—or toward any women for that matter. One day she made a comment about not understanding how lesbians could give up intercourse. I responded by saying that the majority of women I dated were very much into intercourse, and that it was just a matter of using the right techniques. Selena became curious and asked more questions.

Within days, Selena said that she had dreamt about the two of us. She was not the first straight woman to develop an interest in me. And while it always felt like an initial victory—to be momentarily swept onto the competitive playing field with other guys—it usually ended up in betrayal. While I was thinking she sees the boy in me, the woman was going through a process of questioning her own sexuality and thinking this was some sort of a novel "lesbian" experience. So what started as a gain became a loss, as I not only lost out on the male validation but also had to deal with the additional baggage of the woman's angst over the societal implications of our relationship. It became easier to just stick with the one percent of lesbian/bisexual women who were feminine enough to attract me, and who responded to my male energy, but had already confronted all of the societal tensions.

So while I joked and flirted with Selena, I didn't go out of my way to make a move on her. But when she invited me over a week later—under the guise of working late on a case—I accepted. I remember sitting on the floor by her couch, and she *was wearing a thin, filmy dress that was showing off her best parts. At one point she was sitting very close to me and I thought, That's it and grabbed her and kissed her. In that moment, there didn't seem any reason not to go for it. I kissed her again, and she ran her hand up my leg. I was wearing shorts and I remember thinking she had the softest hands I had ever felt. But as she got close to my crotch, I stopped her. I had been enjoying the fantasy that I was an ordinary guy on a date with a girl, but her hand on my crotch would be the end of that fantasy.*

Selena brought me back from my memories. "When are you going to break the news to people in the office?"

"I don't know."

The question was a tough one for me. While the little kid in me wanted to run and tell the whole world about my discovery, the adult was aware it might put too much stress on me to do it this early—before I had the body and face to back me up.

During this time of waiting, it was my fantasies that helped me to make it through each day. While I was walking through the courthouse halls and hearing female pronouns directed at me, I was inside my head, picturing my future pecs and beard. It was as if I was a soldier stationed far away from home and I had this old, crumpled photo tucked away in my breast pocket to remind me of what was waiting for me. To tell everyone at work would be to invite them into those fantasies—fantasies they might soil with their opinions and judgments.

And yet I had to tell them sometime—sometime before the changes started to come through and they began to wonder what the hell was going on.

After several days of further agonizing, I finally found a middle ground. I decided to break the news to my two immediate supervisors so that they could be in on my plans early enough to prepare a course of action.

We met in one of my supervisors' office, and I remember feeling self-conscious during the meeting as people walked by the glass wall and saw the three of us sitting down, engaged in conversation. I also remember feeling a sense of apprehension as I sat down to talk to these two women.

While the social climate in San Francisco was accepting of gays and lesbians, gender change was a whole different issue. And having been in so many feminist or female-centered circles, I assumed that I would be seen as a "sellout," or someone attempting to access male "privilege" or—worst of all—as someone who hated women. After all, if I couldn't accept my own female body, how could I proclaim to love women at all? So, while I knew they wouldn't say anything intolerant out loud, I was preparing myself for resigned acceptance at best.

I remember saying something to the effect of, "I'm going to be going through a sex change." I wanted to use another phrase because the term sex "change" felt like a lie, at least to the boy who had been there from the start. But it really wasn't the time or place to get into semantics; I just needed to get the point across.

"Well, I wasn't expecting this to be the topic," said my head boss, and we all laughed. She added that she knew people who had gone the other way (male to female) and they were much happier afterward. My immediate supervisor, Sarah, said "Congratulations, that's exciting."

They then started asking about the timing of the changes. I told them I didn't want to make any announcements until visual changes from the testosterone began to show, which I figured would be in January or February at the earliest. Sarah offered me the option of working at home part-time during the transition if it would make things easier for me.

But what I remember most is this warmth that began to slowly expand inside my chest. The more they spoke, the more it grew. And I became aware of the sense that in the two years I had worked there, this was the first time I truly believed that they cared for me. I didn't fully understand it at the time, but what I know now, after having had many more of these experiences, is that until I was able to expose my true self, there was always a sense that the love that came my way was not truly meant for me. It remained stuck on this hardened outer shell, unable to penetrate through to my heart. But here, during these initial days and first few cracks in the shell, I was already feeling the difference.

Three

SEPTEMBER 1997

> I am dreaming I am on an escalator, heading up to the sky. Music is playing below. There are two blimps overhead with messages, but I cannot quite make out what they say. I hear a voice behind me and I am aware that the voice is causing the stairway to continue moving upward. As I go higher and higher, I start to become afraid. Afraid I am going to keep moving forever—that I will go so far into the sky, I will lose all contact with the world below. . . .

Toward the middle of the month, I came home to find a message from my mother, saying that my aunt and uncle were coming to visit from France, and that she had given them my number.

I felt a moment of panic. I was tempted to just tell them I was too busy. I hadn't seen them in more than ten years and couldn't imagine sitting through an extended evening of personal conversation, enduring a barrage of female references without blurting out my news.

But then I thought, What the hell? If I am to start this new life, why not tell the truth and let the chips fall where they may? It was an emerging philosophy and was quickly becoming my litmus test for identifying which connections were true.

I arranged to pick up my aunt and uncle at their hotel and drive them to a restaurant. They had chosen a hotel with a French name and when I walked into the lobby, I laughed as I realized I had once stayed there with a woman from law school. I paced the lobby back and forth, remembering fragments of that evening.

My uncle was the first to arrive. He took one look at my square-cut Italian man's suit and short hair and said, "You look so manly."

His tone was more observational than hostile and the comment made me smile. He embraced me and as I looked over his shoulder, I saw my aunt, looking stylish as usual. She had once owned a clothing boutique in Paris.

She looked at my suit and said, "You look so chic—this is the modern look now, isn't it?"

We headed toward an Italian restaurant and, once seated, made small talk about my uncle's early retirement. Because it had been so long since I had seen either of them, it was now like sitting with casual acquaintances.

About halfway through dinner, I decided to go for it and told them I had something to tell them. We had been speaking partly in English and partly in German. Although I was not as comfortable speaking in German, it had the advantage of preventing eavesdroppers from hearing us. Like so many restaurants in San Francisco, this one was quite full and the tables were close together.

I don't remember exactly what I said, but it was something like, "I am going to go through the medical procedures to become a man."

I remember their asking some questions, and then commenting, "This is irreversible."

Neither made any dramatic statements or exclamations, nor did they seem overtly shocked. I didn't know them well enough to know whether this was simply a matter of polite etiquette on their part, whether it was because I wasn't their child and they weren't really that invested, or whether they were just being open-minded. My uncle asked some questions about whether there were any health risks and I told him what I knew.

My aunt had been quiet for a little while, then spoke up and said, "You know, now that I think about it, there was something never really female about you. You never seemed to really take on womanhood."

When I was fourteen, my best friend and I visited my relatives in Europe for a summer. My aunt and uncle had just purchased a little country home in the south of France, and we went to stay there for a few weeks. Every day my aunt put us to work fixing up the place. We cut the waist-high grass with a scythe, and sanded and painted the attic room. The work was absolutely grueling but satisfying; it reminded me of the childhood summers I had spent on my grand-parents' farm in Germany, helping out in the fields until my muscles were sore and tired.

When we got back from our trip and developed the many rolls of film we had taken, the pictures from my aunt's house were the ones that took up most of my photo album. In those photos I was wearing faded jeans, a jean jacket streaked with paint, and a baseball cap. And in some of them—taken from a reasonable distance, with my face partially obscured—I could have been taken for a man.

After a few more questions about my transition, we moved on to other topics. After dinner, they asked me to join them for a nightcap in a bar across the street from their hotel. As we sat down, my uncle asked me for advice on dealing with a broker he was using in the United States. And while I leaned back in my chair and answered his question, I remember feeling a new sense of ease that had periodically made an appearance since my time in Los Angeles.

I thought about it on the drive home, as I imagined how the dinner might have gone, had I kept my upcoming transition a secret. It wasn't a difficult scenario. All through the evening, I would have carried a rigid dis-trust, self-righteously confirmed every time they made a comment or asked a question that held the implication that they saw me as female. In short, I would have resented them for looking at me through a distorted lens and, in turn, would have seen them through my own.

AFTER I ARRIVED HOME THAT NIGHT, I SAT DOWN TO WRITE a letter to my parents. They were divorced by this time and it had been several years since I had seen either of them in person. My mother had moved back to Europe and was living in Germany, while my father had retired early and now spent half the year with my grandparents in India and the other half in Florida where he shared a home with my brother.

While my parents knew and accepted that I was romantically involved with women, they did not know that I had been struggling with my gender identity. And how could they? I myself had only just recently begun putting the pieces together. And yet I couldn't help but wonder whether they, like me, would reexamine events in my childhood in light of this news.

During those first few years in Europe while my parents were still married, my mother arranged elaborate birthday parties. We had streamers of candy hanging as prizes for the various games, including sack racing, and in the photos of those parties, I am boisterously jumping alongside the sack racing contestants in cutoff shorts and wearing no shirt.

Whenever my mother tried to put me in a dress, I cried and yelled and refused to wear it. When she brought back a kimono from Japan, she insisted I try it on so she could take photos. I was grimacing unpleasantly in every shot. But when I insisted on having a cowboy outfit and a toy gun, my mother finally relented and got me both. And in those photos I am clearly content with my outfit.

My father used to bring home jewelry from his business trips and affectionately called me "Dolly" in his Indian accent. I loved his attention and affection, but I shoved the jewelry into an unknown corner in my room until my mother finally took it out and kept it somewhere safe. When I saw a male rock star in a white suit, I begged my parents for months to buy me one like his. When they finally acquiesced, my father filmed me while I stood on the coffee table, gyrating in my white suit and singing "Rock Around the Clock"—just like the guy on the album.

But my frequent proclamations that I was a boy or—after having been referred to as a girl—that I wished I was a boy, seemed to hold no deeper significance to any of them.

A week after I sent the letter to my parents, I received a letter in the mail, but from my aunt. She must have written it shortly after our visit. And something clearly had changed.

The letter was addressed to "Madame" Khosla and it was twelve pages long. It began with her telling me she loved me and that she would understand if I decided not to go through with this change. It then progressed into a lengthy sermon on how my "homework" in life was to learn to make peace with that woman, and that the new millennium is all about the resurgence of the female spirit. At one point she noted that she had once taken hormones for medical reasons and that they made her very depressed. Finally came the section where she said I needed to see that no matter what I did, I could never be a real man.

My blood was boiling as I tore the letter into shreds. I pulled out a piece of paper and wrote in return that she should never write to me again, and that her "homework" was to learn that I am not interested in her misguided attempts at love.

When I addressed the envelope, I ignored the hyphenated form she had placed on the return address and just put down my uncle's last name. If she wasn't going to acknowledge *my* identity, I would not acknowledge hers.

That act was my first taste of a new rage that I would confront over the next few years.

When I was a child, I was madly in love with my mother. On the nights she and my father went out, she seemed to take on the image of a glamorous movie star. Her hair and face looked completely different from those of the daytime mother I knew. And when she reached down to kiss me good-bye, showering me with her German-accented "darlings," she left fresh lipstick marks on my cheek and a cloud of Chanel No. 5 that clung to my pajamas long after she had left.

During the day I had her to myself. Every afternoon I would come home after school and sit at the kitchen counter while she cooked and told me stories. Sometimes she would put on the sound track from West Side Story *or* Jesus Christ Superstar *and sing along to her favorite songs. Or she might play an Abba album and do her own rendition of "Fernando."*

But mostly she told stories—stories of the men who had chased her and the ones who had broken her heart. Sometimes she would cry as she told her stories. And through the undistorted eyes of a child, I saw the depth of my mother's empty sadness. And I wanted to be the one to fill it.

I showered her with poetry that contained fierce and dramatic proclamations of love, such as, "I love you more than there are grains of sand in the world." And I inundated her with attention. I pictured myself as her knight on a white horse, rescuing her from this dungeon of ordinary—and unromantic—life.

She wrote me poetry, too. But her lines were about mothers and daughters and the secrets they share. And whenever she saw an aspect of my personality that she particularly liked, she would proclaim, You're just like me. And while my own proclamations that I was a boy appeared to escape her notice, my pain was mitigated by the fact that I seemed to have landed a special place in her heart.

When she and my father fought, it was me she chose to confide in while she slept on a mattress on my bedroom floor. And during our kitchen talks, she would sometimes lean in conspiratorially while telling me that, deep down, most men were little babies. To punctuate her point, she would tell of the time she and my father went for a walk and a truck driver whistled at her. My father shook his fist threateningly at the driver, and the driver pulled over to the side of the road. When he came up, my father backed down and apologized. Whenever my mother reached the end of the story, she would break into peals of raucous laughter as she described how my father was "shitting in his little pants." And as I laughed with her, I remember feeling grateful that I was not one of those men—that I was in on the joke.

Four

OCTOBER 1997

In my dream I am flying over a row of Spanish houses, singing joyfully from deep within my chest. All throughout the neighborhood, men are standing outside the front doors of their houses, looking up and singing back to me. I call out a passage in my deep baritone voice, and they respond with the same passage. Their echoed responses fill the sky as I soar on. . . .

It was a warm, sunny afternoon and I was in a good mood as I headed south. I was going to meet with the hormone specialist who would be prescribing my testosterone after the chest surgery. In my tape deck was a recording of the song I had written in Los Angeles—"Would You See the Man." It had become a mantra of sorts—a reflection of what had brought me to this point. And today, as I listened to the painful lyrics, there was joy in me because I was on my way to a place that would bring relief from that pain. I had noticed lately that whenever I did something concrete for my transition—such as making a medical appointment or setting up a surgery—I was left with the sense that I had done something really kind for myself. I had always been good at buying myself nice toys or good food, but this felt different—like a truer, deeper act of kindness.

I exited the highway in San Jose and realized I was very early for the appointment. Because of the insane and unpredictable traffic situation in the Bay Area, I was often either extremely early or extremely late for meetings. I pulled into a diner and ordered a sandwich.

While I ate, I overheard a conversation between the two guys next to me. I wasn't really a conversation, actually. It was more a series of unrelated monologues delivered in turn and never responded to. As I listened to them, I felt a sense of familiarity and my mind drifted back to the time I was studying psychology as an undergraduate and worked as a counselor at a detox center.

After numerous workshops on how to actively listen to others, I started to feel that I was becoming reasonably decent at it. And yet, even after specialized training, I continued feeling guilty after conversations with some of my female friends. The ability to follow the flow of the conversation seemed to come naturally to them—especially among the very feminine. But for me it was a cultivated skill. Not only was I prone to constantly interrupting the other person, I had to consciously fight against the tendency to direct the conversation toward an end point that I had predetermined.

Then there was the issue of equal time. Halfway through a conversation with a female friend I would think, I've been talking about myself for a while; now I should stop and ask her some questions about herself. Or I would start the conversation with questions about her to rack up points up front, before I started my turn. But always, at the back of my mind, was a nagging fear that if I didn't stay on top of the situation and keep an active score count—if I let my guard down—these women would see the real me. And compared to them, that person was a self-absorbed, narcissistic asshole.

The doctor's building was not far, and the waiting area was empty when I walked in. There were two young women working the front and I told them my name. I had recently filed papers for a name change at the local courthouse, so I made my appointment under the name Dhillon. It was still a bit foreign to my ears, and saying it brought out mixed feelings. One part of me felt that the name belonged to my future incarnation—after the changes. But the other part of me saw it as part of my preparation. For if

I could start getting used to the name now, then it would be familiar to me by the time I looked like the Dhillon I had imagined.

The doctor was a short guy with a round, friendly looking face. Knowing he had worked with many transsexuals—both male and female—made me feel at ease. After the usual questions, such as medical history and illnesses in my family, he asked about the history of my gender dysphoria. I gave him a brief synopsis of what I had told the therapist. In passing, he wondered how my parents felt about my decision and I told him about the response I had just received from my mother.

The letter was written on purple paper with computer-generated hearts outlining the border:

My dear Asha/Dhillon,

Thank you so much for your letter. I don't know how to convince you that I am proud of who you are and what you are planning to do. You have guts and are true to yourself, to who you are. Perhaps a few years ago I would not have been quite so open as I am now, but I would at all times have stood behind you, even if I would not have understood why you need to take such a step. But increasingly I have less understanding of people who live a life that society expects of them, and they are not brave enough to live life the way they really want. Then they are 70, 80, 90 years old and they are full of aggression, bitterness, and anger as they realize they have not really lived their lives, but what was expected of them.

Who is it that expects something of us? Who the hell is it? Why should we care? How we want to live is only a decision between God and ourselves and no one else's business.

So you see, Asha, I am just in the right frame for your decision. In fact, I hope you don't mind, but I am proud to tell people about it—especially such people who are doing what is expected of them, or they imagine is expected of them. . . .

Will end now and send you all my Love, M.

After the type, and below a row of computer-generated hearts, she added the following words in pen:

Hope to hear from you soon and would be happy if you shared the transition with me, how it goes, and how you feel. Love you, M.

The doctor muttered something like, "That's Europe—they seem to be more open-minded about this than Americans." He then talked about the process of administering testosterone. The optimal dose seemed to be 200 mg every two weeks—the same dose they give genetic men when their testicles don't produce adequate amounts of testosterone—but he liked to start with 200 mg every three weeks. His goal, he said, was to give the least amount necessary to get the desired effect.

I was very disappointed. I knew the changes would be gradual, but I didn't want to delay the process or end up on a dose too low for me. He sensed my concern and said if the testosterone ran out of my system before the three weeks was up, I'd feel it and we could adjust it. I tried to appreciate his caution.

We moved to the examining room, and he listened to my lungs, checked my reflexes, and then said an assistant would come in shortly with my testosterone shot. A huge surge of excitement went through me; the little kid in me was clapping his hands and saying, Yeah, we get it now, we get it now! It took a lot of restraint on my part to quiet down and tell the doctor I was not scheduled to start until November, after my chest surgery, when I got the letter of approval from my therapist.

Later, when I went to the reception area to pay my bill, one of the women said something about my chart to the other woman. I heard her use the word "he" in reference to me, and it took me a few moments to notice. The "he" had felt so natural and appropriate, that it had breezed by without any reaction on my part. What finally brought it to my attention was an unfamiliar relaxation that surrounded me. It was then that I realized I had automatically braced myself for "she." After all of the continued trauma around hearing "she," I had expected to feel jubilant at my first "he" in the outside world. But I didn't. I just felt calm. And I had a new understanding of the saying, "Pleasure is the absence of pain."

As I was walking out the door, a tall, attractive, blond woman walked in. I immediately wondered if she had previously been a man. There was nothing in her face to suggest it, but the combination of her height—as well as her presence in a doctor's office that dealt with transsexuals—put the thought in my head. While the thought was still there, I watched her approach the desk, flip back her hair, and flash a winning smile.

It was the kind of smile that said, "This is the place where dreams come true."

MEANWHILE, MY RELATIONSHIP WITH SELENA WAS BECOMING increasingly difficult. The incompatibilities that lay between us when we first began dating had resurfaced. While my preoccupation with this transition—and her unwavering support—had formed a bond between us, it was really just a temporary reprieve from the reality that our potential as a couple was ultimately limited.

When I was in the throes of intolerable pain, her compassion and her understanding made me want to dispense with my dissatisfactions and consider myself incredibly lucky. But as soon as that pain was resolved and I felt stronger, my doubts returned. In a clear state, I could see that her focus on my struggle into manhood gave her a much needed distraction from her own constant "boredom"—as she called it. During the times that I had followed the thread of that boredom, it had revealed itself as a deep sadness. But within moments of touching the truth, Selena seemed to want to bury it away and instead return her focus to something outside herself. And so as long as I sought out her company and support, we were fine. However, when I needed to be alone or take some time for myself, she would become angry and call me selfish. And, while having her angry at me for wanting to spend some time alone was frustrating, it was not the most compelling reason why I knew we were not going to last. Most vital was the realization that my strongest emotion toward her was that of gratitude—gratitude for seeing me in a way that the world had ignored for so long. During this time of limbo she was my refuge, my bridge between where I was and where I wanted to be. But someday the whole world would see what she saw. And then what would pull me toward her?

———

TOWARD THE END OF THE MONTH, I FOUND MYSELF BACK IN the Victorian-style office of my San Francisco therapist for my third, and final, appointment. I was looking forward to getting those two crucial referral letters—one for my hormones and the other for the chest surgery. My second appointment had gone smoothly enough, but toward the end I found myself becoming agitated.

I had asked my therapist whether she knew specifically how hormones changed the face. Did the face shape change or was it just facial hair that made one look male?

She answered that she thought it was just the facial hair and then volunteered that I could do specific things to make it easier to "pass" as male, such as cutting my hair even shorter and removing my one earring. Her suggestions echoed some of the criteria I had read in the ethical guidelines for transsexuals. They often wanted you to "live" as a man for six months before you started any surgeries. The notion that I should have to dress up to "pass" as the real me seemed wrong.

Today the therapist was holding a piece of paper in her hand. "I have prepared the referral for your chest surgery," she said. "But I didn't prepare the letter for the hormones. I spoke to your former therapeutic bodyworker and she said she was worried about you taking hormones. What do you think? Would you be willing to put this off for a while and think about whether you really want to do this?"

Her words sent a surge of panic through my chest. I felt the color drain out of my cheeks and my legs grow weak. I was once again that second-grade boy in gym class, being led away by those who knew better. Why was my bodyworker doing this to me?

I had begun working with a therapeutic bodyworker during my third year of law school. She practiced a kind of bodywork called the Rosen Method, which was based on the notion that there are parts of our body where we store pain or hold back emotion. A skilled Rosen worker gently focuses on those parts of the body with gentle touch and energy until there is a release or discharge.

I was instantly attracted to the idea because I often had the sense that conventional therapy kept me too much in my head. I found myself caught up in loops of self-analysis and trying to outsmart the therapist instead of working to uncover a deeper self.

I spent three years with her. Every week I lay on her massage table as she gently worked the areas of my back that had stiffened in protection over the years. About a year into my work, I began to have gender-related memories of my childhood. They weren't traditional mental images, but were more sensorial, like when you enter a room and are overwhelmed by a scent that pulls you to a different time and place. As my bodyworker gently passed her hands along the muscles of my upper back, I could almost feel myself as a little boy running around shirtless, anticipating my chest getting broader and more defined as I grew into a man.

One day my bodyworker was talking about how she didn't work with male clients. Without thinking, I immediately responded, "Well, you're seeing one now."

But before I even finished the sentence, my defiance had turned to reticence; it sounded silly to my ears. In the body I was in, how could this statement be taken seriously? And what did it mean?

To my bodyworker, a lesbian, it just meant I was letting go of a socially imposed feminine appearance in favor of a more butch, or androgynous, identity. But for me, the act of cutting my hair or reducing my breast size didn't seem to resolve the mystery. In fact, I felt more lost than ever.

I now stared at my therapist in disbelief. "No," I said. "I cannot wait. You said you'd have the letters today, that everything was okay." I felt a terrible sense of desperation.

She coolly watched my reaction and said, "Look at you—you seem really agitated. You are leaning all the way forward out of your seat." Her analysis was both cerebral and detached.

It made my blood boil. I wanted to yell, "How dare you sit there and analyze me. This is my goddamned life. You know nothing about me and I have to pay you a hundred fucking dollars an hour so you can sit there and decide what I should do with my body? Of course I'm fucking agitated. Wouldn't you be if you were in excruciating pain and someone was holding back your medication?"

But I didn't say it—none of it. Just as my rage was about to break the surface, a strong, swift survival instinct kicked in, sweeping aside all emotion. I pulled myself back into the chair and spoke in calm, measured tones.

"I am just frustrated because I lost my gender identity early on due to the inability of others to see it." I looked her directly in the eye, but kept my tone even. "It is very easy for me to become distrustful and afraid that it will be taken away from me again. I am absolutely sure that I am ready to start the testosterone and I do not want to delay it any more."

I watched her recede into her chair as she mumbled, "Well, I'm not here to stop you." I noticed we were very near the end of our session and I felt a growing sense of desperation. I now only had a few minutes to get that letter. I again looked her directly in the eye and said, "So, could I please have the hormone letter now as we discussed?"

She became a little flustered and then said, "Yes," as she reached into a nearby folder and pulled out a blank referral sheet. I made a very conscious effort to look indifferent as she began to write the recommendation, reaching down for my coffee cup and taking a few slow sips. Then she handed me both letters and wished me good luck on my surgery. I thanked her and said something about calling her after surgery to see her for another appointment. But I was lying. I was still playing the game, ensuring a smooth good-bye so I could walk out of there without fear that she would revoke her recommendation.

When I was finally inside my car and safely out of her sight, I let out a huge sigh of relief. I truly felt as if I had narrowly escaped disaster. And I remember saying out loud, "My God, I have a degree in psychology, have worked as a counselor, and I am an articulate lawyer. I have all the hallmarks of a functional member of society. And yet I almost didn't make it in there."

MY FATHER'S LETTER ARRIVED FROM INDIA ON THE USUAL blue airmail stationary that folded into an envelope.

My "Dolly,"

I was so glad to receive your letter after such a long time. I read and reread your letter many times. Let me assure you that I will always love you and support you as my son. There is no question of me disowning you; you are my flesh and blood. As you had never mentioned your thoughts to me before I left the United States, naturally your decision came to me as a lightning bolt. You have obviously given the matter a lot of thought, and I can well imagine the strain you must have been going through. Naturally it is not easy for me to have a daughter for twenty-eight years who, in physical form, will be a different person in the future. Inwardly, I know you will be the same person. Most important is, of course, that you be happy, in which case I will also be happy and will continue looking after you to the best of my ability.

You are right when you say that I do not know much about these things except that, as a child in India, I remember reading that the first person to have a sex change was a U.S. Air Force Officer Robert Cowell—name changed later to Roberta Cowell.

Well, Dolly (I'll have to think of another nickname for you!), I was hoping you could come to Florida for Christmas, though now it looks impractical with the medical treatment you will have to go through. Let me know. In any case, I'll telephone you when I get back home. If you can't visit at Christmas, I'd like to visit you in the New Year. If it is not practical for me to park myself at your place, you could book me a motel for my stay.

I would like to say a lot of things but just putting it on paper in a letter is so cold. Now that you have made a major decision, I hope you will be inwardly calmer and be happier in life. I am always there if you need my support. (I was often too busy with my work during the working life.) I have always loved you and will continue to do so till the day I leave this world. As old age begins to creep on me, life takes on a different outlook. All the best with the operation—look after yourself. Love you and all that. . . .

Hauf [nickname for my father]

P.S. Continue with the music and your singing. Look forward to listening to your album.

37

Shortly after we moved to America, my parents divorced. My father moved into an apartment three miles away and I spent alternate weekends visiting him. One of our favorite things to do was to watch the old *Mission Impossible* episodes on Saturdays. I remember being most fascinated by the way the undercover agents were able to manufacture these thin face masks that allowed them to look exactly like someone else.

One day I asked my father, "What would you do if I was kidnapped and they changed my face? How would you know it was me when I came back?"

He seemed completely unconcerned and continued watching television as he casually answered, "I would know it was you."

I found his lack of concern troubling and became more insistent. "But how? How would you know it was really me?"

He shrugged his shoulders and said, "I just would," as if there was nothing more to discuss.

But I wouldn't let it go. "But what if they changed my whole face so that I was completely unrecognizable? How would you know I was not some evil impostor?"

My dramatic tone made my father laugh and he turned to me and said, "Because you are my child. I will always know you."

Somehow that answer satisfied me and I relaxed back into my chair.

Part Two

BUILDING

THE TEMPLE

Five

NOVEMBER 1997

I am standing in the middle of a green meadow when a man walks by, looking vaguely familiar. He is carrying a suitcase and I wonder where he's going; there are no houses in sight—only miles and miles of tall green grass. He seems oblivious to this as he strides by without even glancing in my direction. My curiosity gets the best of me and I begin to follow him. As we climb over a small hill, a house suddenly appears to the right and the man confidently walks inside. As I watch him disappear, I say out loud, "I guess he knew where he was going all along. . . ."

When I found out that my chest surgeon's office was in an art gallery, I thought, how perfect. He was, after all, a sculptor of sorts.

I had been referred to Dr. Michael Brownstein by one of the clinics mentioned in *The New Yorker;* then later I had seen some pictures of his work in a book published by a transsexual man. Dr. Brownstein was a plastic surgeon who did many of the usual surgeries, but when it came to transsexuals, he only did chests. I liked that. In my own profession I know it is generally wiser to go to someone who specializes in one area as opposed to someone who dabbles in a bit of everything. I figured that went double for surgeons.

The art gallery/office was in the Potrero Hill district of San Francisco.

Upon entering the building, I was surrounded by metal sculptures filling the lobby. Upstairs I found several suites of offices lining the walls around the open staircase.

Dr. Brownstein opened his own door and when I saw him, I thought he looked a bit like Harrison Ford—tall, fit, with silver hair and steel blue eyes. His deep voice beckoned me inside, and I sat down with him as he explained various surgical techniques for doing chest reconstruction surgery.

The first two involved going in through the nipple and liposuctioning out the tissue. The advantage was that this left no visible scarring, but the disadvantage was that you might be left with loose, excess skin that had been stretched out from the former breast tissue. Your chest could look like two deflated pancakes unless you had very small breasts prior to the surgery. The final technique—and the one he most commonly performed—was to cut a straight line under the breast, take out the tissue, cut away the excess skin, and fold the ends down to the pec line, leaving a tight, flat, sculpted chest.

I told him about my prior breast reduction and showed him the "T"-shaped scars. He explained he would cut out those scars along with any excess skin, adding that while many doctors knew that T-shaped scars signified a breast reduction, a long flat scar along my pec line would not reveal anything, as most doctors didn't know about this type of surgery or what it looked like. When he touched my scars to show me where he would do the incision, he looked down at his bruised fingernail and said in a sheepish tone, "I guess it doesn't look very impressive for me as a surgeon to have this bruised nail, does it?" I knew then that I liked him.

He then explained that postsurgery I would have bandages wrapped tightly around my torso and there would be one drainage tube from each pec. I remember wanting him to be clear that I wanted all the tissue out. I wanted absolutely flat pecs, and I didn't want to be disappointed a second time.

When we were finished, Dr. Brownstein and I chatted informally for a few minutes. I found out that he was semiretired and spent most of his time on his ranch in Montana. Lately, however, he'd been getting more requests for the chest surgery and was finding himself in San Francisco more frequently than usual. As I listened to him talk about some of his patients, I got the distinct impression that he felt a personal sense of responsibility toward us—almost like a protective parent would. It was a feeling that I would have many more times in my encounters with the doctors and surgeons along my path.

As I was leaving the doctor's office and driving to work, I thought about whether I should do any sort of ritual before the surgery. But every time I tried to conjure up something, it all felt so contrived. Years earlier, before my breast reduction, my bodyworker had warned me that I should prepare myself for feelings of loss or grief because I was letting go of a part of my body that had been with me for years. But as soon as I had the surgery, all I felt was the pain of knowing there was still too much there.

THE MORNING OF MY SURGERY, SELENA AND I ARRIVED AT the hospital and noticed that it didn't look like a hospital at all. It was an outpatient surgery center that looked more like a small motel.

Selena was nervous and anxious about my going under the knife, but I felt an unusual sense of calm. When the receptionist handed me the paperwork, I saw that my sex had been labeled as male. I felt relieved to see it there, but it also made me a little wistful. Most people who come in for this surgery have been on six months of hormones, so they have the benefit of appearing male. Seeing the word "male" on my chart made me wish even more that I were truly one of them. And it got my hopes up that the hospital staff would refer to me with male pronouns. But without any testosterone under my belt, that hope was a setup for disappointment.

A nurse led me to a small room and told me to get undressed. I asked if I could keep my boxers on and was grateful to hear him say it was okay. Then, I was led to a gurney where I was covered with a warm blanket, and my IV drip was started. I asked if my girlfriend could come back, and I heard him ask another nurse to get my "friend." My hopes of being seen as male were immediately dashed when I heard the "friend" reference. It was the classic way of dealing with a lesbian couple.

When Selena came back to see me, I told her about the exchange and she said one of the receptionists had referred to her as my "wife"—probably based on seeing the word "male" on my submission forms. I found it interesting that based on who they thought I was, she was either demoted to "friend" or promoted to "wife." And none of it had anything to do with her.

Dr. Brownstein arrived, wearing the obligatory white lab coat, and pulled out a magic marker. He outlined where he was going to cut and where he was going to fold. The markings were dotted lines that reminded me of the origami books my brother and I had as children. He finished his markings, and the anesthesiologist came to prep me for surgery. Within minutes I was drowsy. The last thing I remember was looking up at Selena as they were wheeling me away. She was crying and looked afraid. I remember feeling confused by her reaction. It was so opposite of what I was feeling.

When I woke up, I was back in the same area where I had begun the day. I remember feeling really happy—giddy. There was a slight throbbing in my chest and I went to touch the bandages to make sure all was flat.

A nurse came over and told me to keep my hands away. I watched as she picked up the plastic drainage bulbs coming out of each side and checked the amount of blood in each of them. She had a British accent and as she did her work, I remember babbling, "Were you sad when Princess Diana died? Was she popular among the British?" I was in one of those euphoric moods where I just wanted to reach out to anyone who came by. I remember babbling some more until I passed out again.

When I came to the next time, Selena was at my side. I immediately asked her to see if my bandages truly looked flat. She lifted the blanket and said yes, they definitely looked flat.

An hour later, the nursing staff determined I was ready to leave. By that time, the mild throbbing in my chest had become a strong pain. Someone brought a wheelchair to transport me to the car, and I remember thinking it was ironic that they were willing to let me go home a few hours after surgery in my bandages and drainage tubes, but wouldn't let me walk a few feet to the exit. If I really couldn't stand on my own now, I wasn't going to develop a sudden burst of strength in the car.

During the drive to Selena's, the strong pain in my chest got worse. As soon as we arrived, she got me a glass of water and brought my pain medication. While I was in surgery, she had gone to the hospital pharmacy and filled a prescription that Dr. Brownstein had given her. As it turned out, he made a mistake on the form for the stronger pain medication and tore it up. He didn't have another form with him, so he just called in a regular prescription for Tylenol with Codeine.

I took the pain pills and waited for the relief. A half hour passed and the throbbing became really intense. Another half hour passed and I still felt no relief, so I had Selena page Dr. Brownstein. It took another hour before he called back, at which point I asked him to call in a pain medication I had used after my breast reduction. It wasn't technically any stronger but it had worked for me before. Selena went to pick it up. Within twenty minutes of taking the new medication, I was no longer in pain. I finally fell asleep.

THE NEXT DAY I WAS SCHEDULED FOR A POSTOPERATIVE visit. I slept most of the morning and Selena emptied out the bulbs, carefully measuring how much blood had drained. Whenever she did this process, she got a very serious, studious look on her face. It was a look that made me picture her in a lab coat, surrounded by beakers and charts.

As Selena now pulled out a piece of lined paper and meticulously recorded the amount she had emptied, I said to her, "You're really getting into this; I think you missed your calling." She smiled a shy, slightly embarrassed smile—as if I had caught her at something.

ON THE DRIVE TO DR. BROWNSTEIN'S OFFICE, I BEGAN TO feel nauseated. I don't know if it was because I hadn't eaten enough before my last dose of pain medication or if it was the motion sickness from the ride, but the nausea was definitely there.

When we reached Dr. Brownstein's office, I sat on the floor, hanging on to a small trash can, ready to vomit at any moment. Thankfully, after a few minutes, I felt a little better.

Selena helped me take off the oversized sweater I had on. I lay flat on my back, and Dr. Brownstein unraveled the bandages. I raised my head to look and saw my nipples were covered with small square gauze pads. Across the bottom of each pec was a line of black stitches. But what caught my attention the most was that my chest was entirely flat!

Compared to my shoulders and biceps, my chest looked really scrawny since I had never been able to build it up. In fact it looked like the chest of a twelve-year-old. I realized I had my work cut out for me, but for now I was just relieved that my wishes were finally carried out. And I couldn't help but imagine what it would feel like to wear a tight T-shirt for the first time across my new chest.

But that would have to wait at least another two weeks. Although the tubes would come out in five days, I had to keep the bandages tightly wrapped around my torso for a full two weeks. I had read some stories about people getting chest infections and the image of green pus collecting in my chest made me a very cooperative patient.

ON THE FOURTH DAY, WHILE I WAS STILL BANDAGED AND tubed, I got my period. It was not just physically uncomfortable— weakly stumbling to the bathroom to insert a tampon with this contraption of bandages and tubes dangling from my chest—it was psychologically jarring. Here I was in the most tentative stages of developing my male body only to be shocked back into the reality of my female one.

I was twelve when I got my first period. But unlike those girls in the Judy Blume books, I was not eagerly awaiting this transition into womanhood. And it wasn't for any lack of preparation.

Two weeks earlier, my mother had said, "You're going to get your period soon—I just have this feeling." She explained that it was the most natural thing in the world.

But that's not how it felt. As soon as it happened, I felt disappointed. Not scared or shocked—just disappointed.

This time, it was more than just disappointing—it was difficult for me to bear. When I finally emerged from the bathroom, I immediately went to the phone and scheduled an appointment for my first shot of testosterone.

ON THE DAY I WAS FINALLY SCHEDULED TO GET THE BANDAGES on my chest removed, Sarah, my boss, called. Somehow news had leaked out in the office that someone was having a sex change, and several people had gone to our head of personnel asking whether it was me. She thought they should send out a memo and nip it in the bud.

My immediate response was anger. Here I was, still tubed up and bandaged, and I had to deal with inconsiderate people at work. Who were they to think they had the right to know my business?

Sarah asked if I wanted to write a note or give some explanation to the office to accompany any memo they would circulate. I said I would think about it and call her later. As soon as I hung up, I walked around Selena's apartment, ranting and raving about how cruel people were. They didn't care about me as a person, but as a source of gossip for their rumor mill.

At some point, I went to use the bathroom. I remember sitting on the toilet, looking at the floor and seeing a recent issue of the *Enquirer* that I had bought on a whim. The image stopped me cold as I confronted my own hypocrisy. Here I was, buying a gossip rag, just so I could peek into the lives of strangers. I was no different from those people at work.

The more I thought about it, the more I examined my own fears and reactions. I was afraid someone else would take control of my story and decide they knew my motivations better than I did. It was an old wound. I was also afraid that the more mainstream people in the courthouse would label me a freak—just like those audiences did on the talk shows that presented transsexuals as guests. But that fear was somehow much less pronounced than the first.

WHEN I ARRIVED FOR MY APPOINTMENT AT DR. BROWNSTEIN'S office, he carefully unwrapped the bandages and then began to pull out the stitches along the bottom of my pecs. He placed a thin strip of surgical tape over the scars and told me to continue to do that for several months so the scars would be less likely to thicken while they were healing. I remember feeling hurried; I wanted to get back to Selena's place as quickly as possible.

When I made it back to the apartment, I immediately threw off my sweater and walked over to her closet mirror. I stood there, looking at my chest in the reflection of the mirror. And for the first time, it looked right. True, it was a relatively small chest and there were long red lines along the bottom—but it was flat and tight. Not one bit of loose tissue remained. Dr. Brownstein had kept his promise.

I started to rummage through Selena's drawers, searching for plain T-shirts and simple-style sweaters. I didn't own any formfitting clothes because, up until now, I had only worn loose shirts that de-emphasized my breasts.

Everything I tried on—no matter how tight—looked right. Finally, the material fell flat and smooth.

Within a short time, I had created a pile of clothes on the bed and I began to feel tired from the effort. My chest started to ache in the places where the stitches had been. I took a pain pill, and climbed on top of the bed, lying among the sweaters and T-shirts.

As the medicine kicked in, I started to think about work and about Sarah's offer to write a memo. And the more I thought about it, the more I realized it was my best chance to confront my fears head-on. If I told my own story, then no one else could claim to be the expert on the issue. Those people who went to my boss demanding to know who was having the sex change would no longer have the power of being among the few who held this secret. And if I admitted that I was afraid of being judged, it would probably take some of the fun away from those who wanted to judge me. It's like someone taunting, "You're a chicken—you're scared," and your saying, "Yes, you're right—I am scared."

I slowly got up off the bed, made my way to Selena's computer, and sat down to write.

Dear Coworkers:

As you know, I am currently undergoing sex-reassignment surgery and hormone therapy. This decision comes out of a long history of gender dysphoria and subsequent consultation with and treatment by various professionals. Because it is my experience that exposure to the foreign and unknown can lead to discomfort and misconception, I want to take this opportunity to provide you with a bit of background information.

There is now scientific evidence to indicate that this condition (1) is biologically caused by prenatal distribution of hormones, in that the brain receives a different message than the body and/or (2) arises out of the genetic DNA structure itself in that the DNA of some individuals is actually unclear when tested (this resulted in several women having to drop out of the Olympics when they did not "pass" the sensitive DNA testing).

I don't think I could ever fully describe the pain and anguish of hearing "she" and "ma'am" and "miss," and feeling invisible—to the point where isolation became less painful than socializing. The additional difficulty for me has been that, because I love women and feminine energy, I thought it would be unfair for me to reject the physical female attributes in myself. However, what I have come to see is that by simply bringing my body in alignment with my internal reality, I can accept all of myself.

The decision to undergo this physical transformation is in actuality a culmination of a struggle; it is not an initiation of one. However, having said that, I know that the transition period will be painful to the extent that I fear judgment and reactions from others. Because I will already be vulnerable during this period, reactions from others will most definitely make the transition even more difficult. And while I do not expect the kind of unconditional love and support that I receive from friends and family, I do hope for the same kind of warmth and respect that I have felt fortunate to experience from this office in the past.

Thank you,
dhillon (Asha) khosla

The next day, Selena called from work and told me that every division was having a meeting in the afternoon. She figured it was going to be about me—and my transition—and said she would keep me informed. I hung up, feeling nervous with anticipation—like an expectant parent. I felt as if people would be expecting me to look dramatically different when I returned to work, and all I would have was a flat chest that would be noticeable only if I wore tight clothing. I was already impatient enough on my own, and facing these people as "Dhillon" made me feel more pressure. I just wanted to get through the next few months as quickly as possible.

I sat around the rest of the day, reading magazines and watching bad television, until Selena finally called with an update. She had gone to our criminal division meeting where Sarah told people that I was undergoing a sex change and then gave out the memos. She also offered a copy of the *New Yorker* article for those who were interested. The memo given out by my bosses said that "malicious gossiping" would not be tolerated. Selena said that during the meeting no one said a word.

About an hour later, I was checking my e-mail when I saw there were messages from my coworkers. As soon as I saw the subject heads, such as "moral support," the tears welled up in my eyes. But it was this one, written by a female coworker, which impacted me the most:

Dear Dhillon,

Having just heard of your ongoing transformation, I wanted to offer encouragement and emotional support. To be honest, I was surprised. However, my surprise immediately transformed into enormous respect for you and the courage you have to trust us, your coworkers, with your very personal decision. I cannot even begin to imagine the internal turmoil you have experienced, and the fear you must have in returning to work. It takes guts.

*As a friend, I sincerely hope you will find the inner peace you so deserve. You are
a brave, sensitive, thoughtful, intelligent, warm person, and this is the person I choose
to see. If there is anything you need, please let me know.*

I understood she was saying that regardless of what sex I was, it was the
person inside for whom she cared. And because she also accepted the fact
that I needed to do this, I was able to believe her.

WHEN SELENA ARRIVED HOME FROM WORK, WE DECIDED TO
go out for dinner. I had not been outside since the surgery and was excited to get out of the house and celebrate my new torso. I went into the
bathroom to get ready and pulled out the shaving cream and razor I had
recently bought. It was a hopeful purchase in anticipation of the facial hair
that testosterone might bring. It all depended on genetics and time. Even
people who got a full beard said it took years, and they first started out with
peach fuzz. But I was shaving now in case the old myth was true—that frequent shaving would make the hair grow thicker and coarser. I was also
hoping that shaving would roughen my skin. Ironically, I had the kind of
soft, clear skin that most women envied. When Selena heard that testosterone caused acne, she was excited, perversely hoping my face would finally carry some blemishes.

When I emerged from the bathroom, I lay on the bed, wearing only my
jeans. I called Selena over to me and she climbed onto the bed.

"Please, lie on top of me," I said.

She was a bit cautious about hurting my healing wounds, but I convinced her to go ahead, and she gingerly climbed on top and put her
hands on my pecs. I lay back and closed my eyes: "That's it. That's what I
have been waiting for."

*One rainy weekend when I was about eight or nine years old, I was sitting in-
side, watching a B movie. The hero of the film had been sliced in the abdomen and
torso during a fight. A beautiful woman was sitting across from him, gently cleans-
ing his wounds. I remember being mesmerized as I watched her soft, delicate hands*

gently trace across his broad, brown torso and stomach. When he winced in pain, I
could actually feel what it was like to be inside his body—the warmth of his torso,
the stinging of the alcohol, and the cool, healing touch of the woman's fingers.

Selena and I finally got up out of bed and headed out the door, walking hand in hand down the street to a nearby Italian restaurant. As soon as we sat down, our waiter appeared. And the first thing he did was ask if he could get us two "ladies" a drink.

It hit me like a sucker punch—like everything I had just gone through had been ripped out from under me in one fell swoop. His words knocked me right back to square one. As if I were just fooling myself. Like there really was no way out.

We continued the dinner, and toward the end he referred to us as "girls." I tried hard to shake it off and let it go. This was our first outing and Selena had taken care of me the past two weeks, so I wanted us to have a good time. We continued on to a movie but I don't even remember the plotline. Slowly, throughout the next two hours, I felt sadness seeping in. The images on the screen flashed by, but I was not able to get into the story. The sadness took its hold and I sank deeper and deeper, as it wrapped itself around me like a thick, winter blanket.

When we got back home, I dropped into Selena's sofa. I started to take off one of my shoes but halfway through I lost all motivation and just let my foot fall to the ground. My head dropped into my hands and I began to sob.

"This is all bullshit. How am I supposed to have people call me 'he' at work when I still look the same? How fucking stupid. I cannot celebrate any of this until I no longer look like a woman. Until then I am trapped and dying."

And at that moment, that's exactly how I felt—as if I had a fatal disease and the cure was coming way too late. . . .

Six

DECEMBER 1997

I am driving over the Bay Bridge when the wind suddenly picks up. The bridge starts to shake, and I realize a storm is coming. I can't see anyone else and consider turning around when I come upon a number of cars that have crashed into one another and are completely totaled. I hit the brakes and swerve to avoid them but start skidding across the bridge. This is it; I'm going to die, I think, as I continue skidding and spinning around. But somehow I get by the other cars. By this time I am more than halfway across the bridge, so I keep going—figuring I now have a better chance of making it across than I do of turning around and heading back.

It was hard to get excited about my first testosterone shot. I was still smarting from the sting of entering the world with my new pecs, only to be greeted by a slew of female references. And I was anxious about my upcoming return to the office as I imagined facing people with so little of my emerging self in place. All of these events were taking their toll, and I knew that first shot of testosterone would not magically cure the problem. It would not turn me into a man overnight.

When I arrived at the doctor's office that I'd been referred to for my injections, I noticed it was just down the hall from my former doctor's office. I hadn't explored the option of using my own physician to help me with the shots because I didn't want any of this to be in my medical files under my health insurance. I wanted it all confidential and separate.

The nurse arrived and I walked with her to an examining room. She brought out a small vial of golden liquid and opened a packaged needle. When I saw her draw some of the potion into the needle, I finally felt a momentary surge of excitement. She told me to drop my pants and outlined the area directly above the buttock where she would inject. It was an intramuscular injection so no vein was involved, which made me a bit more relaxed—especially since she told me that the next time she would teach me how to inject it myself into the muscle of my leg. I couldn't quite imagine sticking a needle into myself, yet some part of me liked the image it conjured in my mind—the image of my using the needle as a tool to sculpt my own body.

The nurse finally stuck the needle in my buttock and slowly injected the solution, wiped the area with alcohol, and put a Band-Aid on it. As I pulled up my pants, I felt a sense of relief that I was finally on my way, and I asked how long it would take for the changes to take hold—for me to look like a man.

"Oh, maybe seven months," the nurse said.

I was shocked. Seven months? It seemed an eternity.

I went back to the reception desk and made an appointment for three weeks later—as set out by the prescription—and left. On my way out, I brought my prescription to the pharmacy and dropped it off so I could get my own vial of testosterone. I found the notion of having a ten-dose supply in my possession comforting—like once I had it in my hands, no one could take it away from me. Somehow, at the back of my mind, was the continuing fear that someone would stop this before I made it home.

The next morning, I prepared to drive Selena to the airport. She was flying back east for a visit with her family. While she was packing, we talked about the inevitability of our separation.

It was clear to me that I was heading toward a period of prolonged hibernation. As one older and wiser FTM had said when I told him I was looking forward to transitioning so I could finally talk about something else, if you think you are consumed by gender now, wait until you start your transition. He was right. And I could see that I was heading directly into the eye of the hurricane. It seemed to be the only way. Only by letting go of all obligations and responsibilities could I find answers to that crucial continuing question: how much more surgery do I need to feel complete?

It was good timing on both sides. In January, Selena would be taking a leave of absence from work to study for the California bar exam. We decided that upon her return, Christmas would be our last time together.

I remember feeling nostalgic as I dropped her off at the airport. I knew that someday I would have the energy to fully appreciate all she had done for me, and I wanted to somehow make sure she knew that.

"You know," I said, "even when you are not with me, you are with me."

Without missing a beat, she responded, "Even when you are with me, you are not with me."

We both burst out laughing. And then we kissed good-bye.

THAT NIGHT I WENT TO SLEEP AT MY USUAL TIME, BUT WOKE up around 3:00 A.M. with a surge of energy. My heart was racing quite fast. It was very rare for me to wake up like that, and I started looking for explanations. I remembered this was the second day of my testosterone shot and supposedly the time when I hit my peak levels. The testosterone was suspended in sesame oil so it would stay in my body over the next few weeks, but it was not a perfect science. People often hit very high peaks the first few days and then some low points (called "troughs") the last few days before the next injection.

My mind interpreted the racing heart as anxiety and started forming corresponding thoughts. All of a sudden it struck me that I had this new substance in me that I really didn't know that much about. What if my body reacted negatively to it? What if I developed some unknown side effect? What if I had to stop taking it?

One night in college, a friend brought over some hallucinogenic mushrooms. While I drank a lot and smoked my share of pot during my teenage years, hallu-

cinogenics always made me nervous. I didn't like the idea of losing control over my mind or losing my grip on reality. And yet I admired people who could do it. I felt they were freer for being able to let go and still trust they would return. When my friend suggested the mushrooms, I figured they might be a good middle ground since they were supposed to be much milder than acid.

We made some macaroni and cheese and ate the mushrooms—which were stale and dry tasting. About twenty minutes later, we took a walk. I started to feel strange, as if something were about to happen inside me. I started to panic and thought that I'd better stay on top of this or it would take over. When we passed by a bush, I went behind it and threw up. I said I wanted to be alone and went back to my apartment to finish throwing up the rest of what I had digested.

Now, my mind continued to race around thoughts of testosterone, and I began to reason with it. The hormone was deep inside my system, so even if something were wrong, vomiting was not going to get rid of it. I was just going to have to ride it out. I got up and turned on the television to distract myself. An hour or two later, I ran out of steam and went back to bed.

ON THE MORNING OF MY FIRST DAY BACK AT WORK, I WAS filled with nervous anticipation. Knowing that everyone had heard about my surgery made me feel as though they would expect me to walk through those doors looking like a new person. And yet I looked no different. Except for my chest, that is. As I got dressed that morning, I thought to myself that the one good thing to come out of this early announcement was that I could wear a tighter shirt without having to worry about arousing suspicion.

As I approached the courthouse, I found myself wishing for a secret underground route directly to my office, so I could hole up in there and stay hidden. I just didn't want to face anyone, feeling so exposed. I was afraid people would mirror back my biggest fear—that this "sex change" was just wishful thinking on my part, that I would never really look like a man.

Lately, every time I heard a female reference, it nailed that fear right on the head.

I somehow managed to get to my office without bumping into anyone in the hall. And the first thing I noticed was that someone had changed my nameplate to Dhillon. I was profoundly struck by the gesture, and my fear momentarily dissipated into gratitude. When I walked inside, I found a tray of cards that had been placed on my desk. I sat down and opened them. Several were from people with whom I had barely spoken, except for the occasional greeting in the hallway. And as I read the words on those notes, I started to realize that these people were silently rooting for me. I had totally not expected that:

> *Dhillon,*
>
> *After reading that very touching and informative memo/letter to the court staff, I've spent the last twenty minutes trying to think of something even remotely empathetic to say, and for the first time in my life I'm drawing a blank.*
>
> *Although I know we're not "close friends" and in fact, our encounters have never been much more than a "Hi, how's it goin?" approach when we crossed paths in the hall or in the gym, I did want to say that I respect and support your decision(s) for personal happiness both from within and from without.*

As I was catching up on e-mails, a few people came by my door to let me know the memo I wrote was really helpful. I told them the hardest part of announcing this was the fact that the changes took such a long time. Some part of me really wanted to get that out there so they would pass it on. Then no one would expect anything from me.

When I later headed toward the bathroom, a woman from my division stopped and asked how I was. I said I was okay and started to continue on, but she looked after me with these searching eyes, as if expecting more. I remember feeling guilty, and thinking that by writing my memo I had invited her in, and now I owed her more information. But I had already reached my limit of attention for the day. I felt too exposed in the open hall and just wanted to scurry back to my office.

Stepping into the women's room did not help matters. My bosses had explained to people that I would temporarily be using the women's room—and yet people were supposed to start getting used to referring to me as "he." It was all too much. Walking into the women's room with my pecs—as well as my male identity exposed—felt awkward. And yet I couldn't very well walk into the men's room when I couldn't get away with that in the outside world without being stopped because of my female face. I remember that Sarah had offered to let me use her private bathroom, and I very quickly decided to take her up on it.

Later in the day I was down in the records department, looking for the transcripts of one of my cases, when one of the guys there came to help me out. He called over to another guy, saying, "Dhillon needs the record in 'X' case. Can you get it for *him*?"

I remember feeling deep gratitude toward him, followed by sadness. The sadness came from the sense that it was a charitable act. He was calling me "he" because he had read the memo, not because I looked like it. It was like getting a compliment I didn't deserve. And while it was far better than the stinging pain I felt after the "she" references, it wasn't where I wanted to be. For once I wanted to know what it was like to have someone look at me and call me a "he" based on what they saw—not because of what I had told them.

TEN DAYS AFTER MY TESTOSTERONE SHOT, I STARTED TO FEEL irritable. That surprised me, for after the initial night of panic, a solid feeling of well-being had entered my body. While I was dealing with many varying emotions throughout this transition, the sense of well-being provided a pleasant backdrop for it all. It was a firmer foundation. I had been aware of it the past few days, but hadn't necessarily attributed it to the testosterone. I figured it could be from the support I felt at work, or the lessening of anxiety from my resolution to let myself sink into hibernation during this transition.

But over the next few days, the irritability continued. It was as if I had something good and it was being taken away. It occurred to me that it might be in my head, since I had wanted to do the shot every two weeks from the start, so maybe this was my way of justifying that. But on the fourteenth day I got my period—a week earlier than usual. I was livid. I figured I must have had a large drop in testosterone for the period to kick in. I immediately called my specialist who said it could take several months for menses to stop, but on the whole it was likely my levels had dropped. He agreed to let me get a new shot.

When I drove down the next day, I told him I wanted a new prescription for every two weeks so I could continue that schedule with the nurse near my house. He agreed for the time being, saying maybe later down the line we could change it back to every three weeks. He once again acknowledged that every two weeks was the optimal dose and most doctors start their patients on that schedule, but he reiterated that he was a bit more cautious.

When I walked out with my new prescription in hand, I felt the same as when I left the therapist's office with my letters of recommendation—like I had won an important victory. And I made a mental note to change doctors before I had to renew my prescription.

SHORTLY BEFORE CHRISTMAS, MY CLOSEST FEMALE FRIEND, Sue, came to make dinner. She was heading off to the Peace Corps at the beginning of the New Year and this was going to be the last time I would see her. It was strange timing to watch her leave just as I was beginning my transition. She would come back to find me looking completely different, having missed the changes along the way.

The pork chops were frying as she unpacked the mushroom soup she was planning to use for the sauce. As she took out a small container of milk from her grocery bag, I said, "You know, I have milk. You could have used that."

"And how long has it been in there?" she retorted. "I've been your roommate. Not all of us have ironclad stomachs like you."

I laughed. "You know, you just didn't seem that shocked when I told you about this transition. How come?"

"I don't know," she replied. "It just makes sense. There were so many things that just didn't quite fit with you."

"Like what?"

"Well, for one, the extreme slob you were when we were roommates."

"Come on," I said, "you can't be serious. Plenty of people are messy. That's a personality trait, not a biological sex trait."

"Not in the way you were a slob," she said. "That was definitely male."

A few years ago, I was visiting a girlfriend who was working for a year in Hawaii. One night, we were getting ready to go out and had just showered. She was clearing away some dishes in the kitchen and I came in to talk to her. I was holding a toenail clipper in my hand and I jumped up on the counter, grabbed one of my feet dangling over the edge, and began to clip my toenails. She looked over at me in horror and said, "What are you doing?" I was confused by the question but when she looked at my feet I figured it must be the toenail clippings that were bothering her. I said, "What's the problem? I'm hanging over the edge so all the clippings land on the floor."

But she didn't seem to hear me. She had slowly started to pace back and forth and appeared to be talking to herself, as if she was figuring something out. She suddenly stopped, turned to me with narrowing eyes, and said, "It's not just that you're a slob—you're . . . you're a pig!"

Sue was continuing with her line of observations, "Plus, the way you wore those Jon Bon Jovi rocker outfits—like that silver paisley jacket. Or the way you would apply eye shadow."

"Oh, come on," I said. "I had really big hair at one point and I even wore dresses."

"Yeah, but you still had to wear cowboy boots when you wore the dresses." She put down her spatula. "Okay, you know what it really was?"

"What?" I asked, curious.

"It was the gifts you gave. They were the kind of gifts I got from my boyfriends. I mean, I loved them all because you gave them to me, but, God, some of them were terrible."

I started laughing as she described some of them, including my recent gift of a journal with a thick quilted flower pattern on the outside.

She continued, "It's as if you'd walked into a store and tried to conjure up an abstract image of a woman in your mind and what she might like—like you just couldn't think from that perspective."

Seven

JANUARY 1998

I am at an island retreat for people who are going through gender transitions. After several days there, I notice a small, thin, timid-looking man in an old white shirt who keeps to himself but looks as if he's been there forever. I ask someone who he is and I'm told that once he completed the process, he didn't want to leave, so they gave him a small stipend and let him live there. I feel sad when I see him and think, "Poor guy, he just wasn't able to make it back out there. . . ."

I've heard it said that what you do on midnight of New Year's Eve sets the stage for the rest of the year. If that's true, then I was definitely entering a long period of hibernation. I spent all of New Year's Eve alone; by midnight I was in bed.

The next morning, I put on my running shoes, bicycle shorts, sweatpants, and a thick sweatshirt and drove to a nearby beach for a run. There was a bit of a winter chill in the air, but the sun was out, and the water glimmered as the rays bounced off its surface. I was just a few yards from the water, jogging along a sidewalk that ran parallel to the beach, separated only by a short, wooden fence.

I had started coming to this beach for jogging breaks shortly after I began working at home three days a week. The beach was private, quiet, and best of all, located in a small neighboring town where I was not likely to run into anyone I knew. With my Walkman on, I could escape into my favorite songs without interruption.

After about two miles, the sidewalk curved to the right and led into a green, grassy park with picnic tables facing the ocean. I was winding my way through the park, hitting my peak stride, when I felt an interesting sensation.

The bicycle shorts under my sweatpants were tightly hugging my crotch, and with each movement of my legs, the material pulled back and forth, tugging at the underside. As my attention was drawn to the friction, I had a sudden impression of what it would feel like to have testicles. It was a clear, definite physical sensation—almost as if they had been there once before and my body was simply remembering. And it was totally unexpected.

While I had often dreamed of having a penis, I had never given any thought to having testicles. After finally getting rid of my sagging, fleshy breasts, the last thing I had on my mind was adding another set of pendulous sacs of skin.

But the sensation was not in my mind. It was right there—between my legs. And it was there that I left it, trying neither to understand it nor push it away.

When I arrived home, I took a shower, then wondered what to do next. I thought about calling a friend, but quickly dismissed the idea. Lately, whenever I spoke on the phone, I found myself becoming increasingly agitated. In that mode of communication, the sound of my voice was the only projection of my identity. As it echoed in my ears, sounding entirely feminine, I felt further and further away from myself. Talking with men was especially difficult as the contrast between their voice and mine was becoming unbearable.

Playing music was also out of the question. As soon as I picked up my guitar or sat down at my keyboard, I wanted to sing, but the pleasure of self-expression was quickly outweighed by the sounds of self-betrayal.

One by one, I rejected each option as quickly as it arose. It was starting to become clear to me that my familiar methods of entertainment were not going to work during this journey through no-man's-land.

I began leafing through a magazine. Partway through, I came across a recipe for scones. I couldn't remember the last time I had actually baked anything, but it suddenly seemed like a good idea. I got out a notepad and started to write down the ingredients, wondering what the hell Allspice was. As I was getting dressed for a short trip to the grocery store, I felt a brief lift in my spirits. I thought, This is not so bad—I can just treat this as one long rainy day. There's no pressure to do anything or be anywhere. I can just lazily fill time.

But a few hours later, shortly after I had stuck the tray of scones in the oven, I was desperately poring through my research books and pamphlets, trying to find out how long the changes were supposed to take. All I found were a few vague comments in a medical pamphlet about FTMs and testosterone. The author said that there were some vocal changes in the first six months, but real in-depth pitch changes could take up to a year. There was no discussion about the timing of the physical changes, other than a statement about menstruation usually stopping within three months.

I put down the pamphlet and slowly walked over to a Persian rug that lay diagonally across my living room floor. My parents had bought it in India, but it was a Tibetan prayer rug.

I got down on my knees, folded my hands together, and said, "Please, please, God, give me the patience to make it through this time in waiting."

I said that prayer over and over as I bowed my head and hands toward the floor, the words echoing around me.

TOWARD THE MIDDLE OF THE MONTH, I DECIDED TO ATTEND another FTM meeting. I figured this was one place that might cheer me up a little—if only because I was likely to encounter someone who was not even as far along as I was.

I walked in a bit late and saw a few familiar faces from the last meeting. Jack was not there but one of the men at this meeting gave off that same familiar vibe. He was about five-foot-four and had a clean-cut boyish look—like Michael J. Fox.

I sat down next to him and listened to people introducing themselves. In the corner were three guys who were visiting from Nevada. They had all been on testosterone for fifteen to twenty years and, while visiting San Francisco, had decided to drop in on a meeting. They looked like guys you might see in those news segments about motorcycle gangs such as the Hell's Angels. They were wearing worn white tank tops and had long greasy hair, scraggly teeth, and big potbellies. They weren't the prettiest of boys—but no one would ever mistake them for women. It was comforting to see people that far down the road. To me they were living proof that the research about the safety of taking testosterone was accurate.

One guy toward the back of the room began to talk about his new job. It was his first job as a man, and when his female coworkers found out he had previously worked at a domestic violence center, they asked him how he had become such a feminist. We all laughed as he told the story, imagining ourselves in that situation.

But when he later admitted that one of the women had told a coworker she thought he was a woman, I was not totally surprised. He had started hormones about four months earlier, and his face looked androgynous to me. He had not had any chest surgery and was instead binding his breasts. This, in combination with his large hips, made his body look soft and lumpy.

And that made me slightly anxious. I knew I was entering my own androgynous phase, but I wanted out of it as soon as possible. Focusing on guys like Jack, or the clean-cut boy I was sitting next to, gave me an assurance that it really was possible to go all the way. And right now I needed that.

A short, swarthy man a few seats over began talking and he reminded me of an Italian actor in a Mafia movie. He was saying how he didn't feel right until he had his hysterectomy. He held his fists up near his head and said, "Man, it just drove me crazy, having these female parts."

As he spoke, the man across from me looked at me and rolled his eyes. I'd recognized his name during the introductions; he was the guy who had spoken to me on the telephone that night in Los Angeles.

When he rolled his eyes, my automatic response was to smile and acknowledge his reaction. It was the kind of conspiratorial look I had seen a thousand times from women when they were irritated by a statement made by a typically macho man. But halfway through my smile, I stopped. I realized that the part of me that was prone to smile and agree was the same part that had stood in my way in the first place, vigorously believing that only a freak would reject her female body. And I was becoming increasingly suspicious of that voice.

After the Italian guy finished talking, the man who'd rolled his eyes quickly spoke up, saying, "We shouldn't have to have hysterectomies just to prove we are men. If I hadn't had problems, I would never have had my hysterectomy; it was a very invasive surgery."

The man next to him agreed and I recognized him as the guy who had shimmied his chest at the first meeting. I couldn't help but notice that the two men who were speaking out against hysterectomies were identified as gay men. From earlier conversations, I also knew that both of them were not strongly driven toward any type of lower surgery. And I couldn't help but wonder if there was a correlation between their sexual orientation and their gender identity. Were straight men more likely to be psychologically attached to an exclusively male body?

When it came to my turn to speak, I talked about how incredibly painful it was to continue to hear female pronouns—especially the more I got in touch with how false that identity felt to me.

The clean-cut boy next to me, Jared, picked up on what I said and talked about how he had gone home to visit his parents recently to find they still had his childhood pictures all over the house. He said that when he looked at the pictures, he felt he was looking at pictures of a sister who had passed away. He felt really sad when he looked at her face, like there was all of this potential and hope, but she just never really had a chance of making it in there. As he finished these words, his voice cracked and his eyes filled with tears.

I have that same feeling when I now look at old photos. I can see in my face just how hard I was trying to stay in there. And like Jared, I now know I never really had a chance.

After the meeting was over, I spent some time talking with Jared. I found he'd been on hormones for more than three years but had only done chest surgery so far. He explained he had been thoroughly researching the medical aspects of it all—from the use of testosterone to the various surgical options. He then pulled out a thick binder filled with notes and resource lists. As I watched him point to the various pieces of information, I had the same feeling I'd had during a law school class when I had first met my friend and exclusive study partner, Gary. It was the feeling of having just found the perfect ally.

AS JANUARY WAS DRAWING TO A CLOSE, I FOUND MYSELF AT the San Francisco airport, waiting for my father's arrival. He had called a couple of weeks earlier, expressing a strong desire to visit. And as much as I wanted to keep to myself, I also knew it would be better to let him see me before I got too far into the changes.

I watched the door at the arrival gate swing open, and within a few minutes, passengers streamed through the doorway. I spotted my father and was struck by how thin he appeared. I wasn't sure if it was because he had actually lost weight or because I hadn't seen him in a few years and I had just never got used to how thin he was. He was five-foot-six and couldn't have weighed more than 115 pounds. My mother used to jokingly call him "Gandhi legs" whenever he wandered around in boxer shorts.

His face was deeply tanned from the Florida sun, and I noticed that his thick black hair had collected more flecks of gray. His suit looked rumpled, hanging from his narrow shoulders as if it was on a thin wire hanger. In comparing my upper body to his, it was clear to me that I had inherited my body from my mother's German heritage.

He spotted me and waved before he came over and embraced me.

"You look healthy and trim," he said in his familiar accent that sounded more British than Indian. He had left his native country of India shortly after college in order to pursue graduate studies in England.

As we were walking toward baggage claim, I said to my father, "I don't

want to go out that often while you're here; it's just really hard right now because people refer to me as 'she' and still treat me like a woman."

"But you're not," he replied. His response caught me off guard.

After my parents divorced I stayed with my mother, but shortly after I started high school I decided to move in with my father. I had joined the drinking and partying crowd and figured I could get away with much more under my father's unobservant watch.

Sometimes, on weekday afternoons when he was still at work in New York City, I would sneak into his closet and steal white tank tops and boxer shorts to wear to bed at night. I would then move on to his suits, trying on the pants and jacket and practicing how to put on a tie.

One day, he came home early while I was trying on one of his suits—a dark blue pinstriped jacket with matching pants. When he saw me, he said, "You know, on my next business trip to Tokyo, I could have the tailor make a suit for you, if you want."

We found my father's suitcase on the luggage carousel and I helped him lift it off. As we dropped it to the floor, I wiped my hands.

"Damn, what do you have in there?" I asked. "Gold?"

"I brought you some canned mango and cauliflower pickles from your grandmother in India," he said. "And tomorrow I want to stop by an Indian store to get some spices so I can make your favorite *khana*—chicken curry."

We loaded the luggage into my trunk and drove toward the highway. My father asked if he could have a quick cigarette, so I cracked open my window. As we were crossing the Bay Bridge and heading toward my place in Oakland, he said, "Dhills, would you stop by the grocery store so I can pick up some beer?"

The word "Dhills" struck a sweet chord. I guess he had found a new nickname for me.

Once we arrived at my building, I put his bags near the sofa bed in my living room. I had bought my place a few years earlier, but it was not well

suited to guests. The building was a former schoolhouse converted into fourteen loft spaces. Mine was about eight hundred square feet fashioned into one large space, with a small upstairs bedroom loft that was completely open and overlooked the living room.

My father walked into the kitchen area and started unpacking his beer. When he opened my fridge, he exclaimed, "Dhills, you have nothing in here—what do you eat?"

"Well," I answered, "I cook a lot of pasta and sometimes I get takeout at a nearby Middle Eastern place—they even give me free rice."

But my father was only half-listening, focusing his attention on the shelves of my refrigerator. After a few minutes, he moved on to my nearby cabinets, asking for some paper so that he could make a grocery list. When he had finished with the food list, he began asking about kitchen appliances.

"Dhills, do you have a blender?"

"Yes."

"How about an orange juice press?"

"Yes."

"How about . . ."

The next day, we set off for an Indian spice store in San Francisco's Mission District. As soon as we entered the place, the familiar smells from childhood struck my senses: coriander, turmeric, curry powder. There were rows and rows of open bins that held the powders in bulk, and the scent had escaped into the air, filling the store. There was sitar music playing from speakers hanging from the ceiling corners that reminded me of visits to India, when I would accompany my grandmother while she haggled with shop owners in an unrelenting dialogue in Hindi or Panjabi.

My father began filling basket after basket with bags of spices and different assortments of steel cups and serving bowls. I was tempted to stop him, knowing that after he was gone the spices would lie idle, collecting dust. But I didn't because I knew it was his way of showing affection. Plus, I had this recurring fantasy that I would meet a woman who was so impressed with my Indian heritage that she would pounce on my collection of secret family recipes, whipping up dishes while I sat on a stool and played the guitar.

After our shopping expedition we headed to a nearby Indian restaurant for lunch. Because it was early afternoon, the place was mostly empty. We sat at a small table lining the wall, and looked through the menu. My father asked what I usually ate for lunch and whether I had any good restaurants in my area. As I answered, I started to feel a familiar irritation.

We had been together more than twenty-four hours, and all his questions had centered on food; there had not been one question about the transition. And from that familiar place of past experience, I began to fear that the rest of the trip would be like this.

My father came to visit me shortly after I graduated from law school. He had just returned to America after having worked in Europe for the past few years. On the second day of our visit, I took him to a seafood restaurant overlooking cliffs by the ocean. We were quietly having a couple of predinner drinks as I mulled over how to work in some news I wanted to share. I wanted to tell him that I had been dating women, which at that time meant telling him that I was a lesbian.

I remember being aware that the most difficult part was not the information itself—it was how to segue into it. He never asked anything about my personal relationships. In fact, several times during college, I had brought lovers home to Connecticut. He had graciously entertained them, more than happy to have an extra mouth to feed. But the only time he asked me anything about them was right before my next visit when he would say, "Why don't you bring that friend you brought last time, and I'll make tandoori chicken."

But this time I wanted to tell him more. I guess I needed to see if his love was truly unconditional—or just blind.

I started by saying, "You never really talk about wanting grandchildren—how come?"

I don't quite know why I chose this opening line—especially since I had several lesbian acquaintances who told me they were annoyed when their parents responded to their sexual orientation with laments about how they were never going to get any grandchildren. One of them had retorted, "Just because I'm a lesbian doesn't mean I've lost my ovaries."

But for me, my love for women seemed to go hand in hand with the under-standing that I would never personally carry a child.

"I just don't think grandchildren are a big deal," he answered.

"But don't you want your own flesh and blood wandering around?" I asked.

He shrugged, "No—I don't really care."

We weren't really getting anywhere, so I finally just said, "Well, I guess I just wanted you to know that I am involved with women and I wasn't sure how you'd react—whether you'd accept that or not."

His tone immediately changed from disinterest to one of conviction.

"You should never worry about me rejecting you or cutting you off. You are my blood and I will always take care of you—no matter what."

"Well," I eagerly piped up, "this woman I'm seeing—she's part Hungarian and really beautiful—and we want to travel and visit both Hungary and India. . . ."

But his attention was already wavering. In a last-ditch effort to recapture it, I asked, "So if we visit India, can I bring her by the grandparents' house?"

"Yes, fine, bring her by," he said. "Listen, I need to stop by the Schwab office in San Francisco tomorrow and change some things with my account. Can we go there after breakfast?"

When the waiter arrived, my reminiscing stopped and I ordered a beer. The waiter looked at me and then asked for some identification. My father laughed and said, "It's okay, *he's* of age."

In an instant my irritation disappeared.

WHEN WE GOT BACK HOME, MY FATHER SETTLED IN FOR A nap and I grabbed my jogging shoes and headed out for a run. Jogging, like driving, was a meditative experience for me. It was a time when I could digest the emotions that found their way into my field of awareness.

I left my Walkman inside my car and ran in silence. But my mind was far from quiet. Not more than a mile in, the inner chatter reached a most feverish pitch.

"Man, you are so fucking lucky. There are so many transsexuals with horror stories about getting disowned by their families, and here your father's not only accepting it, he's using the "he" pronoun two months into your hormones! What more could you ask?

"Well, that he asks me some questions about myself, for one. I mean, how can he accept me for who I am, when he doesn't even know who I am? Shit, he didn't even know what grade I was in during high school. What the fuck is that?

"You are so ungrateful. Most people in your shoes would be jumping for joy. Why can't you?"

I ran farther than usual, pounding the pavement of the sidewalk, the dialogue fading with fatigue. When only a few stray thoughts remained, I turned around and headed back.

The clean sea air felt good in my lungs, and my body was solid as I pumped my arms. I passed a female jogger with prominent breasts and I thought, That was me just a couple of months ago. I tried to imagine myself running in a jogging bra stretched tightly across my breasts and cutting into my skin. But the image took effort and already felt like a distant memory—as if it had happened to someone else.

When I got back to my place, I found my father awake and sitting on the couch. He was holding a book on transsexuals that I had purposely left out on the coffee table. He was a voracious reader and whenever he was bored, he would pick up the nearest reading material and consume it in one sitting.

"Hey, Dhills," he said. "This book is quite interesting. You should read some of the things the doctor has to say."

LATER THAT NIGHT, I WAS LYING IN THE DARK OF MY BEDROOM loft and listening to the light snores emanating from the sofa bed below. I was thinking about the letter my father had sent in October and remembering the warm calm that had washed over me after I'd read it. And I was wondering why I had not recaptured that feeling since his arrival in California.

My thoughts turned to earlier in the day, when I had walked in to find him reading the book on transsexuals. I had left it there for him to find. Was it because some part of me already knew that the way to reach him was through the written, not spoken word? And if that was the case, what was he doing here?

THE NEXT DAY, I HAD TO GO TO THE OFFICE TO FINISH WORK on a special project and attend a staff meeting. My father opted to stay home so he could spend the day making chicken curry.

As I walked through the library and climbed the back stairs to my office, I felt a sense of warmth and comfort that comes with entering a familiar environment. I closed my door and sat down at my desk, checking my e-mail and sipping my morning latte.

When I entered the library conference room for a meeting, I sat at the far end of the table. Several others started arriving and one of them sat down next to me and gave me a warm smile.

The meeting began, and I opened my notepad to a fresh sheet of paper and started taking notes. A couple of people asked questions regarding cases they were working on, and my natural inclination was to answer them or to mention some relevant case law. But I held back. With so many in the room, I felt like an open target.

Partway through the meeting, Sarah started talking about the project I was working on. The first couple of times she referred to me, she cautiously used my name. But as she continued and got into what she was saying, I could see her start to relax. The more she relaxed, the tenser I became. I knew she was going to refer to me as "she." With her guard down, I knew it was coming.

And it did. But right after I heard that "she," I heard myself quickly pipe up, "he." Sarah smiled apologetically and corrected herself. I sat back, kind of surprised. I felt exposed and self-conscious, but I also felt proud. As my inner critic had started its usual attacks of, "But you don't look like a 'he,' " another part had responded, "Hey, if my own dad can start using 'he,' so can everyone else."

As the afternoon approached, I quickly tired. I first thought it might be from the anxiety of a day at the office. But later I noticed a hoarseness in my voice. It sounded like I was getting a cold. I thought of my father, and pictured him in my warm place, cooking up a storm.

I picked up the phone and called my house. He answered, and I heard the sound of running water in the background.

"When are you coming home?" he asked. "I'm just putting on the basmati rice."

I felt my spirits lift. "Soon," I answered. I hung up and started to fill my briefcase with printouts of cases.

As I emerged from my office, I saw a man rushing down the hall, pulling on his overcoat. He was a guy I knew from law school who was married to a Middle Eastern woman. During the last few times in the office I had envied him at this hour, imagining he was going home to a place where the lights were already on and the stove was filled with exotic dishes. But today, as I walked down the stairs to the library exit, I only pictured my own house.

I stopped at the entrance and unlocked my mailbox. Inside, was a letter from the Department of Motor Vehicles. I had recently gone down and changed my name, after getting a court order. While I could also legally change my gender with a letter from my hormone doctor, I wanted to wait a few months so the photo would match the sex. By the stiff feel of the envelope in my hand, I could tell my new driver's license was inside.

I opened the door of my loft and stepped into the kitchen to find my father hovering over the stove, stirring a concoction that steamed into the air. I walked over and looked into a pot of yellow-tinged chunks of chicken and remnants of tomato coloring the curry.

"When can we eat?" I asked. "I'm starving,"

"We have to wait for the rice to finish."

I went into the bathroom to wash my hands. When I came out, I changed into sweatpants and a sweater, then came back to the kitchen. I grabbed a beer and went back to the stove.

"Isn't it ready by now?" I asked impatiently, knowing it was rude but asking all the same.

His answer brought me back in time; it was an answer I had heard many times before.

"Okay, here. I'll skim some rice from the top so you can get started and then I'll take mine when the rest is ready."

I accepted without hesitation, piling the chicken curry over the rice. I then sat down on one of the stools lining the black bar I had built in the kitchen. Next to me was a bowl filled with salad and heavy cream dressing, a plate of onions and lemon wedges, and a small silver bowl with spiced mango pickle. I filled my spoon with curry and rice, squeezed some lemon juice over it, and then added a small piece of mango pickle. My mouth watered in anticipation of that first perfect bite.

By the time my father joined me I was almost halfway through. I put down my spoon, took a sip of beer, and reached for the envelope that held my driver's license. The card was shiny and new, and when I looked at it closely I was pleased at the sight of my new legal name: Dhillon Asha Khosla. I spent the next few minutes staring at my photo, wondering if anyone would see me as male in the picture. I wasn't objective enough to tell, so I just went back to looking at the name.

"Hey, check this out—my new name," I said to my father.

"Good," he said looking at it. "Hey, by the way, since tomorrow is my last day, I want to stop by an Eastern bookstore."

I put down my license with a sigh. "Sure, there's one by Stinson beach. We can take a long drive and then have some lunch there."

SEVERAL DAYS AFTER MY FATHER HAD LEFT, I WAS TALKING on the phone with Jared. He commented on the deeper pitch of my voice.

"Yeah, it's been like that for a few days, I've been waiting for a cold to develop, but I don't really have any other symptoms."

"That's how the first shift in my voice happened, too—I started out with what I thought was a cold, but it stayed like that and then just kept getting deeper."

I felt a surge of excitement. When I got off the phone, I immediately ran to my recording equipment, picked up my microphone, and recorded a few passages of speech. I then rewound the tape and compared the new passage with the one I had recorded two months earlier. As I listened to the recordings back-to-back, it sounded like my voice had developed a heavy coating that made the pitch a shade deeper. I put down the microphone and jumped up and down, yelling, "Yeah, YEAH!"

My first sign had finally come.

Eight

FEBRUARY 1998

A man and woman are inside a gravity dome, and I am observing from someplace far above them. The woman has on flying gear which lets her fly to the top of the dome. To do this, she has to punch a code. The man keeps asking her for the code so he can join her, but she refuses to reveal it, not wanting him to get any closer. . . .

I was lying on a mattress tucked into the corner of the room, while my teacher sat in a chair next to me, giving instructions.

"Now take deep breaths and, as you exhale, push out your belly. . . . That's it . . . keep going . . . keep going."

I had been seeing this particular teacher for more than a year as part of a spiritual school I was attending. The class met one weekend a month for a combination of meditation and group exercises founded on principles borrowed from Western psychology and Eastern spiritual teachings. A part of the program included one-on-one sessions with a private teacher every two weeks. The private sessions were to allow further exploration into feelings or experiences that might have been triggered during the weekend workshops.

One of the most popular techniques used by the teachers was special breath exercises. When I'd first started, I'd been skeptical, wondering how a few breaths would really do anything. But more often than not, this continuous cycle of forced breathing would unleash frustration that hovered beneath the surface.

But today it wasn't frustration that I encountered. Instead, as I lay there, pushing out breaths, I started to feel a stretching sensation across my lower jaw.

When my teacher asked me to describe it, I said, "It feels like there is a rubber band stretched tightly across my lower face and up to my ears."

The more breaths I pushed out, the tighter the sensation felt.

I lay there, completely baffled by this strong sensation. Most often the physical was just a metaphor for something deeper that would ultimately reveal itself if I continued to observe it. But this time I felt like there was nothing else behind the sensation.

"Tell me more about this stretched-jaw feeling," my teacher said.

"I know that testosterone will make my face broader," I responded with the one thought that had popped into my mind. "Is it possible I'm somehow feeling the beginnings of that?"

THAT WEEKEND I WAS SITTING IN ONE OF THE PEWS OF THE temple where our monthly workshops were held. The stained-glass window next to me filtered in the morning light and I was enjoying its warmth as I settled in for our morning meditation.

People continued to arrive, first filling up pews and then the chairs that were lined in rows in the middle of the room. Our group consisted of about seventy people. Most of the members were middle-aged or retired professionals: therapists, doctors, and professors who were seeking something beyond conventional therapy. And because it all took place in Berkeley, we had more than our share of New Age personalities—the kind of men and women who would coo appreciative oohs and aahs at local poetry readings about peace and love, while pointing expressions of distaste toward anyone who showed the slightest hint of anger or aggression.

I was watching the door when out of the corner of my eye I noticed someone headed toward me. I looked over and saw it was Don, a quiet guy who kept a pretty low profile during our workshops. But since the beginning he had struck me as a really good person—the kind of guy who might spend his time quietly toiling away in his garage.

"Hey, Dhillon, have you been working out more lately?" he asked when he got to the edge of my pew. "Your shoulders look a lot bigger than the last time I saw you."

"Yeah, but I hadn't really noticed any change," I said.

"No, they're definitely bigger than before," he said encouragingly.

He then asked what types of weight-training exercises I was doing and told me about a couple that he found really helpful. We continued talking until the teacher signaled it was time to start.

Don slapped me on the shoulder and said, "I'll talk to you later," before he headed back to his seat.

The teacher lightly struck her hand chime and I closed my eyes as the last sounds reverberated in my ears, then slowly decayed into the background. Over the next half hour, stray thoughts wandered in and out, periodically giving way to a few moments of blank space. Many of the thoughts were remnants of my conversation with Don. Perhaps it was because that conversation was most recent in time. But I suspected it was more because in all the time I had been there, it was the first time we had ever spoken.

After the meditation was over, and before our group exercises were about to begin, we had a short break. I headed in the direction of the bathrooms, feeling a growing sense of trepidation as I neared the two doors. There was no third door—no place for those of us suspended in between. And there was no way I could go into the women's room without feeling the first few fragile signs of my manhood erased.

I walked into the men's bathroom and found a short line for the one enclosed stall. To my right were a couple of guys standing at the two urinals against the wall. When they walked by me on their way out, I wondered if they felt I had invaded their space. Standing there with just my pecs, but nothing else, I again felt exposed and vulnerable. And I felt like a fraud. As long I could not walk into any public restroom without some suspicion from other guys, I felt as if I didn't have the right to go in there either.

It was during these moments that I would literally brace myself in a way that is best expressed as "sucking it up." I would take a breath, bow my head, and just stubbornly push past the feeling. There was no way to really process anything, just an attempt to survive, to make it through.

I finally reached the stall and took my turn inside. When I was finished, there was only one guy left in the bathroom and when I turned away from the sink to make my way out the door, he moved toward me, opened his arms, and pulled me into a tight embrace.

"It's so nice to have you in the men's room," he said. "It feels right."

His embrace caught me completely off guard. Here I was wrapped tightly inside myself, determined just to get the hell out of there, and this comes along. So my first response was one of hesitation and distrust. But after that came a brief moment of opening. For a second, his actual words—that it felt right to have me in the men's room—struck that buried boy who hungrily reached toward validation. I relaxed into the embrace.

But as quickly as the moment had arrived, it was gone. As I walked out of the bathroom, my defenses reassembled themselves, like soldiers in battle. Suspicion took over, as I wondered if he would really feel comfortable hugging any other guy in the bathroom? Didn't he just hug me because he knew it would be safe—that everyone still saw me as female? For all I knew, he was just trying to get some free affection but was pretending it was about me.

BY THE TIME THE DAY WAS OVER, I WAS EXHAUSTED. AS I walked through the chilly evening air toward my car, I couldn't help but wonder whether I had done myself more harm than good by coming here and exposing myself to so much human interaction.

The question stayed with me throughout the drive home, but I felt myself relax with every mile that brought me closer to my sanctuary of isolation. When I was less then a mile from home, I passed by a Blockbuster video store. At first I blew it off, just wanting to make it to my destination without any delay.

But a few blocks later, I found myself thinking how nice it would be to immerse myself in a movie without the constant interruption of commercials. When I weighed the benefits of that against a few more minutes of public exposure, I found a brief spurt of energy. I made a quick U-turn and headed back to the store.

Inside, I walked through the aisles, scanning the covers for anything that looked like a psychological thriller. I especially loved movies where the genius psycho-killer outsmarted the detective. The whole mental game kept me so entertained that I forgot everything else.

I found a couple of videos that fit my criteria and made my way to the cashier. The guy behind the counter asked me for identification and I handed him my Blockbuster card. He rang up the movies and I handed him a twenty. After he handed back my change, he put the movies in a bag, placed them on the counter past the theft detector and said, "Thank you, sir." I quickly grabbed my bag, and got out of there as fast as I could. I wanted to be gone before he had a chance to take that "sir" back.

I flew home, unlocked the door to my loft and ran toward the back where I had a full-length mirror. I stood there, peering at myself, looking for what it was that he might have seen. Could anyone really see me as a guy? I was wearing a brown wool sweater that Selena had given me shortly before our breakup. It fell flat against my pecs and made my shoulders look fairly square. Had he zeroed in on my flat chest before choosing "sir"? I then studied my face, trying to pretend I was seeing it for the first time. I noticed a tiny bit of blond peach fuzz around my chin and upper lip. My hair was cropped short; I had recently cut it even shorter. But other than that, everything looked the same. My face didn't look like it had changed. Maybe, just maybe, if I really stretched it, I could see it as sort of androgynous. But unless I brought in my imagination to supplement the image of my reflection, I could not see that face as masculine.

I looked at my peach fuzz. I touched it, but could barely feel anything. I had to practically put my face up to the mirror to even see it. I then placed my fingers under my chin and ran my fingers backward, as though scratching against the imaginary grain. It was an automatic gesture and it struck a familiar chord.

Throughout the past couple of years at the court, there were a few occasions where I had to work late to meet a deadline for a particular judge. On those nights, I would periodically leave my office to look up a case in the library. More often than not the library was empty at that hour, and my only company was the faint sound of vacuum cleaners coming from distant hallways in the courthouse.

I would wander the aisles, my shirt unbuttoned, and my hair sticking up on the sides from having grabbed at it while deep in thought. As I tiredly pulled out a casebook, leafing to the first page of the case I was seeking, I would rub my dry eyes to clear them for the task ahead. When I reached the main part of the decision, I would stop, look up, and run through the facts of my own case to see how it might be impacted. And sometimes, while staring off into the distance with my forehead deeply creased with concentration, I would reach up and pensively scratch the imaginary stubble on my chin.

After a few more minutes of staring at my reflection, I found myself wondering what it would take to make my face look definitively masculine? A squarer jaw? But many guys had even narrower jaws than mine. How about a fuller face? But again there were guys who had long, narrow faces. I went to my bookshelf and pulled out the book of transsexual photographs I had purchased a few months earlier. There were many black-and-white photographs of men who looked like any ordinary genetic guy. Some had before and after photographs. In looking at them, I could see that their face shape had changed, but it was hard to pinpoint exactly how. Things had been redistributed, but I couldn't quite figure out where. I could spot the obvious—if, for instance, the guy's face had developed some cut, square lines down the center of each cheek in the way that only men do. And then there were the guys who were balding or had a receding hairline.

But the most obvious change was facial hair. Just about every man either had a full beard, a goatee, or a very visible five o'clock shadow. And as I compared their faces to my own, I had an idea.

I went to the bathroom and started rummaging through my drawers. After a short search, I found an old black eyeliner pencil. I came back to the mirror and started to slowly draw the outlines of a beard and then added some additional lines within the borders. I then took my hand and blended the various lines into the smudged look of a five o'clock shadow. When I had finished, I dropped my hands and stepped back from the mirror to study the final results.

Perhaps the final effect would not have looked so natural in broad daylight or the fluorescent light of an office. But here, by the back wall of my darkened loft with only a muted circle of ambient light coming from a nearby lamp, the effect was nothing less than breathtaking. As I looked at the face that stared back at me, I felt a forceful surge coming from my gut and spreading into my chest.

It was the same feeling that I had felt once before—the first time I stepped onto a stage and sang one of my own original songs.

AT THE END OF THE MONTH, I RECEIVED A CALL FROM JACK. He was flying to Oregon to undergo both a hysterectomy and the first stage of his genital surgery.

"First they will remove my vagina and then extend the urethra out to the—"

I cut him off. "They're going to remove your vagina? How do they do that? I mean, it's a cavity, isn't it?"

"Well," he explained, "they just take out the tissue that lines the cavity and then sew it shut."

Maybe it was the cavalier way in which he said it or maybe it was the image of actually cutting out the vagina, but that information touched off a set of reactions. In an instant, my mind was filled with a flood of voices from feminist lectures and the horrific images of genital mutilation in third-world countries. The voices and images quickly gathered speed until they became a tidal wave of judgments and accusations.

"But that's so intense. How can you do that? I mean, isn't that mutilation?"

"I don't know, man," said Jack. "All I know is that I see myself sailing in the middle of the ocean and I am without a vagina."

"Yeah, but what if—?"

But I couldn't finish the sentence. There was a thick lump in my throat, choking off all speech. Somehow his image of that sailboat on the ocean had found its mark. Suddenly all of my questions seemed pointless and silly, like pollution on a landscape. White noise.

I wished him luck, then hung up the phone. I sat there for a long time, feeling disoriented. As I slowly got up and moved around the living room, I remembered the FTM meeting where one guy had rolled his eyes as another guy talked about his hysterectomy and how having "these female parts" made him feel "crazy."

My initial inclination had been to side with the man who rolled his eyes. But tonight, as I compared that experience to the one I had just had, I saw even more clearly that there were two very distinct places inside me. One was the socialized mind that had become conditioned and rigid with judgments of how things are supposed to be, while the other was an entity that had no words—just a sense of "home."

And now it was up to me to decide which one I would follow.

Nine

MARCH 1998

A little boy is sitting in a field. When I come upon him, I can sense that he is extremely sensitive and deeply curious. My brother is standing beside me, and I say to him, "Do you remember that amazing purity we had as children?" He makes a flippant remark and says he doesn't really remember. I suddenly feel very alone. I continue standing there and feel a deep, deep sadness take hold. Looking at this little boy, I have the sense that I lost something important a long time ago. . . .

awoke to the sound of the phone ringing. I reached over the side of my bed, felt around for the phone that was lying somewhere on the floor, and then grabbed the receiver.

"Hello?" My voice sounded cracked and gravelly in my ears.

"Hi, this is Tonya with Pacific Bell Telephone. Is this Dhillon K . . . ah . . . osla?"

"Yes, that's me," I answered. I had been having some trouble with my voice mail and had recently called the company.

"Well, sir, we've been doing some maintenance, and any problems should now be gone."

The sound of that "sir" sent a jolt of excitement through me, waking me out of my foggy state. It was my first "sir" over the telephone.

I was about to thank her, when she added, "I didn't wake you, did I?"

Her tone had changed from professional to teasingly affectionate. And I got so caught up in the joy of that "sir" that my mood, and corresponding tone, went through their own changes.

Suddenly it felt as if I had all the time in the world. I lay my head back down on my pillow, phone still to my ear, and said, "Was it that obvious that you woke me up?"

She laughed, "Well, yeah. You did sound kind of tired."

"Well, at least you had some good news to make up for yanking me out of my precious sleep."

"Lucky for me, huh?" she retorted.

We talked for several minutes, bantering back and forth until we wound our way to the end of the conversation.

I sat up and swung my legs over the edge of the bed. For a moment I just sat there, wearing only my white cotton boxers, looking down at my legs dangling over the edge. They were typical boy legs—thin, but muscular and hairy. I started to feel a young, innocent joy and found myself swinging my legs back and forth, like a gleeful kid. Out of my mouth came the self-satisfied laugh of a mischievous little boy.

I hopped off the bed, strutted to my loft ladder, and climbed down backward, feeling like I was on a playground during recess, crawling down a jungle gym. When my bare feet hit the carpet, I cockily padded over to my stereo, pulling at the back of my loose boxers. I put on the sound track from the movie *Grease* and then padded to the bathroom to brush my teeth. As the music blared from the stereo, I held my toothbrush like a microphone and danced around my bathroom floor.

This young, childlike effervescence remained with me as I took my shower, dressed, and then made my way to the kitchen to put on the coffeepot. A couple of times I was aware of a strange split—that I had this adult life but was really only playing grown-up. The notion of making coffee or having my own place felt ill fitting to that little boy who had taken charge of my body.

I sat down on a kitchen stool by my breakfast bar and started to eat my cereal, taking occasional sips from my coffee cup. As the music continued to blare from the stereo, I bobbed my head up and down, smacking my spoon against the side of the cereal bowl. As I ate, I playfully splashed my spoon right into the milk, spilling it over the side of the bowl and onto my hands and lap. When I was done, I went to the sink, dried my hands on a nearby towel, and brought the towel back to the counter to wipe off the milk. With just my coffee cup in hand, I began to get bored. The nearest object was the latest issue of *Money* magazine, so I started to leaf through it.

As I paused to read excerpts from several articles, I felt in my mind that distant, observing adult slowly make his way back. By the time I was halfway through the magazine, I was pretty much back to normal. All that remained of the little boy was a lingering sense of lightness—like a really good mood.

A SHORT WHILE LATER, I HEADED TO A NEARBY HAIR SALON. My appointment was with Danielle, a guy who had been cutting my hair for six years. Danielle was a gay man who had grown up in Germany. His sexual orientation made me trust him with my hair while the fact that he spoke fluent German allowed us to gossip about personal stuff in the middle of the busy salon. But the thing that brought us the closest was my decision to transition into manhood.

When he was a teenager in Germany, Danielle had seriously considered going through surgery to become female. Although he eventually decided against it, he spent years living as a woman while dating a military man. He had also passed as a woman in heterosexual bars in Atlanta, where he brazenly picked up straight businessmen while managing to escape any violence during his sexual escapades.

"Do you ever regret not doing the surgery?" I had asked at the end of my last appointment, while we were sitting outside, smoking.

"No, I'm quite content now."

"Well, if you had done the surgery, do you think you would have regretted it?"

"Oh, no," he said. "I would have been a gorgeous woman. I mean you've seen the photos of my old days. I had a tiny waist. But it's okay, because if

I had done it, I probably would be married by now to some rich, old, boring man."

I laughed, "Yeah, you definitely would have done all right."

I had seen the pictures, after all. And the photos of his drag years rivaled my own. Almost.

When I was sixteen, our town had its yearly County Assembly dance—a formal affair where the girls got to invite the boys. In our high school, there were several groups of smokers who hung out during breaks between classes. One guy, Bobby, had a good-looking face and a masculine demeanor. He hung out with a bunch of guys who liked to work on cars, drink beer, and smoke pot. And every day at school, he wore the same jean jacket and smoked Marlboro Reds. I picked him.

On the night of the dance, I went over to my best friend's house to get ready. She put on a tasteful dress with a high neckline and a hemline that almost reached her ankles. I, in turn, put on a black dress with a plunging neckline that accentuated my massive cleavage, black fishnet stockings, and long black velvet gloves that went up to my elbows. To top it all off, I added a small silver purse I had borrowed from my mother and a huge amount of purple eye shadow. My long, permed hair had been expertly swept back and sprayed into a stiff bouffant at a local hair salon.

Throughout the night, I played my diva role to the hilt, aggressively thrusting my gloved hand toward others so they could kiss it. After the dance, we went back to a motel room we had rented for the night and continued drinking.

But somewhere along the way, my diva act began to run out of steam. By the time the morning light had arrived, I had changed into a pair of black cotton pants, a tank top, and my black cowboy boots. We decided to drive to the beach to take some "morning after" photos. When we arrived, I asked Bobby for his tux jacket and his bow tie. He handed them to me and I fastened the tie around my bare neck, letting it casually dangle a bit to the side.

As I stepped out onto the sand to have my picture taken, I reached into the tux jacket and pulled out one of Bobby's cigarettes. I lit up and took a deep drag from my Marlboro, squinting into the direction of the camera.

Today, when I arrived at the salon, I said, "I want to go even shorter today—like a square-cut flat top."

"Okay," he answered. "No problem."

Danielle massaged some shampoo into my hair that had the classy scent of a salon product. He towel-dried my hair, then led me to his station on the other side of the salon. When I sat down, facing the mirror, my reflection caught me by surprise. It looked different from the last time I had been there.

My immediate impression was that my face looked almost puffy. The parts that had been a bit angular before—like my cheekbones—were fuller now and made my face look bigger and rounder. The flesh under my chin—and along my jawline—also looked thicker and wider.

"Danielle, my face looks different!"

"Yes," he said, studying me. "Your whole face is changing shape."

I looked back in the mirror. "But why haven't I noticed this at home?" I asked. "Why am I noticing it now for the first time?"

"Because you look in the mirror all the time at home so you don't notice the little changes happening. But you haven't used this mirror for a while, so you remember what you looked like in it two months ago."

As he answered, it occurred to me that he was the perfect consultant in all of this; having traversed the spectrum of gender appearance, he studied his own features in great detail and tended to be quite vain.

I looked back at my face. It definitely was not the face of the man I pictured in my mind, but more that pudgy, androgynous look. But to see that I was starting to shift away from a feminine appearance was a tremendous boost to my spirits. After almost four months of testosterone shots, I now had clear proof that the hormones were working. My blind faith had just turned into a concrete hope.

I relaxed and said, "All right, let's go for that really short haircut."

When I was thirteen, I went to the hairdresser with a picture of Rod Stewart. I told him that I wanted my hair exactly like his, shaggy and rocker wild. When the haircut was completed, I was disappointed. The haircut looked more punk than rock and didn't work with my face the way I imagined it might. I mean, I just didn't look like Rod—or any of the guys I envied.

Within several months of my failed haircut, I grew my hair out and had it permed. I got many compliments from the girls in my class as they enviously asked me how I had grown it out so fast. A few years later, when "glam rock" became popular, I saw all the hard-core guys on MTV with long hair like mine. I immediately went out and bought the same long, funky-looking coats they had in their videos and wore them over my jeans and black cowboy boots.

Danielle pulled out a set of clippers and started to sheer the hair on the sides of my head. As I watched the tufts of hair fall away, I kept looking at my face. When the hair along my temples got so short you could almost see my scalp underneath, my face took on a less round and puffy look and started to become square. When Danielle was done with the sides, he pulled out a pair of funky-looking texturizing scissors. One side of the scissors had a normal cutting blade while the other looked more like a comb. He started to cut into the thickest part of my hair, slicing away chunk after chunk. Slowly, the top of my head changed from a thick, wavy puff of hair, to a square, cropped style with distinct short rows. By the time he put down the scissors and pulled the towel away from my shoulders, I was very pleased.

Afterward, I crossed the street toward an open-air mall. It was a beautiful, sunny day, and the breeze from the nearby ocean made the temperature pleasant. I was wearing the same form-fitting sweater from the night I heard my first "sir" in the video store, and that, in conjunction with my new haircut, put an extra spring in my step.

When I reached the beginning of the small courtyard that ran between the shops, I hesitated, wondering where the nearest ATM might be. Just as I was about to blindly start my search, I heard someone ask, "Can I help you find something, sir?"

To my right stood an African-American woman in a security guard uniform.

"I'm looking for a bank machine."

She gave me detailed directions and I thanked her and started to walk away. As I headed down the courtyard, I once again felt like I was in the midst of an unfamiliar experience. Something about her extreme helpfulness had triggered it.

I was about halfway to the ATM, when a woman to my right with a clipboard in hand said, "Sir, can I ask you a few questions?"

"Not right now," I answered with a smile. As I continued on my way, I felt a warm substance fill my chest.

I found the ATM, retrieved my cash, and slowly headed back to my car. As I passed by the security guard who had helped me find the ATM, she said, "Hey, did you find it all right?" I said, "Yeah, thanks," and continued on my way.

As I drove home, my mind scrambled to make sense of a growing confusion. Why was the behavior of these women so foreign to me? I thought back to the phone call that morning and the recent exchanges with the security guard and the survey taker. The most obvious connection was that all the women viewed me as male. But that alone did not explain things. As a female, I had experienced many women who were very helpful and friendly, sometimes even bordering on flirtatious. And yet these particular women stood out. As I made my way home, I racked my brain for some clue to this mystery. I was almost halfway home when it finally hit me.

All of these woman were African-American. My surprise at their attention could only mean that I had not previously experienced that type of treatment from African-American women before. At least not those I didn't know fairly well. I was filled with confusion. The feminist training in me had always figured that if African-American women were part of two oppressed groups—both gender and race—they would be more likely to bond with white women than white men, having at least one thing in common with the former.

The next day at work, I sought out two colleagues, both African-American women. I told them of my experience and my subsequent reactions. They each had the same initial response, that it was probably just a coincidence. But later in the conversation, and despite the fact I was speaking to each of them separately, they both added this caveat in almost the same words: "I usually don't feel as if I have much in common with white women, but at least with white men, there's some flirtation."

————

IT WAS A THURSDAY EVENING AND I WAS AT HOME, WORK-
ing out my upper body. Twice a week I worked on my chest: one day at
the gym and the other at home. I started with three sets of twenty deep
push-ups, using the portable handles I had bought at a sports store. I positioned them at different angles, allowing the focus to shift from the inner
part of my chest to the outer chest and shoulders. Next came several sets
of chest presses with dumbbells. I lay on my back, legs in the air to get the
maximum stress on the chest.

I moved on to another set of push-ups, this time putting my feet up on
the second step of the ladder that led to my bedroom loft. By placing my
feet on the steps behind me, I could focus more on the lower chest, ultimately bringing out the underside of the pectoral muscle. The entire
workout lasted an hour and fifteen minutes.

And it was worth it. After a few months of religiously sticking to this
routine, my chest was slowly changing from that twelve-year-old-boy look
to one that had some mass and definition. But the most obvious change
in my physique so far was the appearance of my trapezoid muscles. When
I flexed them, it looked like there were these little triangular wings that
popped up on each side of my neck. I had never seen those muscles before, no matter how much I worked out.

But now I had a hormone that was part steroid coursing through my
body. And with it came several changes that were most noticeable at the
peak of my cycle. During the initial days after my injection, I had a huge
amount of energy with some intermittent aggression, which was best released by a vigorous workout or long run on the beach. I also found my
appetite was incredibly high at the peak, causing me to eat every few
hours. If I had dinner too early, I would end up feeling restless and unable
to sleep. More than once I found myself getting up in the middle of the
night to have a piece of steak or chicken to satisfy the craving in my stomach. Right after the meal, my whole system would calm down and I'd be
able to fall asleep. I had the sense that my body was turning into an efficient fuel-burning machine.

After I finished my chest workout, I took a shower, put on some old jeans and a T-shirt, and headed to my nearby video store.

I entered the Blockbuster store with the fond memory of that first "sir" still fresh in my mind. I leisurely sauntered the aisles, scanning through the titles of the latest releases. One movie with a bunch of high-school kids on the cover caught my attention. I grabbed it off the shelf and read the back. It was one of those typical coming-of-age/awkward teenage angst movies. And in the state I was in, it was perfect.

I grabbed the box with the videotape in it and took off toward the front of the store. When the customer directly in front of me finished his transaction and started for the exit, the woman behind the counter looked up at me.

"Ma'am, I can take you over here."

I looked to my left and then to my right. Maybe she was talking to someone else?

But there was no one else. She repeated "Ma'am" again, and I felt an overwhelming surge of rage followed by an immediate sense of inner contraction—like someone had stuck a pin in a balloon and my identity was nothing but the hot air inside. I went to the counter and wearily slapped my video down. I handed her my membership card, and then waited out the next few excruciating moments before I was finally able to get out of there.

As soon as I had made it safely home, I once again stood before the wall-length mirror in the back of my loft. As I studied my reflection and looked for the female she had seen, I felt my rage return. It surged up through my chest and into the top of my head until I found myself yelling.

"Fuck you, God, you motherfucking merciless prick," I cried. "How dare you give me a taste of freedom and then take it away. What kind of a cruel bastard are you?"

On and on I raged, but none of the words seemed to provide any release. They only made me madder. Finally, as I hit about the eighth "fuck you," I balled my hand into a fist and punched at my own reflection. The mirror made a crunching sound under my hand and a series of cracks fanned out toward the corners. As a sliver of glass started to shake loose from the mirror, I walked away.

I began pacing the floor, my mind trying frantically to reassert control. I wanted to erase what had just happened. I wanted to make sure it never happened again. And most of all, I didn't want to face the cold, hard, ugly truth: there was no immediate cure; I was at the mercy of time.

I marched back to the mirror, took another look, and then spat one more "fuck you" at my reflection. The image of my face was now splintered by the cracks in the glass.

I stomped into my bathroom, opened the drawer near the sink, and yanked out the eyeliner. As I pulled off the cap, I said, "See what you've brought me to? Fuck you."

I brought the black liner to my face and lightly colored in a small patch on my chin and above my lip—exactly where the little hairs of blond peach fuzz were peeking through the surface. It was the only way I could convince myself that I wasn't making myself up to "pass" as a guy. I was just darkening my own "beard." Yeah, right.

When I was done, it looked as if real stubble was emerging. I would have been pleased, but I was too angry about the artificial means it took to get there. I pulled open the drawer to my right and picked up the box containing the vial of testosterone. My next shot wasn't due for another two days, but so what? If my body was processing my dose faster than every two weeks, this would help. If not, a little extra in these early months wasn't going to kill me. Not as much as the waiting, anyway.

I pulled out a fresh syringe and tore open the seal around it. I put some alcohol on a cotton ball, wiped the rubber top of the vial, stuck the needle in, and pulled back the plunger, watching the golden, oily, liquid slowly make its way into the syringe. Pulling down my pants, I relaxed my right leg, then plunged the needle into my upper thigh. I watched the liquid slowly leave the cylinder of the syringe and enter my leg. When the syringe looked empty, I waited for an extra second before pulling it out. I wanted to make sure every last drop made it into the muscle.

I started to clear away the cotton balls and used syringe. When I looked up and saw my reflection, I felt a little less angry. I was still aware that my stubble was not entirely real, but the slight soreness in my right thigh let me know I had done something real to back it up.

When I emerged from the bathroom, the phone was ringing.

"Hey, it's me, Kanut," said the voice on the other end of the line.

Kanut was my brother. He had left a couple of messages a while back, but I hadn't gotten around to returning his calls.

"Hey," he said, "I just wanted to be sure that you know I will always love you as my sibling, and no matter what you do, I still want you in my life."

I probably should not have answered the phone, because in the mood that I was in, I was easily irritated. Something about "I still want you in my life" rubbed me the wrong way. It was as if he were saying, Hey, no matter how crazy your actions, I'm still gonna love you because I'm this generous, giving kind of guy. To be loved *despite* this fight for myself didn't feel that generous at all.

"I figured you'd be cool about it," I said, trying to be gracious. "I mean, given that you grew up with me and saw me as a kid, you're probably not that surprised."

He laughed and said, "Shit, if we went by childhood, then I'd be going the other way."

When I was five, my parents gave me a doll for Christmas. When I unwrapped the package and saw what it was, I threw it down in disgust. My brother, who was nine, picked it up and took it to his room.

"That's more about gender behavior, which doesn't always correlate with sex," I said. "I mean, I'm sure everyone has at some point felt oppressed by their gender role, but not everyone has felt imprisoned by their body, you know?"

"Well, I haven't felt oppressed at all. But, you know, have you thought about the fact that being a man is not all it's cracked up to be. I mean, you have to defend your turf all the time, and you're not allowed to be that sensitive."

"It sounds like you're saying that your own gender role is sometimes oppressive."

"Well, yeah," he admitted, "but I don't let it define who I am."

I said, "Well, that's good." I suddenly felt very tired. "Listen, I'm going to go."

We said good-bye and I hung up the phone. I turned off the ringer and walked away.

When I was about seven years old, I was walking home from school alone when I ran into my neighbor, a guy who was several years older than I. As we crossed an open field that led toward our houses, he started to tease me, calling me names and laughing at me. As he continued to taunt me, I got madder and madder. Finally, in a fit of rage, I reached down and grabbed the biggest rock I could find. It took two hands to pick it up and I hurled it at him with all my might. But the rock missed him completely. And he laughed even louder. When I came home, I told my brother what had happened. He went over to my neighbor and rang his doorbell. When the guy opened up the door, my brother punched him in the face.

Ten

APRIL 1998

I am at a picnic, sitting at a table across from two women. The guy next to me takes off his shirt and I become excited as I realize that I can do the same. Suddenly, I notice that I still have some bandages on and, trying not to panic, I surreptitiously start removing them before anyone notices. . . .

I was back on the mattress in the corner of my spiritual teacher's office, pushing out breaths. As soon as I exhaled the last of my air, I heard my teacher saying: "Okay, now again—another breath."

I sucked air deep within my belly, filled my chest, and then forcefully exhaled, pushing my belly out as instructed. I had barely let out the last of my breath when the order struck my ears again: "Okay, another breath."

With each cycle, it seemed I was going faster and faster. My face got flushed and I felt surges of energy coursing through my body. I kept going, sucking in faster and pushing out harder. In and out. In and out.

"Now . . . again," came the order.

The flush from my face started to rise upward until the top of my head felt hot. More and more energy surged through me with no place to get out. I started to feel angry and frustrated. Her orders were pissing me off and I didn't want to go on.

She wouldn't let up. "Okay, keep going . . . take another breath . . . push out that belly . . . harder. Now . . . again."

"AAARGH," I yelled as my face turned flaming hot. My whole body felt like a ball of frustration.

"Okay . . . now . . . STOP."

Finally. I lay back, my entire body tingling from head to toe.

"Now roll your eyes up and to your left."

I rolled my eyeballs up into my head and then down again. It made me feel disoriented and slightly dizzy.

"Now up and to your right."

I switched to the other direction. I felt even more disoriented.

"Now stop . . . and just relax."

I closed my eyes and lay spread-eagle on the mattress. My whole body was tingling, but the frustration had subsided. I was disoriented, unable to assert control. I felt weird—as if something had been shaken loose. Or apart. I lay still for what felt like a long time, not speaking. Just breathing. I kept my eyes closed, staring into the blackness. The space was vast. And quiet. A stillness.

I slowly felt myself let go and the stillness moved in even closer, surrounding me. I remember thinking, how weird. How can stillness *move* in? But it did. It was a pure dense blackness that was so stark it seemed cold—like black ice.

After a while, I started to feel like I was wet or made of a watery substance. It wasn't as if I could actually feel myself dripping water or anything that concrete, but it wasn't just a daydream, either. It was more experiential. There were boundaries around the substance, which looked like a tunnel, and I began describing it to my teacher.

"What is the tunnel made of?" she asked. "Can you describe it?"

I focused on the tunnel. As I did, it changed into a shell that held me inside. It felt like whatever the shell was made of, it was impenetrable to me. I started describing the shell, but before I could finish my description, things had changed again. Within that watery substance emerged an image. It was very tiny, curled up in a position like the images on a sonogram. The fetus was sucking its thumb.

And in between its legs was a tiny penis.

I don't know if I could ever quite describe that experience accurately. It wasn't the kind of experience I had seen in movies, where the person is actually transported in time or space and becomes that image. I never totally lost awareness of my current reality. And yet it was not just a mental picture. It came from a place deep within me and then moved into my vision—as if it had found me, rather than my mind conjuring up the image. And there was a sense of familiarity around it—the sense of having been there before.

WHEN I GOT HOME, I CHECKED MY MESSAGES. THERE WAS one from my mother.

"Dhillon, it's me, Mommy. I was just going through some old letters and poems that you wrote me when you were little and in rereading them I noticed that they were written with the fierce love of a boy, not a girl! I should send some of them to you. Anyway, I just wanted to tell you that. If you want to call me, I'll be up until about midnight, my time. Bye-bye, darling."

I looked at the clock; it was two-thirty. With the nine-hour time difference to Germany, I still had half an hour before she went to bed. I picked up the phone and dialed her number.

My mother picked up on the second ring, "Hallo, Khosla."

"Hey, it's me, Dhillon."

"Ah, hallo. You got my message?"

"Yes, I liked it."

"*Ja,* you should have seen these poems. So forceful in your declarations—like a strong fury. I don't know why I didn't notice before."

"Well, it seems that people in my life have noticed things they are now telling me." I started laughing and found myself becoming animated. "Like my friend Sue said I gave her the kind of crappy gifts that her boyfriends would give her."

My mother roared with laughter, "Oh, my God, that is so true. I remember so many times you gave me these gifts that were so garish, like you had no idea who I was. They really were the kind of gifts a clueless boy would pick out for a girl."

All of her comments spurred me into further disclosure. I added, "And then Sue mentioned my fashion sense as being a bit draglike."

My mother roared again, "Yes, I used to wonder what you were thinking with some of the outfits you put on."

We both laughed as we continued to reminisce. When we reached a pocket of silence, I shifted gears and asked her something that had been on my mind since I had received her letter.

"You know, given your strong feminism and your bonding with me as a daughter, I would have thought that you would have trouble with this decision. How come you've been okay with it all?"

"You know," she said, "I was having coffee with some women and they asked me if I was masculine or lesbian and passed this on to you, and I just laughed at them. I mean, I am one hundred percent woman, so why should I feel threatened? I don't give a crap if they talk behind my back."

I didn't quite see how that answered my question, so I pressed on, "But as a woman it doesn't bother you that I'm letting go of the female parts?"

"No. I am proud you are so brave and have the guts. Most people are too afraid. You will be a wonderful blend of both male and female. Everyone needs to balance the male and female inside themselves, and perhaps that will be your job here. To lead others into the next millennium."

"You know, I'm not sure that I am the perfect blend of male and female. If I were, I don't think I would be fighting so hard to get out of this body. I think there are people who are born more androgynous and then there are people who are more one extreme or the other—at least in terms of brain chemistry."

"Well, maybe you are right."

"I just don't want to get caught in another trap or identity that's not me, I've had enough of that."

My mother became quiet and I got the sense that she was afraid to say anything that would offend me. Feeling a bit guilty, I reached out to bridge the gap by sharing information even more intimate.

"You know, I was with my meditation teacher today and while I was doing these breathing exercises, I got a strong visual image of myself as a fetus in the womb. And I had this tiny penis."

And my mother said, "It reminds me of when handicapped people talk about how in their dreams their limbs are always normal and they are walking—you know, when we dream, we see ourselves as whole."

THE PACKAGE ARRIVED IN A SMALL, SQUARE BOX WRAPPED IN plain brown paper. Inside was my prosthetic phallus. I had ordered it right after attending my most recent FTM meeting.

The meeting was held at the home of one of the group members, and during the evening we watched videotapes of conferences where surgeons showed pictures of the latest genital surgeries. Jared and I arrived rather late, so we missed the first half of the videotape. However, from the pictures that I did see—and the discussion afterward—it seemed there were two major choices for lower surgery.

The first, a metoidioplasty, involved the use of one's own natural genital skin, transforming it into a very normal appearing set of testicles with a very small penis. The testicles were formed through the use of labial skin, which is stretched, moved lower, and filled with testicular implants. The penis is made from the testosterone-enhanced clitoris by releasing one of the ligaments behind it—the same thing they do in penis-enlargement surgeries—to bring it out more. The final look was scarless and natural, but the penis was at most one to three inches long and looked like it belonged to a little boy.

The other technique was called a phalloplasty. It involved the construction of a full-sized penis made from skin taken from the abdominal region, shaped into a phallus. The most expensive version, referred to as the radial forearm flap phalloplasty, involved the use of skin from the forearm, along with blood vessels and nerves that resulted in sensation throughout the penis. None of us could figure out if sensation just meant some mild, vague feeling through the skin or if it actually meant the potential for orgasm.

The pictures we saw ranged from older abdominal skin surgeries that looked like pasty white tubes of sausage, to more recent surgeries that actually looked pretty much like a real penis. But I had no idea how the phallus was connected to the body or what was done with the female genitalia.

One of the men at the meeting, an older man, had the simpler meta surgery done years before at a clinic formerly affiliated with the Stanford University Medical Center. The clinic, along with its primary surgeon Dr. Donald Laub Sr., was mentioned in The New Yorker. *Dr. Laub had invented the metoidioplasty, but also had done some phalloplasties. As the guy was talking, I took out a piece of paper and wrote down Dr. Laub's name and contact information. I folded the piece of paper into a small square and carefully tucked it into my wallet.*

Now, as I opened the little box, I was immediately confronted with the strong scent of cornstarch. Although the powder coated the clear plastic pouch that contained the prosthesis, I could still make out the outlines of a flesh-colored mold inside.

Before tearing the plastic open, I read the directions that had been placed on top of the pouch. It told me that the prosthesis was made of high-grade silicone that warmed with the temperature of one's body. The substance itself was tacky and had to be left out a few days to completely dry. I assumed that the cornstarch was there to make it less sticky in the bag.

I used a pair of scissors to cut open the pouch. But before I picked it up, I just looked at it. I saw the outline of two balls, fused together. In the middle of the balls was a penis shaped in a way that it folded over and hung flaccidly between the scrotum.

I took my finger and poked at the phallus mold. It felt soft and jellylike, yet it had a firm resistance underneath. I could already tell that it would feel completely real if grabbed through my briefs. At least from the outside, anyway.

I was nineteen when I first started making love to women. My first serious lover was a woman twice my age and she taught me the art of using my tongue and hands as tools of pleasure.

It wasn't until six years later that I even thought about using a dildo. It was in the middle of my relationship with Valerie. One night while making love, she made a reference to my "cock." Just hearing the word sent my libido into high gear. I kept coaxing more and more references out of her as she masturbated me into a roaring orgasm. When she later told me she had given simulated blow jobs to lovers while they strapped on a dildo, I was beside myself.

But my dream never became a reality. She broke off the relationship soon after, leaving me to wonder if I would ever find someone who would fulfill that fantasy. Although my heart was reeling from the breakup, my libido could not shake off the images she had awakened. When I brought up the topic of dildos with my lesbian friends, they teased me, saying, "What took you so long?"

They had drawers full of "toys"—as they called them—usually consisting of purple or black shaped models that looked more like little dolphin figurines than a real penis. When I asked why they would choose something that didn't look real, they told me that the point was to get away from the traditional patriarchal penis symbol. The occasional use of a colorful toy that could be tossed into a drawer was a sign of not being dependent on a penis.

I went alone to a sex shop in San Francisco. I still remember the array of choices propped on a shelf against the rear wall. Of about ten of them in different sizes and shapes, only two caught my full attention. They both were flesh colored and were in the shape of an authentic-looking penis. And they were both large and thick. I wrapped my hand around the one called "Rex," picked it up, and carried it to another area where harnesses were hanging from pegs on the wall.

I chose a harness made of leather with straps that wrapped around the waist and underneath each leg. At the intersection of the straps, in the crotch area, was a patch of leather with a cutout circle. It was designed so the entire shaft could fit through it, but the base would stay trapped behind the leather and not move when the straps were pulled tight.

When I got home, I immediately went into the bathroom, dropped my pants, and strapped on the harness with Rex pushed through the circle in the crotch. I pulled the straps very tight at each location, making the base of the penis fit firmly against my own crotch. But when I looked down, I wasn't that impressed with the visual image. The black straps surrounding the penis made it look like a cheap "S & M" getup. I was, however, pleased with the fact that it was held tightly in place so that

I could thrust my hips without Rex coming loose. I pushed the shaft toward my belly, pulled up my jeans, and walked out of the bathroom.

As I walked from the bathroom, I felt the stiff, firm, erect penis pressing against my abdomen. The bulge in my pants was substantial, and with every step I felt a growing sense of predatory power mixed with lust. It was an "I can conquer the world" feeling which, usually in my head, had moved right into my loins.

That night I had a date with a woman I had recently picked up at a bar. We had done some heavy make-out sessions, but we hadn't slept together. Yet.

I took a shower to get ready for the date, removing Rex before I stepped into the tub. As soon as I got out and had dried myself off, I put him right back on, this time adding some briefs over the harness and letting Rex poke through the fly. With the straps hidden from view and only the flesh-colored dick visible to my eyes, the sight was much more pleasing. I moved Rex down toward my thigh so that when I pulled up my jeans, the bulge was less obvious.

When I arrived at Ashley's place, she opened the door wearing a tight black cocktail dress that hugged her curves. Of all the women I had dated, she probably had the best body. It was straight out of the pages of a Sports Illustrated *swimsuit issue. That body, along with her long, curly, dark red hair and light blue eyes, made the whole effect pretty damn hot.*

When I kissed her, I pressed my body tightly against hers. She pulled back in surprise, looked down, and said, "Well, hello there."

The tone of her voice told me that she was intrigued, not offended. And I knew then and there that we would have sex that night.

We drove to a private club Ashley had heard about. It was run by a couple of women who cross-dressed as men, sometimes entering gay male clubs where they passed as young boys.

When I heard about this private underworld of cross-gender behavior, it didn't strike any chord with me. Nor did it that night. Although I entered the club with a fake dick strapped to my body underneath my Italian tux, the female host who greeted me in her own man's suit and male nickname did not strike me as familiar. I remember thinking she just looked like a lesbian wearing a man's suit. As we walked to our table, Ashley whispered that the host tried to pick her up once, but she didn't have that forceful male energy—as I did.

"That's because she's not really a guy," I answered.

And with that smug comment, I put some distance between the host and me—a distance no less great than the one between myself and my own reflection in the mirror.

We found a table off to the side, and as soon as Ashley and I settled in, I ordered a round of drinks. A band consisting of drag queens played jazz music and some people were slow dancing. I grabbed Ashley's hand, led her to the middle of the floor, turned around, and pulled her close. The song was a slow one, and she wrapped her arms around my neck as I held her waist. I continued to be highly aware of the bulge in my crotch and when it brushed against her a couple of times during our dance, I felt this surge of power.

It was a feeling I would have throughout the night, but in different flavors. When I was kissing Ashley or was sexually aroused, it was a predatory, lustful power. When I was ordering drinks or driving forcefully through the streets, it was more of a dominating power. The feelings were neither new nor created by this hard bulge in my crotch; they were just enhanced and accentuated by it.

Throughout the next few hours we drank and made out, stopping only occasionally to dance or make small talk. At one point Ashley stopped to put on a fresh coat of lipstick and I thought that it just didn't get any better. There is nothing sexier to me than the sight of a woman applying fresh lipstick after I have just kissed it all away. There is just something profoundly, intoxicatingly feminine about that gesture.

After I had erased the last remnants of the latest coat of red, I gave Ashley a purposeful look and said, "Let's get out of here."

On the way to her place, I leaned over and stroked Ashley's thigh, removing my hand just long enough to shift gears. We encountered a few red lights, and I took the opportunity to lean over and kiss her, my kisses becoming more furious as we got closer to her house.

We stepped inside the door, and the second she shut the door I was all over her. I walked her backward toward the sofa, continuing the kiss. When we reached the edge of the sofa, she sat down and I pressed myself on top of her, grinding Rex against her pelvis. I heard her moan and I ground in harder.

Suddenly, she sat up, pushed me back and after giving me a pointed look, started to unbuckle my pants. My pants were halfway down my legs when some part of them got caught on Rex or the harness. I reached down to help her pull them all the way down, when my thumb got jammed in there. I don't know exactly what happened. I just remember an excruciating pain shooting into my thumb. And even though the injury was serious enough to cause a strain that lasted for years, I didn't make a sound that night. There was no way I was going to interrupt what was about to happen.

When my pants made it off my body, she tossed them to the side. She then took Rex in her hand, and leaned down to put him into her mouth. As she wrapped her lips around Rex's head, she looked up at me with her clear, blue eyes.

But there was an aftertaste of pain. The more I watched her mouth, the more I wanted to feel it on my own flesh. This complex mixture of pleasure and pain stayed with me the rest of the evening. It followed me into Ashley's bedroom and hovered as I began a slow, rhythmic thrusting. Pleasure took over when I watched and heard Ashley respond beneath me, when she ran her nails down my back, and when I kissed her while knowing I was inside her.

But pain and frustration simmered just below the surface as I felt the buckles of my harness dig into my skin and the rubber base of Rex press hard against my pubic bone with each thrust, reminding me that it was not really me. It was only my imagination.

In the end, I took off Rex and his harness, dropping them onto the floor by the bed. I was sore and bruised and I wanted to release the orgasm that had been building throughout the entire evening. I lay back and let Ashley slide her mouth down my belly and to my crotch. But this time, I didn't look down. Instead, I closed my eyes and watched her tongue sliding slowly up the shaft of my erect penis. And in my mind, there was no harness.

Three years later, it was Ashley who gave me that *New Yorker* article on female-to-male transsexuals.

Eleven

MAY 1998

I am in Jamaica on vacation with some old college friends. As I talk to a few women I have just met, one of my former friends refers to me as "Asha" several times. The other women look confused, and I quickly say to the college friend, "Just because I used to do drag performances doesn't mean you can call me 'she.'" I then launch into a story about how sometimes I used to wear black cocktail dresses and long gloves and carry a silver purse. As I am telling this story, I realize that it is true—not just the details of what I used to wear but the fact that I had really been nothing more than a man in drag. . . .

Turn a little toward me . . . yeah, that's it."

I heard a click and then the sound of film being rewound for the next shot.

My friend Sandra put down her camera and said, "You know, I no longer see any traces of Asha in your face . . . the feminine features are gone."

"Really?"

Part of me found that hard to believe. There were still so many people who casually slipped into the "she" pronoun. If there wasn't any part of me that still appeared female, then why were they still referring to me as one? I couldn't help but think that something in my face triggered that pronoun.

And yet I couldn't entirely dismiss her point either. In the past few weeks, when I was in the company of complete strangers, I heard nothing but male references. From the guy behind the meat counter at the grocery store to the pizza delivery boy, it was only "Hey, buddy" or "What's up, guy?"

It was those words that gave me the confidence to go to the DMV and get my gender changed to male on my driver's license. When I stepped up to the counter and put my paperwork in front of the clerk, he looked up at me, studied me for a moment, and then said, "You know, you kind of look like Michael Douglas."

But it wasn't until a couple of weeks later that I had the most validating experience of all. And it happened in the most unexpected place you could imagine.

I STEPPED OFF THE ELEVATOR AND TURNED TO THE RIGHT, dressed in a suit and tie, carrying my briefcase. As I approached the doctor's office, I briefly glanced at my watch. I had to present my caseload to the judges that afternoon and I was hoping to get out of there relatively quickly.

When I reached the door, I paused for a moment, looking through the glass wall into the waiting room. On the glass itself, painted in stenciled letters, were the names of several doctors. His was the first one on the list: Dr. Edward Blumenstock, OB/GYN.

I had contacted his office because I wanted to start the process of a hysterectomy. I had been given his number from a nurse practitioner at my old doctor's office who told me Dr. Blumenstock had a stellar reputation as a surgeon. When I called Dr. Blumenstock's office to set up an appointment, the receptionist hesitated a bit upon hearing my voice.

"Can I ask, Is this a medical appointment?"

"Yes," I answered, "but it's a private matter."

After our exchange, I figured she just thought I was a woman with a very low voice. It wasn't how I wanted to be perceived, but it was the only way I could get in to see this doctor. And it was time to move on.

At the most recent FTM meeting, I heard one man say that after two years of taking testosterone, he took a break from his injections and got his period. As soon as I heard him say that, I thought there's no way I could deal with getting a period now. It had been traumatic enough when it happened a few weeks after my first shot of testosterone, while I was starting to build up my newly healed pecs. Now it was five months—and a whole bunch of "hey, man's" later. The psychological impact of a period now would be even more jarring.

I also found that one in four female-to-male transsexuals who take testosterone develop fibrous tumors or cysts. They generally aren't cancerous but can cause cramping and, sometimes, bleeding. The longer I waited, the greater chance I was taking that I would not only need a hysterectomy for physical reasons but that it would be a more complicated one.

As I heard all of this, I began to wonder why these people would keep their ovaries or uterus. I mean, unless you actually felt a connection to these organs, why would you risk your health? Here we were flooding our bodies with testosterone to the point where it was overriding our ovaries. How could that be healthy for them?

I OPENED THE DOOR AND WALKED TO THE RECEPTION DESK. I noticed the waiting room was even larger than it had appeared from my glimpse through the glass. The room was L-shaped and had an extra section that was not immediately visible from the front entrance. Because there were quite a few people within earshot, I lowered my voice.

"I'm here for my eleven-fifteen appointment with Dr. Blumenstock."

"Is he expecting you?" she asked.

"Yes, I have an appointment."

But instead of looking at her appointment book, she asked if I had a business card. I hesitated for a second, wondering if I should give her one of my business cards, not quite sure why she needed one. I couldn't figure out exactly what was going on. I thought the woman who made appointments understood this was a medical appointment so there shouldn't have been any confusion.

"Well, no," I finally said. "I'm just here for an appointment."

She told me to sit down and she would let the doctor know I was here. I walked to a seat and sat down, quickly scanning the room. No one seemed to be staring at me or wondering why I was here alone. I watched one couple in the corner. The woman was in the latter stages of pregnancy. She and her husband had brought their kids with them and were watching them play by the window.

I thought about all the times I had been in gynecological offices in the past. Whenever I had seen a guy in the waiting room, I'd felt a mixture of resentment and envy. I resented the men for being in a very personal female space when they didn't have to go through any of the poking and prodding. And I envied them for getting to be the doting husband. I had my own fantasies of putting my hand on my wife's belly or helping her out of her seat and into the exam room where I would hold her hand throughout the procedure.

But now, as I looked at this man, I felt different. There were no judgments or competitive thoughts running through my mind. I just felt relaxed and comfortable. Even the fact that I was becoming the outsider to these women relaxed me—as if what I had been feeling on the inside was now beginning to show on the outside. The man in me might not have belonged in this waiting room, but he was beginning to feel like he had a place in this world.

I started to fiddle with my tie as I contemplated whether I should pull out my notes and review my cases one more time. I reached for my briefcase and that's when it hit me. The receptionist had asked for a business card because she thought I was a medical representative who wanted to sell some new product to the doctor.

I figured I should try to clear this up. I just didn't know how to do it in a way that would not feel as if I were betraying myself. There was no way I was going to say, "I'm really a woman." And yet if I didn't say something, I might be stuck out here the rest of the day as they took all of the "real" patients ahead of me. I guess I'd been hoping that I could be

vague with the people at the front desk and save the specifics for the doctor himself.

I walked to the receptionist, leaned in, and quietly said, "I think there's
been a misunderstanding, I have an actual appointment with Dr. Blumenstock for a medical issue—it's confidential."

"I'm confused," said the woman. "I don't really understand."

"I spoke to Beth when I made the appointment." I sat back down and
waited while she found Beth.

I was becoming worried and thought I might have to spill out more information. I figured that because I made a medical appointment, they
would just assume that I was a woman who looked kind of masculine. I
mean it was barely three months earlier that I had heard my first "sir." It
never dawned on me that someone would see me as so definitely male that
they would completely reject the notion that I could be here as a real
patient—even after I had clearly made an appointment. But now that it had
happened, it felt so good and so right that I didn't want it to end.

A few minutes later, the receptionist leaned her head over the counter.

"Sir? Beth is on her way out to speak to you."

"Thanks," I said as I waited for the next scene to play itself out.

Although I was kind of nervous, I couldn't help but enjoy myself. Each
bit of confusion and each "sir" gave me more confidence in my male appearance. It was much better than a friend telling me that I looked male
or a person in a grocery store referring to me as "sir" after a brief glimpse.
Nothing says you are a man more clearly than women in a gynecology office asking, "What the hell are you doing here?"

After a couple of minutes, an attractive woman appeared around the
corner.

"Mr. Dhillon? I am so sorry. When we were talking on the telephone,
I made a regular appointment for you."

"It's okay. It really is a medical matter."

But my subtle attempts to clear up the situation fell on deaf ears. She
continued to apologize and then started to laugh.

"The other girls will never let me live this down." I heard a couple of
receptionists giggle in the background.

She then squeezed my elbow affectionately, leaned in close, and said, "Well, what the hell—while you're here, we may as well give you a pap smear." She threw her head back and roared with laughter.

And I couldn't help but laugh with her, for every word brought me pure joy. To have someone not only apologize for assuming I was female but to suggest it was the most absurd notion in the world was an incredible vindication. Whatever had been off-kilter was suddenly being set right. And like a love-starved puppy, I lapped it all up—her words, her flirtatious manner—all of it. I wanted to stay in this moment forever.

"I do really need to talk with the doctor about something," I said when things had finally quieted down.

"Sure. Just have a seat and someone will get you in a few minutes."

I went back to my chair and sat down. I was relieved that she'd let me go without pressing for more information. I figured that I had now gone from prospective salesman to some guy with a personal question regarding his relationship with his wife or girlfriend. Hopefully, the latter status would be enough for me to get the few yards down the hallway and into the doctor's office.

After several more minutes, another woman came around the corner and said, "Sir? Come this way, please."

I grabbed my briefcase and followed her past the receptionist's desk and down a small hallway. We stopped before the last door on the left and she knocked on it, popped her head in for a moment, then stepped back to let me in.

The doctor was standing behind a desk, and the first thing I noticed was that he was really tall. He shook my hand and beckoned me to sit down. I was relieved to hear the door shut behind me. Now that I was before the one person who needed to know my entire situation, I felt ready to be specific.

"I heard about you from Jackie Moore [a nurse practitioner I knew]. I'm a female-to-male transsexual and I wanted to talk with you about a hysterectomy."

"Excuse me, you're transitioning from which direction?"

"From female to male."

"Well, I've never met anyone who went that direction," he said. "But when I was a resident, we learned how to do pap smears on male-to-female transsexuals."

"Well, I've been on testosterone for six months, I've had chest surgery and before I move on, I'd like to have you do this particular surgery since it is your area of expertise. I know the removal of the ovaries is less expensive than a full hysterectomy, but from what I understand, if I kept the uterus, I'd actually have to go through pap smears to check for health issues?"

"Yes," he said. "That's true. But in your case we could probably do a full hysterectomy vaginally, which is far less expensive."

I asked him to explain the procedure and he told me that while most women with problems have it done through the abdomen, which is much more invasive and leaves a scar, there is a way to just make a couple of tiny incisions in the lower belly, cut the support structures, and pull out everything through the vagina. The procedure could be done at an outpatient surgery center.

I remembered a woman at work who once told me she had a hysterectomy with a simpler procedure and it messed up her ability to urinate normally. I mentioned that to Dr. Blumenstock, and he said if she had serious problems, like tumors or an enlarged uterus, it would be a bad idea to pull it through vaginally, but in my case, the tissue was probably not only healthy but the uterus would have shrunken from the testosterone.

I asked, "So you'd be willing to do the surgery on me?"

He responded, "Well, since I would be removing healthy tissue, I would need to check what kind of ethical guidelines I need to follow. Is there someone I can call and ask about that?"

I told him that I would get him the number of the therapist I had worked with for my other surgery, as she had information on the ethical guidelines.

He said, "Well, good. I'll check and we can go from there. By the way, is it all right if I inform my staff of your situation? If you come here for treatment, they will need to know so they can schedule you."

I said, "Well, I guess so."

"I'm sure they'll be professional about it," he said, catching my hesitation. "Since they don't know anything about this issue, there will probably be some snickering behind your back. But I imagine you're used to that."

I gave him a puzzled look and he added, "Well, maybe only if you tell people, since you look so male."

I wasn't too fond of the "snickering" comment, but I let it go. It wasn't malicious or patently offensive, just an assumption from someone who was facing a situation that was new to him.

There were gynecologists who worked with surgeons who did genital reconstruction for female-to-male transsexuals. But the way I looked at it, just because a gynecologist has worked with a number of transsexuals doesn't mean he is necessarily good at doing a hysterectomy. My only goal here was to find someone who was the best at a particular job. Now that I was more confident in my appearance, I would rather suffer through some awkward moments of social interaction than risk a hysterectomy with complications. The comments would fade over time, but my body would be around for the rest of my life.

Dr. Blumenstock had an excellent reputation. And now I was finding that because of his expertise, I was also about to save some money. The regular price for an abdominal hysterectomy was about fifteen thousand dollars and required a three-day hospital stay. The clinic in Palo Alto that performed genital reconstruction surgery on transsexuals did only abdominal hysterectomies.

I asked Dr. Blumenstock if he could give me an estimate of what the surgery would cost.

"There's my fee, and then there is a separate fee for the surgery center and the anesthesiologist," he said. "My fee is normally three thousand, but since insurance won't cover this, I'll lower it to eleven hundred."

Hearing him say that made it even easier to blow off his earlier comment. Here he was, faced with a stranger asking him to take a leap of faith and remove healthy tissue. Not only was he open to doing it, he was willing to cut his fee by more than half. All of that spoke volumes to me.

I stood up to leave, and he said, "Just a minute. I have to fill out a code sheet so the receptionists know how to bill you for this visit." He looked down at the sheet, moving his pen over the various choices. He seemed to be having trouble deciding which one to pick. When he finally stopped and circled one, he laughed, "Here we go. I circled contraceptive advice. How's that?"

I laughed with him and said it was fine. After all, the bill wasn't going to any insurer, just to me. I took the sheet of paper, and headed down the hall to pay my bill. As I wrote the check, the receptionist smiled warmly and asked if I got what I needed. I said I had. Then I thought back to Dr. Blumenstock's comments and found myself wondering: will these women treat me any differently once they know?

IT WAS EARLY SUNDAY EVENING AND I WAS PACKING MY briefcase and gym bag, preparing for the upcoming week. As I crammed the last bit of paper into the bag and zipped it closed, I felt a growing apprehension.

The next day, when I stepped back into the courthouse, I would once again be at the mercy of the perceptions of others—perceptions that were distorted by past history and prior knowledge. And no matter how much they cared for me or wanted to support me, they just could not see me as clearly as my local grocery store clerk. For what took my colleagues effort came naturally to the strangers who saw me only now, and not then.

The more I anticipated the next day, the more restless I became. I walked into the kitchen and started to busy myself with the task of preparing dinner. I was about to pour a bag of dry noodles into a boiling pot of water, when I stopped. What am I doing, I thought? Here I am about to have another dinner alone at my place, when there is a whole world of people out there who have no connection to my past. I don't have to hide from them. I put down the pasta, turned off the burner, grabbed my car keys off the counter, and walked out into the evening air. I had no specific destination in mind. It didn't matter what direction I took as long as I ended up in unfamiliar territory.

I caught up with the highway and found myself heading toward the Bay

Bridge. But when I crossed into San Francisco, I ignored the exits that led into the city and instead followed the signs that headed south. After a short while, I joined up with Highway 1. It was the same highway I had taken all the way to Los Angeles the previous year. It was dark, but at points where the highway or neighboring towns were well illuminated, I caught glimpses of the ocean to my right.

The signs to Santa Cruz caught my eye. I had been there a few times before and had always found it to be charming and quaint. It reminded me of Boulder, Colorado, where I had gone to undergraduate school. And I wasn't the only one. I had once stopped in a tourist shop in Santa Cruz, only to find a poster with a picture of Boulder superimposed against the Santa Cruz coastline.

It was after nine when I arrived in Santa Cruz. I drove down the main strip toward the wharf, passing motels and gas stations. When I reached the pier lined with seafood restaurants, I kept on going. I was looking for something less touristy and crowded.

By this time it was close to nine-thirty, so I doubled back and returned to a larger street that was close to the highway. After passing several brightly lit diners, I noticed a brick building set back from the street. There was an Italian name on the awning across the entrance, and I saw lights from the windows peeking out above the basement floor.

I opened the front door and found myself facing a staircase that led down. I started down the steps and when I reached the bottom, I saw several tables covered in red-and-white-checked tablecloths. I stood at the entrance for a few moments and looked around. There were a few families scattered throughout. To my left was the entrance to another section with high-backed booths and dimmer lighting.

"Can I help you, sir?"

I said I'd like a table for dinner. As the hostess walked toward the square tables to my right, I stopped and asked if it was all right to take one of the booths in the other section. I followed her and time seemed to slow down. My movements felt very deliberate and I found myself taking in more of my environment than usual.

The hostess stopped in front of the first booth, put down a menu in front of one of the place settings, and said, "Enjoy your meal."

I began to read through the choices, pausing to enjoy each entry as though it were a character description in a short story. I was about halfway through when a waitress walked up to my table.

"Good evening, sir. Can I start you off with something to drink?"

I noticed her long brown hair and warm smile.

"Yes, I'll have a glass of your house red wine."

As I watched her walk away, I was once again aware of a sense of slowness. And there seemed to be a connection between that slowness and my own relaxation. The more I settled into my surroundings, the more it seemed that time was expanding to accommodate me.

I reached into my coat pocket and pulled out a blank notepad and a pen. Whenever I went to a restaurant alone, I either brought a book to read or an empty notebook for songwriting. I tapped the pen against the blank paper.

The waitress returned with my wine and proceeded to take my order. As I gave it to her, I noticed her name tag: Adrianna. After she was gone, I lifted my pen and wrote "Adrianna" on the top sheet of my notepad. I reached over, took a sip of my wine, and returned to my paper. My pen was poised, ready for the next word. But nothing else came. My mind was as empty and clear as the page had been before she arrived. And it was an unfamiliar experience.

I was used to a mind constantly filled with running thoughts and ideas and strategies. I was used to a mind filled with creative images and escapist fantasies. But I was not used to this thick stillness that enveloped me. It almost felt as if I was succumbing to the influence of some sort of drug. The texture of the air actually felt different—velvety and golden, like molasses. I remember later thinking that this is what people must mean when they say, "Time stood still," because in that moment, the world seemed to go from spinning to stillness. And I was profoundly aware of my own existence.

As I drove home later that evening, I realized for the first time why people in my situation move to a new town. Until then, I had always thought that people who disappeared from their old life were cowards. Why, I thought, would they leave behind people who love them? Why would they reject their past? Isn't our past part of who we are? Isn't this whole journey about integration, not rejection?

But that night, as I left the warmth of the restaurant and drove into the thin, night air, bracing myself for the coming days, my old judgments once again gave way to a deeper understanding.

Twelve

JUNE 1998

I am walking out my front door to my car. As I get closer, I notice that the window is smashed and realize someone has broken in. I look inside and see that all of the contents are missing, and I get angry and upset as I stand there, assessing the damage, then pull out my wallet and head to the house to make some phone calls. When I look down at my license, which has my new gender on it, I feel an immediate sense of relief. And I say to myself, "At least I still have this. . . ."

It was ironic, really. Six months into my transition—as I was getting consistently recognized as male in the outside world—I received my first crank phone call at work.

It was a Monday morning when I walked into my office to find the message symbol lit up on my phone. I dialed the message center and when I pressed "one" to retrieve my new message, I heard an unfamiliar male voice: "Nice message, you fucking queer."

The words hit me quick, like a fist—it was a pure sucker punch. And that's what pissed me off the most. Here was this guy questioning my masculinity when he was the biggest coward on earth. Who else would insult me through a voice mail left on my machine at the office—over the weekend—while I was away? Can it get any weaker than that?

I gripped the receiver tightly in my hand, clenched my jaw, and punched the keypad to replay the message, trying to identify the voice. I must have played that damn message at least ten times. I was determined to nail the guy. In retrospect it probably wasn't the smartest move—to hammer myself repeatedly with his words. By the time I finally erased the message and hung up the phone, there was a cacophony of "fucking queers" in my head. I spent the rest of the morning knocking them out with images of smashing his face against the concrete wall.

But once the anger finally subsided, I was surprised to find myself feeling pretty much the way I had before the call. There were no real lingering effects. When I thought about it later that night, I realized that it all came down to his choice of words.

His attack had been mean. But it had also been imprecise. He could have attacked my male identity much more savagely and directly, by saying something like, "You're never gonna be a guy," or "You need a real dick? I got one right here, bitch."

Had he said any of those words, he would have hit the bull's-eye. He would have immediately exposed the weakness in my foundation: that it was still incomplete. But instead he chose an expression that men generally level at other men—granted gay or effeminate men. But men. And that made all the difference.

IT WAS BARELY A WEEK LATER, WHEN I RECEIVED MY SECOND blow. This was not turning out to be a good month.

I was on the telephone with a representative from my mortgage company, looking into rates for refinancing my loft. Throughout the conversation I was feeling comfortable and relaxed; he was, after all, a stranger, and I was several months into hearing "sir" over the phone.

At the end of our discussion, I thanked him for his help. And he responded, "You're welcome, ma'am."

My first reaction was one of denial. I tried to explain it away, thinking maybe he really said, "You're welcome, man." But in the end, even I couldn't buy that. The entire tone of the conversation had been too formal for that type of "hey, man" tagline.

But I wasn't ready to give up. My next strategy was to look for alternative explanations: Maybe he had the paperwork from my original mortgage and had seen the "Ms." on it. Maybe we just had a bad phone connection. There was only one way to find out.

I picked up the phone and dialed the number to my bank. As I was waiting for a customer service representative, I came up with a couple of questions to ask about my account. I pulled out my checkbook and opened it to the most recent transactions.

This time I got a woman on the phone. I told her my name and then proceeded to ask her whether certain checks had cleared my account. She answered all of my questions, but didn't make a single reference to my gender either way. When she asked if there was anything else she could help me with, I couldn't think of another question.

"No thanks, that'll do it," I answered.

"You're welcome . . ." And then I could swear she added, "Ms. Khosla."

I fought it again. Maybe I didn't hear that right. She said it pretty quickly. Maybe she said "Mr." but it sounded like "Ms." to me because I was still paranoid from the first call. On and on my mind raced, trying hard to come up with something, trying hard to reshape each experience—anything to avoid facing the most painful explanation of all: that my voice did not sound male.

But much as I tried, I could feel myself losing the battle as the evening wore on. My mood became darker and there was an underlying frustration setting in. I felt as if something had been taken from me. And I wanted it back.

Around one in the morning I was still awake, watching television. An infomercial came on. Partway through the advertisement, a telephone number was flashed to call for a free video and brochure about the product. When I saw the number, I thought, Here's my chance to get back that "sir" before the day is over. It's not too late. I can still turn this around. I felt like a desperate gambler, determined to break even with that one last bet.

I picked up the phone and dialed. When the operator answered, I told her I was interested in having a brochure sent to me.

"Okay, may I have your address?"

As I started to give her my address, I was aware of a sense of distrust and distance.

When I finished, she said, "Is there a daytime number where we can reach you?"

"No," I snapped, "I don't give out my telephone number." I was hard and defensive.

"Okay," she answered. "We'll send this out to you."

I slammed down the phone so hard, I thought it would break. I grabbed the glass next to me and threw it across the room, yelling "Fuck!" The glass bounced against the wall but didn't break. Somehow that made me even madder. Not only did I not get that "sir" back, I couldn't even break a glass when I was pissed.

And so, once again, my rage turned to God. I couldn't help it. If I didn't have control over my life, someone else did. And they were fucking with me—giving with one hand and taking away with the other. It was a cruel mind fuck, and I didn't like being a powerless pawn.

As I got into bed that night, I found myself thinking, Maybe it's because I picked up my guitar and sang last night. I must have knocked my voice up a notch. That's it. I'm not singing anymore.

LATER THAT MONTH, ON A SUNDAY AFTERNOON, I FOUND myself crossing the Bay Bridge on my way to an FTM meeting in the city. My spirits were muted from the events earlier in the month, but my hopes were high. I thought an afternoon in the company of others who were fighting the same battles would leave me feeling reinvigorated.

The room was close to full when I arrived, and a few guys were bringing in additional chairs from neighboring rooms. I grabbed one of them and put it down next to a man who looked vaguely familiar. I looked around and recognized a few more faces from past meetings. Some looked more male, having several more months of testosterone under their belt. But I couldn't help noticing how many men appeared overweight. Not only had many retained the wide hips and large butts from their female era, but some of them had now added a significant male gut to top it all off.

As I was feeling guilty for being judgmental and reprimanding myself with a "Jesus, can't you focus on something other than looks," the moderator started the meeting.

"Due to a number of requests, we're going to open this meeting with a discussion around testosterone and weight gain."

A guy a few seats over spoke first: "Since I started testosterone, I've gained thirty pounds and I just don't know what to do about it."

Someone asked him if he went to the gym.

"Well, not that often," he said. "I'm just not comfortable enough with my body to deal with the locker room stuff. I mean, I'm still binding my breasts."

As the man continued talking about the depression surrounding his weight gain, I remembered how concerned I had been when I started taking testosterone. Everything I read seemed to contain some comment about how people gained a lot of weight when they first started the injections. But now, after six months of gaining muscle, not fat, I began to wonder if it was all just a matter of weight training.

Testosterone is classified as an anabolic steroid; some genetic men inject it for bodybuilding. So my thought was, if you work out, the testosterone gets used up and turns the body into muscle, but if you don't work out, it turns into fat. I mean, isn't that exactly what happens to genetic guys who are all beefy and muscular? When they stop working out as they get older, they often end up with breasts and potbellies. There had to be a connection.

A short while later, a guy at the other end of the room started talking.

"When I first started testosterone, I was all excited about the changes and I started working out for the first time in my life," he said. "I lost weight and started to feel good about my body. But now it's been over four years and I still haven't had my lower surgery. And depression and anger over that have put me back to my old eating habits and I've just stopped working out."

He went on to explain that he was a city employee and had been waiting for the city to change its policy on health coverage for transsexual surgeries so that he could get his operation paid for.

"You know," another man said, "a lot of us come into this with bad eating habits because we never connected to our bodies, but then we continue the bad habits while taking testosterone."

Several others nodded in agreement, and another guy started talking about his lifelong battle with bulimia and anorexia. As I listened, I felt the mood in the room get heavier and heavier. All around me it seemed people were trapped in some state of despair or frustration. And as they continued to speak, I found myself beginning to wonder: where were all the men who had gone through lower surgery? I couldn't help but think that the fact that they were not here was no coincidence. I couldn't help but think they had moved on; they were living ordinary, normal lives. I didn't know for sure, but in looking at these guys around me, especially the ones who had been here for years, I started to become anxious.

I started to see my own writing on the wall.

When I got home from the meeting, I put on my jogging shoes and drove to the beach. As I sprinted down the sidewalk, my feet pounding the pavement, I knew I was not just running to stay in shape; I was running to get away from something.

I OPENED THE DOORS TO THE TEMPLE AND STEPPED INSIDE to take my shoes off before the morning meditation. It was the beginning of another weekend workshop at my spiritual school.

As I stood in the alcove and began untying the laces to my boots, the area quickly became congested. A group of people had arrived all at the same time, and the task of removing our shoes and placing them on the nearby shelves was creating a bottleneck. Everyone seemed to take it in good stride, chatting with one another and embracing in the doorway.

Several people sent smiles my way or touched my shoulder as they passed, and I acknowledged their greetings but stayed close to myself. The more I felt people milling around me, the more nervous I became. I had a real sense of unease.

I stacked my boots on the nearest available shelf space and darted to a seat in the rear pew by the stained-glass window. I closed my eyes and waited for the meditation period to begin.

When the gentle sound of the chime reached my ears, I took a couple of deep breaths and exhaled. I wanted to let go, to sink into a sense of relaxation. I concentrated on putting my attention deep in the center of my belly. But everywhere I turned there was an underlying tension. I was anticipating something—something to come. And it wouldn't let me go.

When the chime rang again, signaling that it was time to return, my eyes popped right open, letting me know I had never left in the first place. I reached to the floor, picked up my notepad, and waited for the lecture to begin.

Today's topic was "the beast"—that part of ourselves that is so disappointed in infancy at not getting loved in the perfect way that it grows to reject all love and goodness in an attempt to avoid being betrayed once again. I felt myself being drawn into the lecture. I couldn't help but review some of my past relationships and the way in which, as soon as I realized people's love or caring was actually motivated by their own needs or wants, I rejected the whole package.

When we later split into groups of three for a monologue exercise, I found myself eagerly participating. I spent my fifteen minutes delving into my past, comparing my love relationships to the relationship with my mother, and making the connection between love and the need to be needed.

The other two members of my group, a gay man and woman, did the same. And during the five-minute feedback session that followed each monologue, we pulled on threads from one another's discussions, noting patterns and acknowledging important insights. By the time the hour came to a close, I started to feel like a normal member of the group again, bonded in our common goal of taking ourselves apart and examining the pieces. I felt my morning reticence and isolation slipping away.

The teacher signaled it was time to return to the large group for comments and questions. The gay man stood up, turned to the woman and to me, and said, "Well, thank you, ladies."

When he saw the expression on my face, he said, "Oops." Then he casually shrugged his shoulders and walked away.

Had he looked even slightly remorseful, I might have stayed where I was. But he didn't. So I didn't. I got up and followed him to the kitchen. He was getting a glass of water when I walked up and said, "Is there some reason you referred to me as 'lady'?"

"No, just habit," he said. He kept his eyes averted but added, "I hang out more with women, and it's also a term I use with my friends."

I knew what he was talking about. In the gay community, a lot of gay men refer to one another as "girl" and use the pronoun "she" toward other gay men. But I was not one of them. And more important, I had spent a lifetime hearing the wrong pronoun. Without that history, I might have been able to shrug off his reference as nothing more than a slight annoyance.

But right now it was my life we were talking about. And he knew that as surely as I knew that the word "fag" would hurt him. So for him to walk away, without showing one single ounce of compassion—or even a willingness to look me in the eye—made me want to take him out back and beat the shit out of him. I wanted to hurt him like he had hurt me.

But we were not inside a bar. We were inside a temple—a temple filled with spiritual teachers who had been telling me that these types of situations were all just fodder for growth, that they represented the "edge" of my work.

I was trying hard to believe them. I really wanted to be here. The material was so rich and so true and had already awakened so much in me. How could I let a few words get in the way of that?

And so, in a final effort to clear the air and let go of my resentment, I said, "I know that a lot of female references are used by some men in your community, but I don't have that luxury. For me, it really brings up a lot of stuff, so it feels like a deep attack."

He continued to ignore me, but as I said the words, I felt a small release—just saying it got it off my chest. When I was done, I walked away with the hope that the moment had passed, that I could now move on and get back to my "higher" spiritual work.

I went back to my pew and sat down. An assistant started to roam around the room with a microphone, and various people began to share what they had learned or observed during the exercise.

One woman talked excitedly about her relationship with her father and the way there was an aspect of that dynamic she had never seen until now. One guy cried as he told the group he kept a distance because he was afraid to open up to any warmth or let in any love, and he had never really understood until now that this was an actual choice he had made very early on in life.

All around me people shared their experiences. And with every passing moment, I felt myself getting angrier and angrier. The more they spoke, the more judgmental and hateful I became. But it wasn't until the woman next to me took the microphone that the dam really burst.

She started telling us how safe she felt in this room, how it was so different from her own family. She was held and supported here in all of her vulnerability.

The defiant, jealous little boy in me took over and I found myself thinking, "Fuck you. You get to come here and relax and open up while I end up tenser and more hurt than when I arrived."

It was true. Every single time I did an exercise someone used the wrong pronoun. And every single time, I was the only one to correct them. No one else stood up for me.

I could feel my whole body getting hotter and hotter; there was no turning back now. When the woman next to me was done, I grabbed the microphone. I felt like a prosecutor about to hand down an indictment.

I started by describing my dinner in Santa Cruz and how incredibly present and relaxed I had felt there, knowing that I didn't have to brace myself for any pronoun attacks. I then said how hard I struggled to come in here, to let down my guard, open myself up, and be vulnerable so that I can continue with my work. But each time that inevitable "she" comes my way, I am left stunned and bruised. And now that I know how it feels to be in a place where I hear the right pronouns and references, returning to a place like this every month had become more and more difficult.

Throughout my statement, there was an underlying self-righteousness; I was wagging my finger at them all, saying, See what you are doing to me. But below that was a naive kid who was still hoping, thinking, If I can just make them see—really see—how much it hurts, they will stop.

"You really need to look at why this is so unbearable," the teacher interrupted, "because people aren't really doing anything to you."

"Would you say that to someone who was constantly being called 'faggot' in here?" I asked.

"But this is not intentional. People aren't trying to hurt you."

"Even if people trip over you, it can leave a wound," I said. "And if they do it over and over again, you start to become suspicious, whether the trip was intentional or not."

And that was the part that I felt the teachers were missing. This whole "people don't mean it" argument didn't fly. Why were there some people who always used male pronouns, while others never used them once? Why were there some people who apologized profusely when they slipped up, while others made it clear that they didn't give a crap? The only logical explanation was that some people had a serious resistance to accepting the transition, while others did not. And in a place that was all about seeking truth and exposing the shadows, I resented being dismissed with superficial platitudes, left alone to bear all the responsibility.

As soon as they announced a break for lunch, I grabbed my running shoes and headed out the door. As I sprinted through the streets, passing rows of small houses, I felt a sense of fierce determination. It was almost a sense of duty, like I was making a pact of some sort. A promise.

THAT EVENING I WENT TO ASHLEY'S HOUSE FOR DINNER. SHE and her new girlfriend had moved into my area and were living just a few miles from me. When I arrived, Ashley was in the middle of making a pumpkin-squash soup. I walked into the kitchen and sat down at the table in the corner.

I opened the wine I had brought and poured us each a glass. As we began talking, I felt warmth permeating the air and enveloping me in its embrace. The smells of the soup, the familiar feeling of sitting near Ashley while she prepared a meal, were a part of that warmth. But it was also more than that. It was the sense that what I had been wanting at the spiritual school was right here. The safety that people spoke of in that temple was inside this kitchen.

I felt my whole body slowly exhale as I said to Ashley, "Hey, how come you don't ever slip up on the pronouns? You have tons of memories and associations with me from the past, but you never use the female pronoun."

"Well," she said, "I just made the decision to refer to you as 'he' with everyone—even when I talk about us dating in the past. It kind of confuses people who know me as a lesbian, but I figure, Let them think what they want."

By the time we sat down to dinner, Ashley's girlfriend had arrived. We spent the evening exchanging stories and savoring Ashley's cooking, and I could feel the tension continue to wind its way out of my body.

Every "he" that casually floated through the air found its way to my wounds, becoming a soothing, healing salve. With each passing hour, my shoulders relaxed a little more, and my tight guard loosened its grip. It was as if some part of my brain was sending back a message saying, "It's okay. It's over. You're safe now."

LATER THAT NIGHT, AS I WAS GETTING READY FOR BED, I stripped down to just my briefs. With my prosthetic phallus firmly in place, I climbed under the covers. I lay on my back and looked up at the fluorescent stars pasted on my bedroom ceiling. My hand was resting on my naked chest and the bulge in my crotch felt comforting. I reached up and ran my hand down my chest and over the rough ridges of my scars. As I continued looking up at the stars and stroking my chest, I began to feel as if I were soothing a little boy, resting beneath my protective wing.

I heard myself whisper, "I'm sorry. I'm so sorry."

As I continued to repeat these words, tears streamed down my face, spilling out onto the sheets.

The tears I cried that night came from a well so deep and so vast that its very discovery brought forth shades of sadness and grief. For in finding my own compassion, I had to face the realization that I had spent so much of my life being unloving and unkind to myself in a most profound and fundamental way.

Every time I listened to those outside voices that said I should let this go; I should accept what I've been given, that this does not matter, I was turning away from that sweet, precious boy.

Every time I tried to tell myself it's just a pronoun—don't get so upset; don't be so angry—I was telling that little boy to shut up, that he did not matter. Even something as subtle as trying to take my mind off things or cheer myself up had been, in actuality, a turning away.

Because in each and every moment of frustration, of pain, of sadness, of rage, and of hurt, that little boy had been trying to reach me.

Thirteen

JULY 1998

> I am walking down the street when I notice a group of people crowded around something. I push my way forward to see what is going on and see that in the middle of the circle two men are on top of a woman. I rush up and pull them off.
>
> All of a sudden, I realize that I might not know the whole story. I lean in and ask, "Is this what you want? Is it your will to be with them?" She says yes. I stand up, apologize to the other two guys, and leave.

The criminal case we were discussing at our office staff meeting was the type of case that always divided the sexes right down the middle: an incident involving rape allegations. We were engaged in our regular task of going over the latest published cases to come down from our court when we encountered one involving a defendant who had been convicted of raping a child. He had challenged his conviction on the grounds that certain hearsay statements made by the victim should not have been let into his trial.

The women in the meeting were saying, "Of course they should come in; they are relevant to the issue of guilt," and "How can this court overturn a conviction when twelve jurors found the evidence sufficient beyond a reasonable doubt?"

The men, on the other hand, were making statements more along the lines of, "Hearsay statements are not the same as hard evidence" and "Sexual crimes usually come down to one person's word against another, and statements from a child are subject to a great deal of manipulation."

Until this point I had always understood the makeup of the female perspective in this debate. Having been an insider in the female culture, I had been entrusted with some of the most personal and painful experiences told to me by women in every conceivable setting—on my night shift at the detox center where I worked as counselor during college, at a party during a drunken, vulnerable moment in the bathroom, or in my bed after lovemaking. And through these experiences, I came to understand that women not only have to face the fear of becoming a potential victim, they then have to face the fear of not being believed.

But I had never understood where the men were coming from. Instead I just assumed I knew. I assumed that any man who expressed his caution or disbelief over a rape case was a man who hated women, or a man who wanted a world where it was easier to get away with rape.

But today I found myself feeling differently. Not toward the issue itself, but toward the men who were sharing their views. The same judgment or anger was not there. And I was trying to figure out why.

As the debate intensified, I continued to hang back and watch everyone. And after observing a few more conspiratorial looks and frustrated glances, I got it. I got what was softening my reaction toward the men. It was my own shifting boundaries.

Recently I had begun to notice a totally different reaction from women when I was walking down the street—especially at night or in an isolated area. Whereas they used to smile at me before in a completely open and relaxed manner, there was now a sense of guardedness. Their eye contact was limited and their entire body movements were tighter—almost as if they were pulling themselves inward and away from me. Almost as if I were a potential perpetrator.

A few of those experiences and I was already feeling a sense of separation. How would I feel after thousands of moments like that? And what about social situations where the boundaries were even less clear? Would I have to change my old aggressive behavior or risk an accusation?

THAT MEETING WAS THE BEGINNING OF MY UNDERSTANDING that the debate among the sexes was not one of good versus evil or right versus wrong, as I had always assumed. Instead, it was simply a reflection of the fact that we all see through the lens of our previously accumulated experiences. And while women may live with the fear of becoming a potential victim, men live with the fear of being falsely accused of crossing that line.

So far, I had never had to face the fear that I would be seen as a predator or rapist. I had been sexually aggressive, forward, blunt, and nasty without a single repercussion or misperception. As a woman, my motives were never questioned.

But what about the fear of being raped or assaulted? Had I, as an attractive-appearing woman, had that same hypervigilance that I now sensed from women?

Several years prior to beginning my transition, while at the height of my female appearance, I was walking down a dark alley at around 2:00 A.M., making my way from a closing bar to my nearby car. As I walked through the alley, a grungy guy stepped out and said, "Can I have some change?"

"No," I answered.

He started to follow me and said, "How about some sex then?"

In an instant, I had turned around and said, "Bend over, motherfucker. I'll fuck you up the ass."

His mouth dropped open as he stared at the blond, buxom "woman" who had spat these words out at him.

It was not the first time that I had done something like that. When my female friends heard about my behavior—or witnessed it—they asked if I wasn't afraid I was going to set someone off.

"I don't know," I remember responding. "I don't really think about that at the

time. It's like a switch gets flicked, and my rage comes faster than I can process anything else."

I could hear my phone ringing as I opened the main door of my building. I quickly unlocked the door and managed to pick up the receiver just before voice mail kicked in.

"Hello?"

"Hi, this is Dr. Ann Singleton, you left a message about setting up an evaluation?"

Despite the first name, the voice that struck my ear was distinctly deep and masculine. And I found my mind automatically conjuring up the mental image of a man at the other end of the line.

Dr. Singleton was not only a gifted therapist who worked with transsexuals—she was a transsexual herself. But while I could make my vocal chords thicker with testosterone and naturally lower my voice, she could not unthicken hers with estrogen. I remember thinking I was going crazy just from the fact that my voice was not deepening fast enough. How did she deal with the fact that hormones didn't change her voice at all?

The reason for my contact with Dr. Singleton was because she had become the next step on the way to my hysterectomy. A few weeks earlier, Dr. Blumenstock had telephoned to let me know he had received the ethical guidelines for transsexuals, and it appeared that they required two separate letters of referral. Since I had only received one—from the therapist who recommended me for chest surgery—I now had to find a second.

I called Jared in the hope that the large binder he carried to FTM meetings might have something useful in it. As it turned out, Dr. Singleton was listed as a resource. From my initial discussion with her, it appeared that one appointment would probably be enough for her to make her recommendation.

IT WAS A BRIGHT AND SUNNY AFTERNOON WHEN I STARTED the drive toward Marin County. As I crossed the Richmond Bridge, I looked down at the ocean and saw several sailboats making their way toward the bridge. Seeing them made me think of Jack. I pictured him on one of those boats in the middle of the ocean. Without a vagina.

Shortly after he returned from his first stage of surgery, Jack stopped by my house. During his fourteen-hour surgery, the medical team had performed a full hysterectomy, removed the entire vagina, sewn the area shut, and rerouted his urethra through the tip of his micro-penis/testosterone-enhanced clitoris.

At this point, his genitalia did not look that different since the major work was not really visible to the naked eye. But the next stage would bring dramatic visual changes. When Jack stopped by, he had just got back from Oregon and was still wearing a catheter—or I should say, catheters. He had a small catheter coming through the penis, so the newly formed urethra would stay open and heal without urine passing over it, while another catheter was coming from his lower abdomen and draining urine into a small bag strapped to his calf. When I saw the whole contraption, I couldn't believe he had traveled on a plane from Oregon, let alone driven to my place. But he didn't seem uncomfortable. He just seemed happy.

When Dr. Singleton opened the door, my mind was still imprinted with the image of a man from the voice I'd heard on the phone. And that image was not immediately dispelled on first sight.

Although the doctor had long hair and was wearing a dress, her facial structure and her lumbering walk had strong remnants of the masculine. As we entered her office, I wondered how she could be happy. She must constantly confront people who see her as male.

We sat down and first made some informal small talk. I found out she was in her sixties and had made her transition to female more than twenty years earlier. At one point, she said, "I think my life is quite like that of any other woman."

I found that statement striking. Here I was, less than eight months into hormones and I looked and sounded more like my true gender than she did after twenty years of hormones. And yet she seemed so content. Did her comfort come from the fact that she had female genitalia under that dress, while I was still incomplete beneath my appearance? Was that the anchor that kept her calm?

She began to ask questions about my background and the transition itself. About twenty minutes into the conversation, she said, "I must say, although I've only spent a short time with you so far, I'm very impressed—you know very much what you want and you strike me as a very authentic person."

As soon as she said this, I relaxed. I stopped feeling like I had to prove something and started feeling she was already on my side. As we continued talking, our conversation veered into potential surgeries. At one point, I asked if she knew anything about the removal of the vagina among FTM patients—such as what happened once the lining was removed and whether it would affect orgasms in any way.

"From what I understand, once the vaginal lining is taken away and the area is closed, the tissue and muscle eventually heal together, becoming thicker and stronger. It's why some people describe their orgasms as different—or more intense—after the surgery."

As I listened to her, I felt a surge of excitement. The notion that I could end up with one large pumping male muscle was awesome to me. And I marveled at how surgeons were able to mimic what should have transpired in the womb. It was as if the basic foundation were already in place.

The more we talked, the more I relaxed. I completely forgot my agenda of hitting all of the relevant points and proving just how functional I was. It was a totally different feeling from my early visits with the other therapist where I had constantly felt the need to justify myself.

Maybe it was because Dr. Singleton had been through this, too. Or maybe it was because she had entered her later years with acceptance and grace. All I know is the calmness that emanated from her not only permeated the room—it made its way into me. And somewhere in that there must have been some quality about her that struck me as feminine. For later, as I was driving home and thinking back on various things she had said, the accompanying mental image was exclusively that of a woman. Somehow, without any conscious effort on my part, her presence had transformed my mind.

A few years ago, I briefly dated a woman I met at a housewarming party. She had been with men most of her life, but while she was working at a strip club, she had fallen in love with one of her customers—a woman who came regularly to watch her. After the relationship ended, she moved to San Francisco and began to explore the lesbian community.

When we met at that housewarming party, she was on a date with another woman, but gave me her number anyway. On our first date, she said, "You know, I pursued you at that party because your energy struck me as totally different. You stood out."

"What do you mean?" I asked

She responded, "Well, your energy is clearly male."

"How can you tell?"

"When I gave a massage to a woman I was dating, I felt the absence of any boundaries between us," she said. "It was like I got lost in her—like we were sisters. But when you were standing next to me and I touched your arm, I felt a definite separation. A clear boundary."

"What did that boundary feel like to you?" I asked.

"Like warmth and protection."

Sometimes, after a woman complains about being approached by men on the street, people ask what she was wearing. But they never pose that question to a man.

I was wearing black jeans, black boots, and a white tank top that revealed the tribal tattoo wrapped around my biceps. It was late in the afternoon and I had just walked Ashley back to her car, which was parked near the curb outside my building. I was heading back, when out of the corner of my eye I saw a van coming up the street.

As the van pulled alongside of me, I looked over and saw a thin-faced, seedy-looking guy at the wheel. As soon as he saw me, he stopped his van, practically screeching to a stop in the middle of the street.

The man rolled down his window and said, "So, ah . . . what's that building over there?"

I told him it had lofts and condos.

He looked off to the side and then said, "Well, ah, there any up for sale?"

"No, not that I know of," I answered in an abrupt tone. I was becoming impatient, wondering why he was bugging me with his questions.

He continued to linger, saying nothing, so I headed toward my building. As I reached the front door, I heard his engine as he continued up the street. It wasn't until I was all the way inside that my mind started to piece together what had just happened.

During our conversation, I felt an irritation. It was that old anger, left over from the days when men constantly talked to me on the streets, interrupting my space. And yet while the scenario was similar, it felt incredibly unfamiliar. Something about his approach was different. It was much more indirect and careful—like he was testing the waters. And he had been very, very nervous.

That's when my mind kicked in to the present. This wasn't then. This was now. The man wasn't coming on to me as a woman; he was cruising me guy-to-guy. The second that realization struck, whatever irritation had been there was gone. And all that was left was validation.

Shortly before I began exclusively dating women, I had my last one-night stand with a guy.

I was at a college party, standing in a room full of people, when I saw him standing in the back corner. He stood out as the best-looking guy there—dirty blond hair, a square jaw, and muscular build. I walked over to start a conversation. He had a really good sense of humor and we ended up cracking jokes the rest of the night, and drinking a lot of liquor.

As we became more intoxicated, the conversation turned to sex. I remember saying something about my attraction to women. He lowered his voice, and told me that he considered himself bisexual; he had slept with several men. As soon as he said that, I felt closer to him, like we were bonded somehow. I offered him a ride home and we ended up at my apartment.

When we got into bed, I was so drunk that the room was spinning. I got up and went to the bathroom, shut the door, and threw up. When I came back, the room had stopped spinning, but the large amount of alcohol still in my system helped me relax enough to get through a brief period of intercourse without tensing up too much.

There's not much else that I remember about that night. But one thing that does stand out is the fact that the next morning I did not feel the anger I was used to after one-night stands. Nor did I feel as great a distance with him as I had with other men. And it had something to do with my knowing that this guy, who had gotten into my bed, was attracted to men.

Fourteen

AUGUST 1998

I am sitting in a room full of people. They are passing around my under-wear with my prosthetic device in it to see if my male genitals are real. I think to myself, "Obviously, if it is attached to my underwear and not my body, it can't be real, so they must see that." I then pick up some photos I have had developed and notice that only a couple of them have come out fully developed. All the others have faded ghostlike images overlapping one another. . . .

It was a month before my hysterectomy, but instead of taking it easy, I was on my way to the hospital for another surgery: the revision of my chest scars and nipples.

At my last follow-up appointment with Dr. Brownstein, he commented on the thickness of the scars running along the underside of each pectoral muscle. He said sometimes with a second procedure—in which the surgeon cuts out the scars and resutures the skin—the resultant scar is much thinner and less visible.

I asked if we could also relocate the nipples, as they felt too high on my chest. Dr. Brownstein said he could relocate them but each time he moved them, there was a risk that the grafts would not connect to the blood supply of the underlying skin. In short, there was a risk they would turn black and die.

It didn't take me long to make my decision. After several more weeks of lying bare-chested in my bedroom during hot summer weather and running my hands over nipples that were pasted almost in the middle of my pec muscle, I said, "Let's go for it."

Although this was a much smaller surgery, the building in which it would take place was much larger; it was a full-sized hospital in the heart of San Francisco. And this time it was Ashley, not Selena, who was bringing me to the front door.

AS WE PULLED UP TO THE HOSPITAL, I TURNED TO ASHLEY and told her I should be out by early afternoon. I got out of the car and headed through the double doors that led to the lobby. My first stop was the payment of my fee. When I looked down at the registration form, it had my social security number and name on it. Next to "sex" there was an "F."

The instant I saw it, my defenses went up. I felt as if I was suddenly in a hostile environment and had to watch my back. I handed the clipboard back to the receptionist and said angrily, "This has an error on it; it says 'female' here."

She took the clipboard, looked at it, and immediately said, "Oh, of course that's wrong," and went to print out a new form on the computer.

As soon as I saw her response, I relaxed. And I realized no one was out to get me; it was simply an old piece of information in the computer. One of the smaller buildings on the hospital grounds contained the office of a physician I had seen during law school. He probably shared the same computer system and they had pulled up old information.

When I finished paying, they sent me to the second floor and an empty room. I started to undress, but when I got to my underwear and prosthesis, I hesitated. I didn't understand why I had to take them off if I was just having chest surgery, but I did it anyway. I waited for Dr. Brownstein; several minutes turned into twenty, and then half an hour. There was still no sign of him. And the longer I lay there without my underwear, the more exposed and uncomfortable I felt. I had become used to the presence of my bulge and now that it was gone, I felt an emptiness down there. And without any underwear to cover me, I had a heightened awareness of my own genitalia.

Even before I had my prosthesis, I never got into bed without at least wearing my underwear or boxers. But here I was, wearing a gown that fell around me like some sort of nightgown. And I had nothing underneath. Nothing at all.

Dr. Brownstein finally arrived, wearing his white lab coat and greeting me with a cheery, "Hello, Dhillon."

Right away, I asked about my underwear.

"Yes, of course you can keep it on," he said.

I felt like he was my dad and had just given me permission to do something I really wanted. I immediately jumped off the bed, went over to my gym bag, and pulled on my underwear and prosthesis under my gown.

Dr. Brownstein took out a marker to prepare my chest. I had some pictures on the dresser that I had brought from magazines. I wanted him to make my nipples smaller and I showed examples of other guys. He looked at the pictures, then pulled out a nickel to use as a guide.

I said, "No, I really want them smaller than that."

He put the nickel back in his pocket and took out a dime, "How about this?"

"Perfect," I answered.

He put the dime on my chest close to the pec line, where I had indicated, and drew a circle around it. He then did the same for the other pec.

"Now, you realize," he warned, "if we move the nipple lower, there will be a scar from where it was before? It will be a thin line because I'll close it up, but there will be a mark."

"Then I guess I'll have another scar, because I want the nipples put where they should be," I said, "where I feel they belong."

A few minutes later, a male nurse arrived to take me to the operating room.

"Just hop on this, man, and we'll wheel you down there."

I WAS FEELING QUITE ANXIOUS WHEN I WAS FINALLY ROLLED into the operating room. The room was extremely cold and I started to shiver. They pulled a heavy, heated blanket up to my waist, but then opened my gown and exposed my chest. Then, as if I wasn't cold enough, they put circular pads all over me to monitor my vital signs. The pads were cold to the touch. To top it off, they rubbed an antiseptic lotion across my chest. My teeth were chattering by this point.

A voice said, "You'll feel relaxed in a few seconds."

I was hoping they were right, when suddenly I felt the sweetest sensation. It was a slow, mellow tide rolling in, leaving me lucid but very relaxed. I stopped feeling cold—or maybe I just didn't care anymore.

Dr. Brownstein started injecting the local anesthetic along my chest. The needle stung a bit as it went in, but not too bad. After he had completed several injections, he put the needle away. Within moments, I felt a tugging sensation on my chest.

Whatever drug they had given me was one beautiful concoction. After a short while, my mood began to shift from relaxed to euphoric. A couple of times I started to feel a sharpness to the tugging on my chest and I said, in this really mellow tone, "Hey, you might want to add some more novocaine." I saw the needle come back into view and then the sharpness was gone.

At one point I heard the doctor say, "Pass the dime" and I just cracked up, laughing. But sure enough, someone passed over a dime that had been sterilized.

The more I felt Dr. Brownstein working on my chest, the more I got into the sensation. The whole experience began to strike me as warrior-like. And I felt as if I was participating in an important rite of passage—as if I was offering myself up to be branded and scarred. And brought into manhood.

It was the first time I had ever felt a tremendous sense of authority and control over my own body.

———

A FEW DAYS LATER, I MET DR. BROWNSTEIN IN HIS OFFICE and he removed the cotton he had taped over my nipples. Underneath, the nipples were blackened and bruised-looking, but he said, "I can tell they will make it. The grafts have taken."

Although I had not let my mind imagine myself losing my nipples, it was still a relief to hear those words. But I barely had time to let them sink in before I was off to prepare for my next surgery.

I WAS NERVOUS AS I STEPPED OFF THE ELEVATOR AND approached the doors to Dr. Blumenstock's office. After having just come from an experience of power and control, I now was entering a place where I was about to relinquish some of that—or so I thought.

I walked to the reception desk and found myself face to face with Beth—the woman who had apologized during my last visit for making a "regular" medical appointment.

Although she had now been informed of my story, Beth was as warm as ever.

She smiled and said, "Hi, Dhillon. The doctor is running a little behind, so have a seat and we'll get you in a bit."

The room was even more crowded than the last time I had been there but now there were no men in the room, only women. Noticing that, I felt some of my unease return. Knowing that everyone around me was an actual patient reminded me that I was one, too. It highlighted the fact that in this moment—and for this purpose—I was one of them. And that re-alization made a part of me feel invisible—fragmented.

I heard my name being called and I walked with a nurse who led me to an exam room and took my blood pressure, which she noted was a bit high.

"You must be nervous about your pap smear," she said. "The doctor will be here in a few minutes but you can stay dressed for now."

I was hugely relieved. Something about being able to first greet the doctor fully dressed—before having to put myself in a vulnerable position—was important to me.

A few minutes later, Dr. Blumenstock entered the room, greeting me with such open warmth that it surprised me. I remember wondering if he had been reading up on this stuff since I last saw him.

Unable to wait, I said, "Will this be my last pap smear ever?"

He said yes, and when he saw the expression of joy cross my face, he smiled.

"Do you want me to bring a nurse in during the procedure?" he asked.

"No. I don't want anyone else in here."

"I didn't used to ask that question," he said, "but recently I had a female patient who was very attractive and after I commented on her tan, she thought I was being inappropriate and asked for a nurse."

I tried to imagine myself in his position. But it was hard. I'd spent my life making much more personal and intimate comments toward women. If I were to take over his job right now, the patients would be asking for a nurse every second.

Dr. Blumenstock first started to feel the tissue on my chest. That part felt comfortable to me.

"Does the chest reconstruction also include building and shaping the muscle for you?" he asked.

I felt a sense of pride as I said, "No. I had to do that on my own."

The doctor then sat at the foot of the exam table, instructing me to place my feet in the stirrups and to move down. As he was slipping on his gloves, a shift took place inside me. The first reaction that surfaced was the old familiar desire to disappear, to check out just long enough to endure this.

But as that was arising, so, too, was something else. And that something else was a taste of the power I felt during my recent chest surgery. As it emerged, I asked Dr. Blumenstock to wait a second.

"One thing," I said, "that will really help me during this exam is if you don't stop to ask me how I'm doing or feeling, or if I want a nurse to come in, or anything like that. It will just delay the process. If you need me to relax because you're having trouble, just tell me, and I'll do my best. But other than that, no matter how uncomfortable I seem, just keep going and finish up, okay?"

The doctor agreed and picked up a speculum to start the exam.

"People have said I'm really gentle," he said.

"As long as you're quick, too," I replied.

And he was. Really quick.

AS HE WALKED OUT OF THE ROOM, I REMEMBER FEELING A bond with him—like we had just accomplished something as a team. It was the sense that I had actually participated in what had happened rather than just letting it happen to me. And that was a new feeling.

Shortly after graduating from law school I signed up for a new health insurance plan. I was in the process of selecting a physician, when a lesbian acquaintance suggested I choose a family practitioner that she knew.

When I arrived for my first appointment, an assistant led me to the exam room. The door between the exam room and the adjacent office was ajar, and I caught a glimpse of the doctor on the telephone. She was an older, slightly round woman with gray hair. As I put on the gown, I caught pieces of her conversation. She was having an argument with a family member.

Eventually she came into the exam room, sighed, and said something about children and the problems they cause.

As she examined me, I became more and more uncomfortable. I was anticipating the pelvic exam and something about her was not putting me at ease. She seemed totally distracted, and her movements were abrupt and too firm. Finally, she was ready to start the pelvic exam.

"Would you like me to bring in a nurse to hold your hand during the exam?" she asked.

I quickly declined. I didn't want another stranger in the room. Exposing myself to one person was tough enough. She slipped on her gloves and then brought over the speculum. She had barely gotten it near my opening, when I tensed up.

"You're nowhere near relaxed," she commented. "Why don't you let me bring in a nurse and she can be with you?"

I said that, no, I really didn't want someone else there.

But she wasn't listening. "I really think it would help you," she said.

Again I declined. I tried to relax, but something about her demeanor made me even tenser.

The doctor finally said, "I really think you should have someone here. Why don't you let me bring in a nurse?"

I was so angry at that moment, I wanted to scream, "Goddamn it, I said 'no.' "

But instead I just repeated, "No, please. I just want to continue alone."

The doctor stopped then, sat back, and looked as if she was preparing to deliver an important sermon.

"You know," she said, "when I see this kind of resistance, I wonder what is going on. And I start to think that there is something very traumatic in the past of that patient. I mean, here I offered you, several times, a very nurturing option of having a nurse come in and hold your hand, and you turned it down. It all strikes me as very troublesome."

As she spoke, I thought, "Oh, my God. She's right. There must be something awful that happened. But what was it?"

When I left her office, I felt exposed and shaken and afraid. And violated. It wasn't until a day or so later that the rage really hit. Some part of me realized that she had not only hit upon a dark, hidden place; she had thrust her fist right inside.

When I finished dressing, Dr. Blumenstock pulled out a diagram of the reproductive system and pointed out the organs he would remove during the hysterectomy: the uterus, cervix, ovaries, and fallopian tubes.

As I was signing the consent form, I asked, "I really can't work out for a whole month? Can't I start a little earlier?"

"No. Anything that engages the abdominal muscles is totally out of the question."

He then pulled out that familiar billing form.

"What type of insurance carrier do you use?" he asked.

I told him the name and it was a plan that didn't cover his practice.

When he heard that, he started searching for the cheapest procedure he could find on the form so I could save some money.

I gave the receptionist one check for my current visit, then wrote another to cover Dr. Blumenstock's surgical fee. The rest would be paid directly to the outpatient surgery center. The hysterectomy was going to cost several thousand dollars and I would have to put it on credit cards. I had no more cash left in the bank.

Dr. Blumenstock told me he had called the outpatient surgery center and asked them to give "the guy a break," as I was paying for everything myself. The fact that he was using male pronouns throughout the preparations for my hysterectomy not only filled me with gratitude, it left me with a strong feeling of trust.

AS I DROVE HOME, I THOUGHT OF ALL THE KINDNESSES I HAD recently been shown. Every time one of those moments made its way into my consciousness, my eyes filled with tears, and I had a true sense of wonder and surprise.

In keeping myself hidden for so long, I, too, had been blind. I had never really seen that the world was filled with so much love.

Fifteen

SEPTEMBER 1998

I am moving into a new apartment, but still have the lease to my old one. When I go to the new apartment, there are three pianos; two of them are plain upright pianos and one is a baby grand. I really want to play the baby grand, but the keys are made of glass and are too wide for my fingers. . . .

On the day of my hysterectomy, I woke up feeling calm and relaxed. There was a time when I would have questioned this serenity. But today I was simply allowing it.

Three years ago, as I was approaching my breast reduction surgery, my bodyworker told me I should prepare for feelings of mourning or grief. I was, after all, about to let go of a part of my body that had been with me my whole life.

The night before surgery, I thought about her words. I even started to talk to myself, to my body, in an effort to say some sort of good-bye. But as I was doing this, I knew it was contrived—there was no emotion there. But instead of accepting that, I thought I must be in denial. I must be out of touch with myself. I was sure it would hit me later.

But it never did. There was never any sense of missing, or loss, or letting go.

The same thing happened after my mastectomy. Not only were there no feelings of loss, there was an immediate inability to remember what it felt like to have breasts. And now, when I pulled out old photos of me in a bathing suit or jogging bra, I found myself asking, "God, who was that? Was that really me?" I felt no connection to those images.

And the lesson I was learning was this: before one can experience feelings of grief or loss, there must have been a genuine sense of attachment.

I began the morning by leisurely filling the bathtub with hot water and bacterial soap as the sounds of Latin music emanated from my stereo speakers. When I stepped into the tub, my stomach growled.

I had spent most of the previous day following the doctor's orders and drinking a couple of bottles of an over-the-counter laxative solution. By the time I went to bed, my stomach was completely empty and I was starving. Throughout the night, my dreams were haunted with visions of mouthwatering meals.

While lying in the tub, I found myself picturing a plate filled with fried eggs, sizzling bacon, and buttered toast. And home fries with ketchup. And fresh orange juice. And really good, strong coffee. When I reached the point where I was practically drooling, I wished the surgery was already done, just so I could eat.

I stayed in the bathtub until my hunger pangs subsided and my skin had taken on the texture of a raisin. When I got out, I pulled out a small travel bag from the closet and threw in a few toiletries, some extra underwear, and contact lens solution. I brushed my teeth, being careful not to swallow any water when I rinsed out my mouth—the doctors were really strict about avoiding liquids so close to general anesthesia.

By this time it was 10:30 A.M.—half an hour before I had to be at the surgery center. Although it was only a fifteen-minute walk to the clinic, I decided to leave. A few more minutes and I might be tempted to open the refrigerator or use the espresso maker.

I turned left and walked down a residential street lined with mature trees and quaint-looking houses. As I passed by a park, I felt a slight breeze and I flashed back to a time when I was about seven and riding my bike on a street near my house. It was early fall and I had just taken off my sweater and wrapped it around my waist. And I distinctly remember coasting down an incline, enveloped by a warm, subtle breeze of the most perfect temperature.

After a few more minutes of walking, I arrived at the small square building where my surgery was to take place. I opened one of the double glass doors and stepped inside. Because there were several people in the waiting room, I was nervous about going in. I was worried that when they called my name, they would put a "Miss" or "Ms." in front of it. I was, after all, having a hysterectomy.

I finally heard someone call out, "Dhillon Khosla?" Relieved, I walked to the desk.

"Sir, these are your registration papers and the forms we need you to fill out," said the receptionist.

As soon as I saw the "Mr." in front of my name, I breathed a sigh of relief. Dr. Blumenstock must have said something; why else would they list a hysterectomy patient as male? I don't know for sure how it got there—I just know that seeing the "Mr." made me feel I was in a friendly, nurturing environment.

A nurse came to escort me to the pre-op area, so I followed her to a very small room. On one of the chairs was a familiar plastic package with a gown, cap, and my favorite little socks with the skid pads on the bottom.

I quickly changed into the gown and socks but didn't put on the goofy shower cap that came with it. I did not take off my underwear and prosthesis. I had no idea how long I'd be waiting and figured I could quickly whip them off when the time came. I walked to the door, propped it open, then sat down to wait.

As I was looking into the hallway, I saw a well-dressed woman walking in my direction, and I found myself wondering if she was the assisting surgeon. During my last appointment, Dr. Blumenstock had informed me that one of the surgeons in his practice was going to assist during the surgery. When he told me the surgeon was female, I felt a sense of panic. My mind immediately called forth images of articles written by women about unnecessary hysterectomies and made me fear that this surgeon—who had never met me—might have a last-minute moral objection to my procedure.

The fear that something would stop me before I was all the way home was not a new one. It was constantly there, just waiting to be triggered. And any situation that required the help of someone else—especially a stranger—set it off.

The next person to walk down the hall was a tall, friendly-looking guy in a white lab coat.

"Hi," he said, entering my room. "I'm your anesthesiologist. Just call me Larry."

Larry had a strong southern accent and a very warm demeanor. He asked some questions about my history with anesthesia, and then gave me a couple of prescriptions for pain. That surprised me, since it was usually the surgeon who gave the postsurgery prescriptions. But when I heard him say he was writing prescriptions for Valium and Percocet, I found myself actually getting excited. Although I had never tried these drugs, I had heard about the wonders of Valium. I figured a drug with a long history of getting thousands of housewives addicted had to be pretty good. And, hey, how often do you get a chance to be under the influence of drugs—legally?

As Larry handed over the goods, he said, "You know, some people feel they have to be brave and tough it out through the pain."

I said, "Not me. I don't see the point in that." And then I added a term that I'd heard other doctors use. "I think it's important to 'stay ahead' of the pain."

Larry looked at me, his eyes all shiny and bright. "You and I are completely on the same page."

I felt like we were two potheads about to share a bong hit.

Carefully I tucked my prescriptions into the side pocket of my travel bag, and stuffed my underwear and prosthesis under my other clothes.

As they wheeled me to the operating room, I heard the doctors talking about the upcoming surgery. Each time they referred to me, they used the pronoun "he." So far I had not encountered a single female reference. And yet this was the one surgery where I had actually expected it.

When I opened my eyes, I was still in the operating room. I heard voices, but none of them was near. I also heard faint sounds of metal clanking and got the sense things were winding down. The surgery must be over.

I then became aware of a faint scent of perfume. As soon as I noticed it, I thought of the woman I had seen in the hall before my surgery and wondered, "Where is she? Is she still here?"

I was starting to feel heavy and tired, as if I was about to go under again. But I fought it, thinking, "I've got to see her."

I mustered up whatever strength I could and then said, "Please, bring her to me—bring the doctor here."

My voice sounded hoarse from the tube that had been inserted during anesthesia. But somehow they understood, because I heard someone saying, "He wants to talk to you," and the scent of perfume became stronger.

And then she was next to me. I was slipping quickly by then and couldn't even move my head to look at her. I just remember feeling her there. And then I heard myself saying, "Thank you—thank you for doing this."

THE NEXT TIME I AWOKE, I WAS IN A DIFFERENT ROOM. I felt a strong pain in my stomach and I could feel a bulky pad in my underwear. There was a tube coming from my underwear that led to a large bag that was hanging from the edge of my bed.

The pain got sharper and I started to call out, but my voice was still weak. I then noticed another tube snaked around the grill of my bed near my right arm. It had a little plastic box with a button.

I pushed the button and within a few moments a nurse came in and said she'd bring some Demerol. I felt a stinging sensation as the solution went in. She wiped a cotton ball across my buttocks, then pulled down my gown and left.

It didn't take long before I was drifting off into a happy, loopy state. The pain receded far into the background, and I got really drowsy and passed out.

When I awoke again, the pain was back. I reached over and pushed the call button. My efforts were rewarded with another shot of Demerol.

The rest of the night went like that—patches of sleep, interrupted by moments of pain and more shots. At one point I woke up and saw Ashley in the room. It must have been shortly after a Demerol shot because I was so out of it she seemed like an apparition. I vaguely remember her leaning over and gently kissing my forehead while my eyelids felt as heavy as stones. I let them close. When I next opened them, Ashley was gone.

The next morning Dr. Blumenstock showed up. I remember his going over some post-op instructions and my really trying to focus, but I was too out of it. At one point he handed me some prescriptions for pain medication. I told him I already had some and gestured to the coffee table where the nurse had put my prescriptions. He picked them up and as he read them, said that we should just cancel them, that they were unnecessary. Had I not been so drugged out, my response might have appeared less dramatic—or at least smoother. But all I could do was pathetically reach my arm out toward the prescriptions.

"No . . . please, don't . . ." I must have looked like a total junkie.

He smiled and said, "Well, okay. I don't feel that strongly about it." He put the prescriptions on the table and I fell back to sleep.

The hospital discharged me a few hours later and I was cranky from the pain, impatient to get home. When we got to Ashley's car, I lay my head against the seat and closed my eyes. I was feeling awful. I just wanted it to be over.

When we finally reached my place, I grabbed some water, took a pain pill, and went straight to bed. I spent the next few days in a foggy haze of pills and sleep and occasional visits that left me with Tupperware dishes of food that I would eat in small portions before I took my pills. On one of those visits, a woman from my office made a salad, using the fruit from a gift basket sent by my mother.

FIVE DAYS AFTER SURGERY, I WOKE UP WITH A SURGE OF energy. The pain was completely gone and the last bit of bleeding had stopped. I jumped out of bed and took a quick shower. As I was drying off, I caught a glimpse of myself in the full-length mirror. My reaction to what I saw was no different than usual: I quickly wrapped the towel around my waist and walked away from the reflection. I grabbed a fresh pair of underwear and tucked in my prosthesis, pulling it up tight against my body. Only then did I remove the towel.

I went into the kitchen and made a protein shake with fresh fruit. As I was drinking it, I charged around and collected the prescription bottles. I brought them into the bathroom and tossed them into a bag that I stuffed far into the rear corner of the cabinet below my sink. My movements were rapid and strong; I felt like a bull about to charge out of his stall. I wanted to hurl myself into the world. At the time, I figured it was just a normal reaction to having been cooped up for a while.

I drove into San Francisco and first stopped at my mortgage broker's office. I left a message with her assistant, saying I was interested in refinancing my place. I then moved on to a bookstore where I picked up a couple of books on financial advice. After that, I stopped at a secondhand store and picked up a couple of decent Italian suits for work, a couple of ties, and a pair of jeans. I also found a heavy, oak rolltop desk and decided to buy it, telling the store I'd pick it up the next day.

I continued to run errands without feeling at all tired. At one point I wondered if my increased energy was due to the fact that my ovaries were gone and I now had a higher level of testosterone in my body. I made a mental note to set up an appointment with my doctor to test my blood levels.

When I came home, I unpacked all my goods, including enough groceries for the next two weeks. Then I did the laundry and spent the rest of the evening reading financial books. I stayed up until four A.M., tabbing pages, highlighting passages, and jotting down notes.

The next day, I was just as driven. After less than three hours of sleep, I got up and called a friend to meet me at the secondhand store where we picked up my desk. It was unbelievably bulky and heavy, and it took a huge amount of maneuvering to get it inside the van and then unload it at my place. At one point, as I was sweating and straining, my veins bulging from the weight, I thought, Dr. Blumenstock would kill me if he saw what I was doing less than a week after surgery.

As soon as we were done, I got into my car and headed back to the city to meet with my mortgage broker. She told me she would set up an appraisal so we could figure out exactly how much money I could borrow against the equity in my loft. I left her office, feeling optimistic and charged up.

As I was driving home, figuring how much money I needed to borrow, I realized my excitement was not just about paying off debt. It was about the possibility of getting enough money for more surgery. And with that came another, larger realization. It was the awareness that my recent surge of energy was not just a hormonal aberration; it was a strong, restless, desire to move forward.

AS I WALKED TO THE FRONT DESK IN DR. BLUMENSTOCK'S office, several women in the waiting room looked up from their magazines. On any other day, I might have been self-conscious, trying to imagine the reasons for their stares. But not today. My arms were overflowing with bouquets of flowers and wine. This was my final visit.

As I handed one of the bouquets to the receptionist, she said, "This isn't good-bye forever, is it? You'll come visit us when you're done, I hope?"

I smiled and said, "Yes, I'll be back when this is all over." I handed her the other bouquet and asked her to pass it on to the woman who had assisted Dr. Blumenstock.

When I went back to Dr. Blumenstock's office, I gave him the bottle of wine. He looked at the label and commented, "Hey, this is a really good wine."

I laughed and said, "Well, of course. What do you think—I'm going to give you the cheap stuff after what you did for me?"

He then told me he wanted to do a quick pelvic exam just to see how the stitches were healing. Disappointment washed over me when I heard that—I had thought that no more pap smear meant no pelvic exams at all. I guess I should have been more precise.

We went to the examining room and he quickly put a few lubricated fingers inside me. I took some deep breaths to keep as relaxed as I could. When he pulled out, I had a bizarre sensation. For a moment, it felt as if my vagina were separating from my body—as if it were pulling away from the rest of me.

During first-grade recess, the boys and I would often hang out under the staircase at the far end of the courtyard. One day, we all pulled down our pants and one of the other guys pointed to the area between my legs and exclaimed, "Hey—you're different!"

I remember thinking, "Of course. I know that, but so what?" To me it was like having an unusual birthmark or scar. It didn't change my identity. And at that age, it wasn't a big deal to them, either. They shrugged their shoulders and we continued on as usual.

Dr. Blumenstock told me everything was healing really well, and I told him I had moved furniture a few days after surgery.

"You probably shouldn't have told me that," he said, smiling.

He added that I should be especially careful now because as the stitches weaken, the scar has to become strong enough to take over.

I then asked him about three little holes that I saw on my stomach. He explained that one was the entry point for the camera scope while the other two were entry points for the tools he used to cut the ligaments and loosen the whole structure before he pulled it out through the vagina.

When I told him I had recently read an article that said this type of surgery required a great deal of expertise, he nodded and said many surgeons don't like to do a hysterectomy this way. The surgeon has to work totally from the camera screen, and, because the image is two-dimensional, he has to guess at depth perception by feeling around.

As he was drawing a diagram to show me the organs he had removed, I said, "You know I have no way of knowing that you took everything out. Is there some sort of certificate of authenticity you could give me?"

"Sure," he laughed. "I could make one if you want."

He then put down his diagram and said, "I hope you will keep in touch with us and let us know how things turn out."

I said I would definitely do that. As we shook hands, I found myself thinking, "I'm going to miss him."

It was an automatic response to separating from someone who had come in so close, so quickly. And yet that seemed to be the nature of this journey: strangers who appeared like angels, walking with me just long enough to get me through to the next destination.

When I emerged from Dr. Blumenstock's office, I headed down the hall toward the reception desk. As I was coming around the corner, an office door opened up, and out stepped the woman who had assisted Dr. Blumenstock during my surgery.

She headed straight toward me and without saying a word, pulled me into her open arms. I was instantly enveloped in that familiar, sweet perfume.

When we separated from the embrace, I quickly said, "Thank you for helping me get one step closer to the end."

She looked at me with an incredible overflowing of warmth, gestured toward my appearance, and said, "Clearly, you're there."

And as she stood there, keeping her eyes upon mine, I felt myself starting to close down. And I wanted to get out of there as quickly as possible. It was not until a long time later that I came to understand my reaction:

I had arrived at my final appointment with a specific agenda: I wanted to let them all know just how much their contribution to this journey meant to me. The flowers, the wine, the words on the greeting cards—all were carefully selected to show them my gratitude, a glimpse of my heart.

But the look in her eyes shook up my whole agenda and turned it on its head. For there was more than just an offering of love and kindness— there was the reflection of someone who had been deeply touched and affected. And some part of me could not accept that. Some part of me said, "No, this can't be."

After all, I hadn't done anything for her. So how could she be so moved—by me?

Sixteen

OCTOBER 1998

I am sleeping in a park with my son by my side. Suddenly, a man comes by and smashes my son's CDs into pieces. I throw the man to the ground, and tell him that I once shoplifted and had to pay the price, and so should he. After the fight is over, I sit there thinking about how I ended up with a son from one night of passion, and now things are forever changed. . . .

As I loaded my travel bag into the trunk of my car, I thought to myself, "I'm really going to enjoy this weekend." I was in the right mood at the right time.

I HAD RECENTLY BOOKED AN APPOINTMENT WITH THE GENDER Dysphoria Clinic (formerly affiliated with Stanford University) during which time I would meet with the surgeon to discuss various options for genital reconstruction surgery and undergo a psychological evaluation. My home equity loan had been approved, so there was nothing for me to do but pass time.

I had spent the last week practicing my blackjack skills until my decisions on when to hit were so automatic that I knew I could enjoy the free casino drinks and still play some decent hands. I was heading to Reno, and as I got closer to my destination, I felt an increasing sense of lightness. I was looking forward to a couple of days of total indulgence: greasy food, alcohol, and cigarettes—and, of course, no incorrect pronouns coming my way.

As soon as I checked into my hotel and let myself into the room, I took off my shirt and walked around until I found an ashtray. I pulled out a cigarette and sat down on the bed and smoked as I turned on the TV. By coincidence, there was a report on a news show about the number of thefts in casinos and the tactics used by crooks to take your cash. As images of people gambling flashed across the screen, I found myself getting excited. I took one last drag from my cigarette, exhaled a few final smoke rings, and headed toward the bathroom.

When I emerged from my shower, I put on a pair of cream-colored slacks and a pressed off-white shirt that I left unbuttoned at the neck. I finished the look with a blue Calvin Klein blazer. Then, I opened my wallet and took half the cash—which I wanted to save for the following night's gambling—and tucked the money into the inside slot of my glasses case. My wallet was tucked in the back pocket of my slacks and fastened with the button that closed around the pocket to keep it out of reach of fast pickpocket artists.

I parked my car and headed to Fitzgerald's, which advertised itself as the "certified loosest $1 slots in Reno." My plan was to start with the slot machines, then move on to blackjack. A guy at the entrance handed me a flyer and said, "There you go, buddy." Inside, I was surrounded by flashing lights, and by the sound of coins falling into the slots. I could feel my heartbeat rising and I knew I was being sucked in.

I took a few deep breaths and slowly walked around the casino to get the overall layout of the place. I was very aware that I could lose a large amount of money in a matter of minutes, so what was most important to me was that I fully enjoy those precious minutes.

About six years ago, on my way to California to start law school, I met up with some friends in Reno. After sharing a nice dinner and a couple of drinks, we started our rounds of the casinos. I spent the rest of the evening racing from machine to machine, convinced that I could win big and depressed when I didn't. After losing all the money I had brought with me, I went to the cash machine and continued to take out more. I became oblivious of my friends and more focused on my goal of turning things around. I don't even remember enjoying the process; I was just looking ahead to a great outcome and was angry and frustrated when it didn't turn out my way. The next day, when we stopped at a diner on our way out of town, I left our booth to use the slot machine by the counter.

Now, as I strolled up and down the aisles, I started to feel very clearheaded. I took the escalators to the second floor, then wound my way to the back, where I found the restrooms. As I passed the women's restroom and continued on to the men's, I felt a momentary sigh of relief. The fact that my entry into a female restroom would now cause alarm was confirmation that I had come a very long way. And it was one of those moments that allowed me to see the cup as half full instead of half empty.

When I returned to the first floor, I walked to a relatively empty corner and found a set of dollar slot machines against a counter. Behind the counter was a woman wearing the casino costume I had seen on the cocktail waitresses—black tights, black bra with gold trim, and a green tailcoat. The woman was petite and pretty in a subdued, tasteful sort of way.

I took off my jacket and sat down at the slot machine. But before I put any money in, I looked around for a cocktail waitress. I wanted to enjoy each spin in the company of a drink and a cigarette. The woman at the counter asked what I needed and I said I was wondering where the cocktail servers were. She said one should be around in a minute.

I put a twenty into the machine and began to play. On my third spin I got lucky and was up fifty-seven dollars. I rolled up my sleeves and leaned back in my chair, ready to enjoy a longer playing time. I looked around and still saw no cocktail waitress. The woman at the counter saw me and came down from her post to go hunt one down.

I began to spin again and started losing at each turn. As I watched the numbers go down, I slowed down again, not wanting to let the time slip by too quickly and becoming increasingly annoyed that the waitress wasn't there yet. I then stopped playing completely and waited until someone came by and took my order. When my beer arrived, I pulled out my cigarettes and the woman from the counter brought me an ashtray. I lit up, took a sip from my beer, and began playing again.

The woman behind the counter continued to come by periodically to see how I was doing and at one point she brought me two dollars, saying they might bring me luck. Unfortunately they didn't, and I continued to lose as I pulled out the additional money I had allotted for slots and continued to play.

I was once again surprised by the way I played the slots. Between each spin I stopped to take a breath, or a swallow of beer, or a drag of my cigarette. And I wondered how much was due to my experience with meditation and how much was owing to the fact that I was there as a man and that particular underlying anxiety—for which I had no name years ago—was now gone.

I finished my allotted money for slots and headed to the blackjack tables. I found one with only one guy playing. I took a seat at the other end from the man and asked the dealer what the side "match" bet meant.

"Man, it's way too complicated for you," he said jokingly. "I don't think I can explain it." He then proceeded to give a convoluted explanation in a joking way, saying, "If at two minutes past the hour you get a certain card, you can win a bet."

"I think he's messing with me, man," I said to the other guy. "What do you think?"

The other guy just shrugged. Finally, he said to me, "What do you do?"

When I said I was a lawyer, both of them immediately launched into their repertoire of lawyer jokes.

We continued playing and I had really good luck, holding my own for quite a while. Finally, toward the early morning hours, I slowly started to lose and ran out of what I had won. But it was all right. With a small amount of cash, I had managed to stay alive very late into the night and had not exceeded my budget.

I got up, thanked the dealer, and walked into the brisk dawn air. As I passed the other casinos and their flashing lights without feeling any temptation, I thought, "No matter how much money I win or lose on this trip, I will come out a winner."

Every "Jack" or "bud" or "Hey, man" brought me one step closer to the rest of the world. It's as if I had spent my life staring in through a window at the party, and now people were finally recognizing me and inviting me inside.

As I continued on down the street, I started to laugh as I thought about it in terms of a Visa commercial—Gaming chips: $260; Dinner: $15; Recognition of Manhood: Priceless.

I woke up later that morning, feeling hung over, dehydrated, and unhealthy from the cigarettes. It made me want to detox myself before the next night of gambling—a good sign that my healthy living had been going on long enough that it automatically crept back when I pushed my body.

I drank several glasses of water, did some stretching, a bunch of push-ups, and some deep breathing to clear my lungs. After breakfast, I sat at the table in my room to look over a guide to the area. One particular advertisement caught my eye. It was for a men's club—a place offering dinner and beautiful entertainers, as well as a fine selection of wines and cigars. I was intrigued. I had been to strip clubs before, but they had lacked any sense of elegance or class. And none of them had high-quality food and drinks. In fact, some clubs in San Francisco didn't even have a liquor license because of the level of obscenity involved in the entertainment.

The men's club was only a few blocks from my hotel so I decided to check it out and get some fresh air at the same time. I put on some loose jeans and a T-shirt and headed out the door.

The club was an innocuous-looking, whitewashed building with a menu stand outside containing a glass-covered menu of the various dinner selections. The entrées were somewhat pricey but in keeping with a good-quality restaurant.

I walked to the front door and found myself in front of a host stand with an office to my left. The rest of the place was hidden; there was a small entrance to the side of the stand revealing only darkness beyond.

An attractive woman stepped out of the darkness. When I asked about dinner, she said that she had not put up a list of specials yet, but that they served dinner from 9:00 P.M. until midnight. She handed me a brochure and I walked out, knowing I would return. The hedonist in me could not resist a place that fed all of my needs: my love of high-quality food, my desire to smoke a good cigar and drink fine wine, and my prurient desire to be surrounded by stunning, sexually enticing women—all at the same time. As the brochure said: "A feast for all your senses."

AFTER SATISFYING MY CURIOSITY ABOUT THE CLUB, I RE-turned to my hotel, and took a nap. When I woke up, I was feeling fully detoxed and healthy. I put on the same clothes as the night before, tucked my wallet and hotel key in my pocket, and headed out the door.

I walked to the men's club, slowly enjoying my anticipation with every step. I was also thinking how I had never gone to a bar or restaurant alone in my former life—partly because it was not as socially acceptable for a female to be alone—because it's seen as an invitation for men to talk to you—and partly because I simply didn't feel as comfortable with myself as I do now.

I entered the club, found the hostess, and told her I was there for din-ner. I paid my cover, and walked through the narrow opening and down a short dark hallway which led to the restaurant in the back. There was an-other host stand and a large bar covering the wall to the left. Behind the stand was a darkened room filled with tables of various sizes, and a stage with a woman dancing to one of the latest hit songs. What also struck me was the scent that permeated the room—a very subtle perfume.

A man dressed in a suit and tie met me at the host stand. When I told him I was there for dinner, he said, "Excellent, sir," and led me to a table close to the front of the stage but a bit off to the side, against the wall.

"Would you like to sit here and I can turn the armchair around so you can watch as you eat?"

"That," I said, "would be perfect."

It really was the perfect seat. The chair was plush and high-backed. I was a few feet from the stage, but the first table in line when the entertainers came out the door. And I liked that I was against a wall with no one be-hind me.

Within seconds, my waitress arrived. She had the tall, statuesque, sleek beauty of a chorus showgirl. She asked what I wanted, calling me "sweetie" in a very warm tone, and I ordered a glass of red wine to go with the steak I was planning to get for dinner. I then sank back into my chair and looked around. The place was truly the best club I had ever seen. It was very luxurious, and the women were all really attractive and healthy; their bodies tightly toned.

Soon a woman made her way toward me. She was short and petite, with a formfitting dress, beautiful long hair, and a sultry face.

"Would you like for me to dance for you?"

At that point I wasn't planning to spend extra money on a lap dance—lap dances cost twenty to twenty-five dollars—and I was intending to stick to my budget. But the guy next to me wanted one, so I focused my attention on it. First, the woman sat on his lap and talked to him. When the next song began, she spread his legs, put his arms at his side, and began her dance. I watched as she slid her body up his chest, then turned around and bent over. She sensually rubbed her crotch, cupped her breast, and licked her own nipples inches from his mouth. My own mouth watered as she ground her ass in his crotch and whispered in his ear, then flipped her head over and brushed her hair between his legs.

And with each move she made, I began to see the value of such a dance. I mean, I could lose twenty dollars at the casino and get some little pleasure in the act of playing cards. Or I could pay that same twenty dollars for the feel of a beautiful woman's skin, her attention, and her breathing into my ear.

When she had finished, the woman came over to me and said, "Are you ready yet?"

"I'm getting there," I said, and turned my attention to other women in the room.

Before I could get my bearings, another gorgeous woman came over and slowly leaned into me, whispering, "I would really like to dance for you."

Again I said no. Now that I was letting in the possibility of buying a dance, I wanted to survey the entire selection, watch the dancers, and then make my decision. Plus, I wanted to eat first and have the dance be my desert.

As I was waiting for dinner, I went to the bathroom. When I came out of the stall, I found an older black man working the men's room, selling cigars.

"What's happening, my man?"

I asked about getting a decent cigar. I watched him roll the end in cognac as he explained I should let the sulfur burn off the match first, then warm the head before I lit it. I told him I was saving it for after dinner so he put it in a bag and I brought it back to my table.

My food was ready. And it was delicious. The steak, the baked potato, and the salad with balsamic dressing, along with the taste of red wine and this lush, sweet-smelling atmosphere definitely stimulated all of my senses.

But things were just getting started. While I was eating, the dancer, who had already come by twice, returned.

Looking disappointed, she said, "And now you're eating." She leaned toward me and whispered, "As soon as you are done, I am coming back to attack you."

And as I felt a heat pass through my body, I knew she had me. I started to laugh because I realized that my twenty-some years of having been socialized with women, of having changed with them in locker rooms and bathrooms, and having been treated as one of them had no impact on this moment. As I saw men shelling out twenties for their third and fourth dance, I knew I was next. After having been so disciplined and careful with my budget in those tempting casinos, I was going to blow it here completely. I was no more immune to the power of these women than any other man in there.

And regardless of any intellectual discussion you want to have about the kind of power women have, or the implications or burdens that come with that power, it is a real power. With a few words, a certain look, or just their beauty, women could on a consistent basis do what no other salesperson or brilliant marketing executive could achieve—make men part with the last few dollars of their paycheck for just a few minutes of intangible pleasure.

And, of course, all of this was heightened by the fact that I had broken up with my girlfriend more than eight months earlier and had not had any sexual contact since then. But here I could have that contact—or the fantasy of it—without any of the burdens or commitments of the real world. And even more important, I could have it—for the first time—as a visible man. That made this experience fresh and new and imbued with the wide-eyed innocence of a virgin teenage boy spending his first evening in a strip club.

When I finished dinner, my girl reappeared. I nodded yes, and she sat on my lap, awaiting the next song. She asked my name and then told me hers—her stage name, of course. I then asked if she got to choose her own music and she said, Yes, she did. I asked if she liked working here and she answered that she liked to dance, and anytime she heard a song, even on the street, she began to move to the music.

When the next song began, she stood up, I spread my legs and she started to dance. She took off her top and as she slid her breasts up my torso, I took in her scent—which was sweet. I closed my eyes for a second and inhaled her, trying to memorize every moment before it was gone. She slid up my torso again and bit my nipple though my shirt, then turned around and arched her back against me, sighing in my ear. I loved the moments when she would touch me—on my legs, behind my neck, on my shoulders.

When the song ended, she sat next to me, getting dressed, and we talked a little more. I asked if she had ever had a bad experience here, and she said once a guy tried to grab her crotch and she kicked him. She said she got into trouble for it, but now won't dance for guys who she can tell have a bad vibe. I mentioned that I had dated a stripper who said dancing made her feel more confident, and my dancer now admitted that it did boost her confidence. I said something about the power she must feel onstage, and she scoffed at my use of the word "power."

"I don't feel powerful, just good with myself," she said, and moved on. And that left me with a mix of emotions.

A few years ago, I went to a hard-core strip club in San Francisco and paid for a private room where the girls masturbate for you. The woman I picked was clearly uncomfortable doing it solely for a female customer and—interestingly—insecure.

She kept asking if I was turned on and seemed more comfortable bonding with me as a friend.

Afterward, she lit up a cigarette and immediately began chatting in a warm and friendly tone, saying, "You know, I used to work for AT&T, but this sure beats the full-time hours and the pay. By the way—my real name is Jeanne."

And now I was finally just an ordinary guy customer. Yet I was not entirely satisfied with that, either. I wanted to be recognized as male, but not as "typically" male. I wanted something that gave me an edge over the other guys—something that brought me closer to women. Something that made me special to them.

So here I was thinking about all of this when a guy next to me started getting a lap dance. As the dance was going on, I heard him ask the dancer where she was from and if she liked working there—essentially the same questions I had asked. And I realized I was not the only man who wanted to personalize the dance, or make a connection. No wonder my dancer wasn't instantly impressed with my "sensitive" questions.

A few minutes later, I overheard two dancers talking at the table next to me.

"I was talking to this guy," laughed one of them, "and he said, 'All you want me for is my money' and I was like, 'Damn right, so hand over your wallet.' "

So here I was with my shattered illusions of grandeur, just another ordinary wallet in the crowd. Then I thought, fine. If I'm just another customer I may as well totally get into it and really do my part.

I returned to scoping out my next dance choice. I found myself most drawn to women who would stroke the back of a customer's head when they sat on his lap—there is something very sensual and feminine in the way a woman runs her fingers through a man's hair or strokes the nape of his neck.

As I continued to enjoy the atmosphere, I found myself flashing back to the time when I was four and visiting my grandparents in India. They had several servants, and I remember sitting in my high chair, gleefully banging my spoon on the table and commanding them to bring me an egg.

By the time I returned as a teenager, I had gathered enough Western liberal guilt to feel uncomfortable being surrounded by servants, and immersed in a culture with such a strict caste system.

But now I was thinking that maybe my enjoyment at being treated like a king as a child didn't come from some inherently bad place; maybe it was just a natural desire. Maybe it was unnatural to suppress it on the basis of some intellectual or political principle. I continued to ponder all of this as I puffed my cigar and kept my eye on the dancer with the affectionate hands.

I noticed another dancer heading my way. I was prepared to say no, as she wasn't my type. She had shorter hair and a kind of beauty that was more "cute" than glamorous.

She leaned in, looked directly into my eyes, told me her name—which I promptly forgot—and then asked me mine. I told her and she again looked me directly in the eyes and asked me what had brought me to Reno.

"The beautiful women," I responded.

She rolled her eyes and said, "What else?"

"Gambling."

She moved in closer and asked, "What else?"

I found her persistence a bit unnerving. I was running out of reasons and was certainly not going to say the celebration of my hysterectomy.

And so I said, "A breakup."

"I just went through one, too, and was crying my eyes out last night," she said.

She asked what sign my ex was and then what sign I was. I told her I was a Taurus, and she said her ex was a Taurus but he lacked passion. I responded that Tauruses were supposed to be very passionate and sensual.

"I believe that about you, but he wasn't." She then asked me if I wanted a dance.

I said no, but she didn't leave. Instead, she sat down next to me. I turned to her and asked her to tell me how to spell her name, which was my way of getting around the fact that I had forgotten it.

"My stage name or my real name?" she asked.

169

That surprised me. "Your real name," I said.

"Jennifer," she said. She kept staring into my eyes and I was struck by the intensity of her eye contact—and I liked it because it gave me an intimate feeling.

She then asked what I was thinking.

"Well, I was thinking that I would like to see you work the room and then come back and dance for me."

"The room is actually kind of dead right now."

I looked around and asked how she could tell.

"Very few men are getting dances right now, which means they aren't buying as many tonight."

I then pointed out a guy across from me. "What about him?"

"He's a possibility, because his friend is getting a dance right now."

"And he just arrived, too," I added, "so he hasn't had one yet."

As she got up to go over to him, I watched her work, feeling a little like a proud pimp.

And once again my perceptions of the differences between these men and me were shattered. My growing to like her—even though I wouldn't have selected her at first—was because I, unlike the other men, was drawn by her ability to connect with her eyes. But as I watched her do the same with the next guy—looking into his eyes, stroking his hair, and really listening to him, I watched him change his mind, too, and within minutes he had agreed to a dance. She had ample breasts and a tight small body, and as I watched her use it, I noticed she stroked the guy's hair a lot. I was also aware that despite the few short minutes of our connection, I was already feeling possessive of her.

When she finished, it was her turn to go onstage and I sat back, relit my cigar, and prepared to watch "my" girl do her thing. I enjoyed seeing the men get into her and the DJ was egging on the crowd, saying that she was "guaranteed to put a rise in your Levis" and we needed to "get that testosterone level up in the room." I found him amusing—partly because I was also having such a good time. By now, Jennifer was on her second song—a Prince song I liked—and had taken off her top.

The blackjack tables and the casino atmosphere seemed less and less interesting.

When her dance was up, Jennifer was immediately "hired" by the guy in front of me. As she was dancing, I noticed he had a wedding ring on and for a second I was surprised—not that he was here, but that he didn't take it off. But then I thought, He's not here to pick up anybody or find a date and the dancers couldn't care less. I also didn't feel any judgment toward him; he actually looked like a really nice polite guy, and maybe this was his way of getting a thrill without actually cheating.

When she was done dancing for him, Jennifer came back and sat next to me. She then asked about my ex-girlfriend and why we had broken up. I said my girlfriend was warm and nurturing, but that I couldn't be with someone who didn't have her own passion—someone who lived out her passion through others.

Then I asked Jennifer why she and her boyfriend had broken up, and she said he was a really good friend but the sexual passion wasn't there. We continued talking and at one point she asked what wine I was drinking. I asked if she would like a glass and had the waitress bring one for her. We sipped our wine and talked until the current song was over, and then I said I was ready for my dance. She stood, and as another Prince song began, she told me to "spread 'em" and got between my legs and began.

What made her sexy was the intense eye contact she gave during the whole dance. And I gave it right back. I would take in her body—and lick my lips—as she thrust her breasts toward my face and then return my gaze. In that moment, the bulge in my pants was as real as could be, and her hands running through my hair over and over as she slid her ass over that bulge brought heat in a matter of minutes. I was surprised at how confident I felt, and how quickly the familiar, potent drive broke through the surface.

When the dance was over, Jennifer asked if I enjoyed it and I said absolutely. I asked if she did, too.

"You know I have to say yes because you're a customer, but I think you also know the real answer." She gave me another direct and pointed look and sat down, saying, "So, what is your impression of me from the short time we have spoken?"

"That's tough, since you're asking me to assess you from your work environment, which is probably a different world from the rest of your environment."

"True," she said. "But you must have some sense."

I said I thought she liked to stay conscious—that she didn't like to numb herself out.

She said that was true and that many of the women here did drink a lot or check out in some way. She added that she didn't eat red meat and exercised regularly.

"I have to admit it's really important to me to have a girlfriend who is in good shape," I commented. "But at least I work out so I won't become one of those hypocritical fat men."

I then asked her if any of the women here were lesbians. She replied that almost all were bisexual. I asked if she was, and she said she was, "kind of."

"Is your attraction to women more emotional than to men?"

"No, not at all," she said. "I prefer men emotionally—and sexually. I just sometimes like fooling around with a woman because it's kind of sensual and there isn't as much focus on orgasm."

Then she leaned in again, "Now, since you've told me your impression of me, I'm going to tell you mine of you." I felt a bit apprehensive yet—admittedly—curious.

"I think you have really high standards and that you are a perfectionist. I also think you are really smart but not in a way that is intimidating or conceited because I feel totally comfortable with you."

She then asked how long I would be in town. She also wanted to know where I was staying, and I told her. At this point it crossed my mind that if I was totally functional, like any genetic male, or if there was a way I could have sex with her without having to explain my situation, I would do everything in my power to get her to my hotel room.

"I would get another dance from you," I said slowly, "if you would kiss me."

She said, "You know I can't do that here—but if we weren't here, I would kiss you."

"Come on—there's barely anybody left in here."

"Are you a good kisser?" she asked softly.

"I kiss like I give head."

Her eyes flashed in response and she said, "I give great head, too."

We sat there quietly for a few moments. She then picked up my hand, and put hers against mine.

"You have beautiful hands—and long fingers," she said. "You know, earlier you asked me if all dances were the same for me. Well, they're not—some are very different from others." Then she added, "If you were to stay in town, I would date you."

It wasn't until much later that it occurred to me that all of her flattery might simply have been a function of her choosing the most responsive customer on a relatively slow night.

But I'm glad I didn't think of it then. Because with the many long and difficult miles that still lay ahead, I really needed a night like that.

AS I DROVE HOME EARLY THE NEXT MORNING, THE FAINT scent of cigar smoke and perfume still clinging to my hair and skin, I felt different. I had only been in Reno for two days, and yet I felt as if I had somehow aged. Matured. Like that little boy was on his way to becoming a man.

Seventeen

NOVEMBER 1998

I am standing in the middle of the ocean with my keyboard floating on the surface. My instructor is showing me a specific piece of music and I start to improvise. He compliments me, then steps back and says he wants to further test my skills. He pulls out a cage with a spider in it and holds it up high in front of me. Impatiently, I reach up, lace my fingers around the wire of the cage, and grab to pull it down. The spider stings me and as I feel pain shooting up my arm, I realize I should have waited for the spider to come down on its own. . . .

climbed out of bed and made my way across the living room, enveloped in total darkness. I tried to recall the last time I had gotten up this early. Had I succeeded in conjuring up the memory, I'm sure it would not have found me in a good mood.

But today was an exception. I was going to meet the doctor who would perform my next series of surgeries. As I started my car and made my way through the empty streets, some part of me knew I was about to set into motion a chain of events that would forever change the rest of my life. But it wasn't until later—much later—that I would come to realize just by how much.

———

THE HIGHWAY TO PALO ALTO, WHICH ALSO CARRIED THE
dot.com commuters, was relatively clear and free of accidents, so I arrived
well over an hour before my appointment. I drove toward the clinic, passing stretches of sports fields and buildings belonging to Stanford University. I slowed as the address numbers came closer and closer to that of
the clinic.

Number 1515 was a big building on a square plot of land in a residential neighborhood across from Stanford University Medical Center. My
destination had the typical look of those office-style suites that doctors lease
in nice neighborhoods. The whole area looked like a replica of those plastic models of towns used by architects in presentations, prompting me to
subsequently refer to Palo Alto as "that little toy town."

I continued on past the building until I found my way to a local coffee
shop. I spent the next hour happily sipping a latte, eating a lemon poppy-
seed muffin, and rifling through the latest issue of *Money* magazine. I was
relaxed and excited at the same time. The relaxed part came from knowing I wouldn't have to worry about any initial disclosures or explanations
about my gender status. Not only were these doctors used to people like
me, they specialized in taking care of us. And I had chosen them because
they had been mentioned in the *New Yorker* as one of the few clinics in
the United States that had a long history of doing transsexual surgeries.
Plus, I wanted to go to someone within driving distance; I just didn't feel
secure flying somewhere and then being left on my own to face potential complications.

As the time for my appointment approached, I headed toward the clinic,
parking on an adjacent street. I checked in with the receptionist and was
about to take my seat in a small waiting area by the front door, when I saw
a little, handwritten letter framed on the wall. I walked over and saw it was
signed "Mother Teresa." The letter thanked Dr. Laub for his help in getting medical care for people in need.

I sat down and picked up a black portfolio. Inside were letters from ambassadors to various third-world countries, thanking Dr. Laub for his contributions. In reading them, I learned he was the founder of an organization called "Interplast"—which brings doctors to third-world countries to fix major deformities such as cleft palates. I saw a newsletter in a literature basket that contained black-and-white photographs of third-world children before and after their surgeries. The transition from pain and shame to one of joy and gratitude shone through, and I found myself thinking how rewarding his job must be. *The New Yorker* briefly mentioned Dr. Laub did charitable work, but the article had mainly focused on his long history with transsexual surgery.

As I was rifling through the materials, Dr. Laub walked through the door in green surgical garb. He was an older man who reminded me of some of the judges at my court. He had the look of a stately, robust man who lived a challenging and rewarding life.

He walked briskly to me and extended his hand, saying, "Good morning, sir."

The receptionist came out from behind the desk with a clipboard, and Dr. Laub said he'd see me after I was done with my paperwork. I sat down with the clipboard while he walked into his office and shut the door behind him.

The first few pages were the basic medical history questionnaires common to every doctor's office. But toward the end, questions appeared that were specifically geared to plastic surgery patients. One checklist asked you to rate how happy you were with various features of your body. When I reached a question about eyebrow placement, I laughed out loud. I didn't know you could change that.

As I was still laughing, a tall, blond woman walked in and introduced herself as Judy Van Maasdam—coordinator of the Gender Dysphoria program. In looking at her closely, I could tell she was in her forties, but she had obviously taken good care of herself. And I couldn't help but wonder whether she, too, had gone through any plastic surgery. Given the proximity to an expert surgeon and the likelihood that any procedure might be discounted, if not free, it didn't seem such a far-fetched thought.

She handed me a map with directions to the nearby office of a psychiatrist who would be conducting my evaluation. I was scheduled to go to the doctor at eleven, take a lunch break, then return to see Judy at one.

Shortly after I finished my paperwork, Dr. Laub's door opened and he beckoned me inside.

"I've read through your paperwork, and since you are an attorney, I won't talk to you like a layperson."

I was instantly amused and, admittedly, flattered. Obviously my legal experience didn't give me any greater familiarity with medical jargon than anybody else, but I appreciated the sentiment just the same; he was going out of his way to make me feel respected.

"It is my duty," he said, "to give you as much information as possible so you can make an informed decision." He then launched into an overview of the phalloplasty procedure—the construction of a full-sized penis.

He explained how doctors form a phallus using skin, nerves, and vessels from the forearm and, through the use of microsurgery, connect it all down below.

Before he got very far into his explanation, I interrupted, saying, "I'm most concerned about orgasm and sensation."

"Well, the tip of the phallus is definitely sensitive because when I touch people after surgery, they say they can feel it."

But when I asked, "Do people have full orgasm?" he admitted he didn't know.

"It seems that having this nerve from the forearm running through the shaft would give you some sort of vague sensation," I said, "but not necessarily an erotic feeling or an orgasm."

"Well, the brain is triggered by the nerve ending and then theoretically it would travel back and trigger the same muscles for orgasm."

But it was all speculation; he really didn't know, and I found myself wondering why they did not follow up with their patients and keep better track of such important information. As I probed further, I also found out that he didn't connect all of the nerves from the former clitoris to the new phallus; he just connected one or two, then left the remaining tissue and nerves of the clitoris in place. Hearing that turned me off; the idea of having two sets of genitalia just did not work for me.

But the final nails in the coffin were the photos. The phalli looked to me like big, ugly, disfigured sausages. When I asked the doctor how many phalloplasties he had done, he said about fifteen. And after discussing it further, he revealed that there was a high rate of complication. That was the end of that discussion.

We then proceeded to the type of surgery at which he was the expert and inventor—the metoidioplasty. In this procedure, the surgeons work with the very small penis that has already begun to form from the clitoris through the use of testosterone. Just as a clitoris becomes a penis in the womb through the addition of male hormones released by the male fetus, testosterone added in adulthood will also slowly shape the clitoris into a penis. However, in adulthood the change is much more minute, resulting in a natural-appearing, but very small head and a bit of shaft—sometimes called a "micropenis." During the metoidioplasty, the surgeon not only forms a foreskin around the head of this micropenis but also releases the ligament behind the emerging shaft, allowing for additional length. This is the same technique used in ordinary penis-lengthening surgeries. In my case, I was also going to have the vaginal lining/cavity removed completely and closed off, and then have the urethra extended from where it was, into and through the penis head, allowing for natural urination. Below that, Dr. Laub would form a set of testicles using the former labial tissue, which would then be stretched from the inside with testicular implants that could be injected with saline over time, eventually allowing for the placement of good-sized testicular implants. The final look, as shown in the photos, depicted a completely natural, scarless, male set of genitals from top to bottom. The one drawback—and it was a big one—was that the penis looked like that of a young boy on a cold day. The most someone could expect to get from the surgery was one to three inches.

The doctor then told me something that really threw me for a loop.

"Most people wait about two years after they start testosterone to do this surgery. It can take that long to get the full penis growth from the testosterone and there is a chance the surgery itself, with the releasing of ligaments and repositioning, will cut off any chance of additional growth. So that's something to think about."

Several months old

Behind the childhood home in Luxembourg, at age six

Europe after my parents returned from a trip to Japan, at age seven

Shirtless at a childhood birthday party in Europe

A family trip to
the East Coast,
at age twelve

With Dad
somewhere
in Europe,
at age eight

As a junior in high school,
at the county assembly dance

After senior prom, 1987

With my friend Sue, at my
college graduation party, 1991

With my parents,
following graduation from
the University of Colorado
at Boulder, 1991

Thanksgiving break during law school, 1992

Two years before beginning
transition to manhood, 1995

Six months
post hormones,
May 1998

Approximately one year
after beginning hormones,
January 1999

January 1999

Recovering at the resort Le Résidence in Montreal, April 2001

May 2005, at age 35

Panic raced through me as I thought, But that's more than a year away! How can I make it that long? And is the hope of a few millimeters worth the potential toll on my mental health? What if I suffer through all of that time only to find myself gaining nothing?

He saw my concern and said, "Let's go have a look, and see where we are before we get too worried about it."

I followed him out of the office and into a small examining room. In the middle of the room stood a chair that looked exactly like the kind you see in dental offices. The doctor opened a drawer, pulled out a package with a gown, and handed it to me. He left as I slipped it on, and I could feel my apprehension return. The few times I had looked at my lower body with any sense of real scrutiny, I had seen the tip of a small penis head peeking through, but without any real length behind it. The head was not much wider than the tip of a pinkie. And I now wondered how much length the surgery could give me.

When Dr. Laub returned, he was not alone. Behind him was a petite, blond, blue-eyed woman with delicate features. She was wearing a white lab coat and he introduced her as Dr. Annette Cholon, saying she would be assisting him during surgery.

I didn't like the idea of having a third person in the room while I got naked, but when I saw her move to the side and stand quietly by the wall, I felt better. She was clearly sensitive to the situation and was trying to be as unobtrusive as possible.

Once I was settled in the chair, Dr. Laub first examined my chest, saying he was curious to see another surgeon's work. When he saw my pecs, he said, "Wow, that really turned out well."

He then lifted the bottom of my gown and began to examine my genitals. "Well," he said after a few seconds, "you don't really have much length here; you barely have a shaft. But it is workable."

Dr. Laub realized we were running late for my appointment with the psychiatrist. I quickly got dressed, grabbed my briefcase, and started out the front door. On my way out, I passed a couple of people in the waiting room. One was a woman with long hair, wearing a dress, and the other looked like a butch lesbian wearing an ill-fitting man's suit. As I was making my way to the car, I thought, Why doesn't that person look male? They—or he—must have been on hormones at least six months to be down here for surgery. Then I thought, This is why people have such fucked-up perceptions of us; they think we all look like that.

A few weeks ago, Jack and I were having drinks and he related a story about a guy at another firehouse who had heard there was a transsexual man in the department. The guy drove by Jack's firehouse with his son and pointed to a masculine female firefighter wearing a baseball cap, saying, "There—that's the one."

Jack, however, completely escaped his notice.

A similar thing had happened to me. A new intern had joined our office and, on hearing there was a female-to-male transsexual at the courthouse, said to a colleague of mine that it must be hard to be both a transsexual and a Latino. When my colleague asked what he was talking about, she found he was referring to a genetic male in our office who had feminine features and a pear-shaped body. It never occurred to the intern that I, who had spoken to him on many occasions, might be the one.

As I was smugly singing my praises and distancing myself from the person I had seen in Dr. Laub's office, another memory began to wind its way through, tugging at my conscience. In the corner of my mind, I saw an image of myself checking my voice mail the previous week, only to find a message from another crank caller. This one was even lamer than the first, with the caller just saying, "You're a freakin' dork." But the message of the memory itself was clear: No matter how good I looked, there was always someone waiting to judge. And by focusing my attention on how I am perceived by others—good or bad—I am making myself more vulnerable for that next crank caller.

THE PSYCHIATRIST'S OFFICE WAS LOCATED IN A COMPLEX across the street. I took the elevator to the fourth floor and found the office of Dr. Elizabeth Mahler toward the beginning of a mazelike hallway. I knocked on the door and waited for a response.

When the doctor appeared, I couldn't help but smile. For before me stood another very attractive, petite, blue-eyed, blond woman. It was at that point that I started to wonder whether being beautiful was a prerequisite for anyone working with a plastic surgeon. It was like being in the middle of a magazine layout.

The doctor beckoned me inside and I found myself in a large, spacious office with a picture window revealing a clear view of the thick, green foliage behind the building. I sat in one of two cream-colored, leather armchairs, and Dr. Mahler took a seat in the other. Something about her gentle demeanor and the quiet, graceful way she moved around the room immediately drew me to her. I found myself looking forward to the next hour.

"So what has been your impression of everyone so far?" she asked.

As soon as I heard the question, I felt my old psychology classes kick in and thought she was asking because my impression of others is partly a projection of what I really think about myself. I was irritated by my own thoughts. I mean, obviously I was here to show that I am functional, but I wanted to do this with her in a way that was genuine, not manipulative.

"Well," I said thoughtfully, "so far everyone seems kind and efficient, which I like."

Dr. Mahler then asked some questions about whether I use any supplements or vitamins. I was somewhat surprised; so far no therapist, let alone a psychiatrist, had inquired into my use of health supplements. I gave her a list of the various vitamins I took, as well as some of the powders I put in my fruit shakes in the morning. She made a few notes, then moved on to questions surrounding my transition.

I spent the next forty-five minutes telling her my life story. I explained how hard it was to arrive at this truth when my own feminist teaching had led me to believe that all gender was an artificial construction. I told her how lost and invisible I had felt in the female identity, but how I didn't want to cut off my tender or emotive side just to be seen as male or butch.

At one point, she asked if I had ever been suicidal. I thought back to the night in Los Angeles, and the desperation that led me to break down and give in to all of this.

"No. But I think that's because as soon as I became conscious of this issue, I started doing something about it. But I honestly don't know what would happen if I couldn't fix this. I could easily see entering a permanent state of hopelessness."

When she asked whether I ever wanted to turn toward alcohol or substance abuse during the transition, I said, "Definitely—in the beginning. Being aware of the issue and then having to wait to appear male was unbearable. And many times I just wished I could take a pill and wake up when I was done."

"Well," she said, studying me, "you look good. You clearly pass now."

Hearing the word "pass" made me cringe. The word had a connotation that suggested the male identity was a role rather than the simple truth of who I was. And, of course, it reminded me that there was still a part of my body that was betraying that truth.

When the doctor asked me about past relationships, I explained how some of my lovers seemed to intuitively recognize our "oppositional chemistry." She latched on to that phrase and asked if I could clarify.

"All my life," I said, "I've felt this sense of sameness when I'm around other men—this underlying feeling that I am one of them. And when I'm around women, I've felt this sense of 'otherness,' like they are my opposite. Some of my lovers have noticed it, too, saying they felt this definite boundary of difference. And that difference, or that opposite energy, created a chemistry between us that had a strong romantic—and sexual—pull."

As I was explaining all of this, I saw a look of understanding slowly spread across Dr. Mahler's face. "I haven't ever heard it described that way," she said, "but it makes a lot of sense."

As we were nearing the end of our session, she asked if I had any questions for her.

"Have you ever read the book *Brain Sex*?" When the doctor shook her head no, I continued, "Okay, what do you think about the fact that transsexualism is labeled a psychological condition when it seems to me to be a biological issue—or basic birth defect?"

"I think many conditions that are labeled as psychological have a biological basis," the doctor responded.

As soon as she said that, I thought, of course—she's a psychiatrist. She must dispense medication for conditions such as depression in the belief there is a brain chemistry issue. I then found myself becoming curious about her work and her practice and how she ended up as Dr. Laub's evaluator.

I was gearing up to ask more questions when she said, "What I meant was whether you had questions for me about your own situation."

I laughed as I realized I had gotten carried away. It just felt unnatural to have this one-way conversation with another human being—especially when I wasn't seeking her services as a therapist. She was just a necessary—albeit very pleasant—stop on my way toward completion.

Dr. Mahler wrapped things up. "I don't see any reason not to recommend you for the surgery. You've responded very well to your past surgeries and it seems to me that you have the emotional and spiritual realm very much taken care of. I assume that the social and relationship aspects of your life will emerge more as time goes on—some people like to wait until all of their surgeries are complete before they start a serious relationship."

AFTER A BRIEF LUNCH, I RETURNED TO THE CLINIC AND stood there, trying to figure out how to get to Judy's office, when she appeared from around the corner.

"Why don't you first go in and see Dr. Laub again," she suggested. "We can talk after that."

I was glad to hear her say that, since I had been thinking over a few things during lunch. I opened the main door and saw Dr. Laub's office door was ajar and the surgeon was sitting at his desk. He looked up as I was shutting the door and beckoned me over.

"You know," I began, "I was thinking about the surgery date and I just don't want to wait another year. But a decent compromise that I can live with would be April."

"I was thinking about it, too, and I thought, Hell, why not do it sooner. And what we can do is order some testosterone cream for you to put directly on the penis and that should help promote growth."

Knowing that we had both arrived at similar decisions about the surgery date left me with a greater sense of confidence, and I stood up, ready to move on to Judy's office.

As I was walking out of the building, Judy popped up right behind me again, and I laughed, "This is like a sitcom. You keep popping up at exactly the right moment."

I then told her that I really liked Dr. Mahler and added, "I don't know if it is inappropriate to say this, but she's really attractive."

"For a psychiatrist?" Judy quipped.

"No," I said, "for any human being—no qualification needed."

When we reached the top floor, Judy led me down a narrow hallway and then into her office. I noticed that her window overlooked the courtyard, making it easier to understand why she'd had such good timing in finding me.

I walked to her bookcase and noticed some of the titles were in German.

"Your mother might be interested in some of those," she said.

As I was trying to make out the meaning of one of the more complicated words in the title of a book and sounding it out loud, she said in a teasing tone, "I thought you spoke German." Then she added, "Well, just until age eight, right?"

I was impressed with how detailed her memory was of the background information I had sent to the doctor's office.

"I know you have thought a lot about gender and sex and probably feel everyone should be able to be who they are regardless of gender, right?" she said. "Well, we look at ourselves as doctors who deal with people who have body image issues. And to us, gender dysphoria is the most intense body issue there is."

Judy's description appealed to me right away; it was so open-ended and devoid of judgment. When I read the *New Yorker* article on female-to-male transsexuals, I was most struck by the story of Louis Sullivan, a person who had wanted to transition from female to male but was rejected by multiple clinics. Louis not only knew he was a man; he knew he was a gay man. And before he passed away from AIDS, he used his time to educate the transsexual community about the fact that transsexual men, just like genetic men, fall into a wide spectrum of sexual orientation and varying degrees of masculine behavior.

"I'm not surprised that you have chosen the metoidioplasty because you strike me as a perfectionist, so it would make sense for you to choose this technique as it leaves no visible scarring," said Judy. "I personally think that phalloplasties are not yet where they need to be, but they will get better and the surgery you have chosen will not foreclose you from doing more if you want to later."

She then asked, "What are you hoping to gain from the surgeries?"

"The comfort of being free of my vagina, and also the appearance of externalized male genitalia."

She asked, "How would you feel knowing you probably won't be large enough for full penetration?"

I swallowed hard and said, "Well, I know I will miss it for my own pleasure, but I also know I can find ways to give deep penetration to my lovers, so they will probably mind less than I will."

Judy leaned in, looked me straight in the eye, and said, "That's a really good attitude, because so many men are so focused on their penises. And what you will find is that what women want most of all is to be loved."

Her words stirred up so much, so quickly: a childlike yearning and hope that my handicap really would not matter to any woman I encountered; my gratitude for the women in my life who had already proved that to be true; and a sense that I was holding on to a well of waiting—waiting for this journey to be over so I could finally let go and pour myself into another without the fear that I would forever remain lost.

As Judy and I walked down the stairs of her office building, she said, "Let's book the surgery date and I'll give you an informal tally of the costs."

I followed her back into Dr. Laub's office and she stepped behind the reception desk and took out a payment form. While she was doing that, the receptionists went through the dates and found an open day: April 1, 1999. She hesitated.

"Do you want a different date?"

"No." I smiled. "No. That's fine. I'm not that superstitious."

On hindsight, maybe I should have been.

When I reached the open courtyard, I let out a deep breath. It was not just the release of tension from a long day of appointments and decisions; it was my coming to grips with the fact that a huge medical fee was now my sole responsibility—all seventeen thousand dollars of it. And that was just the first stage.

There was nothing I could do about the fact that none of the costs was covered by my health insurance. Most of the time I didn't really dwell on it. But once in a while, during moments like this, I did think about it, and it bothered me.

My health insurance paid for alcoholics to get inpatient treatment and therapy; for morbidly obese people to get surgery; for depressed people to get drugs and therapy; and for people with sexual dysfunction to get treatment and surgery. But when it came to my condition, the insurers went out of their way to put in their brochure that they did not cover any services, drugs, or supplies related to sex transformations.

So, basically, if I kept avoiding the issue, if I pushed it aside and got more and more depressed, they would shell out the money to keep me doped up and happy. And then, if my depression—and unresolved body issues—got totally out of hand and I started overeating and became obese, they might even pay for the surgery to cut out a part of my stomach, or at least compensate me for the medication to lower my blood pressure and cholesterol.

But under no circumstances would they pay for my little vial of testosterone. Or my pecs. Or, of course, my penis. After all, the castration that had happened in the womb was only in my head. Right?

Eighteen

DECEMBER 1998

I am arguing with a heavyset woman in the middle of the street. In a fit of rage, I call her a "fat bitch." She immediately steps back, and says, "You know, it's unfair for you to call me 'fat' because men don't get as criticized about their weight. And 'bitch' is sexist because there really is no male equivalent." As she says this, I get the sense that she knows about my past, but is not going to use that against me. Grateful, I feel myself softening. . . .

It was early Friday evening and I was aimlessly wandering around my house, dreading the looming weekend. With all the preparations for surgery out of the way, there was nothing left to do but wait out the next four months. And that, as I kept discovering, was the hardest part.

The inadvertent pronoun slips by old work colleagues and friends had now dwindled down to the occasional. But when mistakes did happen, they were a painful reminder of the truth that constantly lay just below the surface: that I was still a prisoner in no-man's-land. And during those pockets of time when I wasn't actively planning my escape with surgical preparations or distracting myself with brief excursions to foreign towns, there was always a measure of pain threatening to seep through the cracks.

As I ambled barefoot across the living room carpet, I felt a darkness nipping at my heels. As a countermeasure, I found myself thinking back to my weekend in Reno, yearning to get away from the familiar reality of my own surroundings. Within minutes of the reverie, I had grabbed my jacket, laced up my boots, and set off on the highway, driving in a random direction. I was like a drug addict, trying to chase an old high in an effort to avoid the clutches of a despair that still remained partially unresolved.

ABOUT AN HOUR INTO MY DRIVE, I NOTICED I WAS APproaching a bridge. Since I had never taken the highway in this direction, I had no idea what lay beyond. But more important, I had no cash in my wallet, so a bridge toll was not an option. I flicked on my turn signal, preparing to get off at the next exit.

As I came down the ramp, I noticed that whatever town I had landed in was a small and desolate one. There were not many lights to be seen through the windshield, and the largest building I could spot was a sugar refinery. I set off in the direction of the lights, hoping to at least find an ATM.

When I came across a neon sign that said SALOON, I parked my car and walked inside. I saw a couple of pool tables and a bar where a few biker types in leather jackets were smoking. Clearly they were not enforcing California's smoking ban here; but then again, this little tavern probably wasn't on anyone's radar screen.

I asked the bartender where the nearest cash machine was and he gave directions that led me toward the sugar refinery. The streets were pretty empty and once I got my cash, I headed back toward the cluster of lights, looking for a larger bar.

As I drove up a small hill, I came across what looked like the center of town. There was a pizza joint with a few teenagers sitting by the large glass window, a couple of stores, and a few neon signs spelling BUDWEISER through the windows. I parked my car and headed into a bar that had a sign that said LIVE MUSIC.

Inside, I saw a couple of pool tables, a few bikers, and an older woman who looked like a seasoned barfly. I sat down at the bar, ordered a beer, and bummed a smoke from a guy a couple of seats over.

After a few minutes, I turned to the bartender and asked, "So where do all the women hang out?"

"Do they have to have all their teeth?"

I laughed and said, "Yeah, that would be nice."

"Well, then, you should really go down one exit to a bar called Jasper's—that's about as much of a meat market as you're gonna get around here."

THE TOWN ONE EXIT OVER WAS DEFINITELY MORE POPU-lated. As I veered off the exit, I saw a much larger cluster of lights. And when I entered Jasper's, the interior confirmed that as well. There was a large L-shaped bar, a dance floor, an area with small tables, and a stage where a DJ was setting up the sound system. There was only a handful of people, but the guy at the door taking the cover charge told me the place usually started to fill up around ten. It was a little after nine, so I took my seat at the short end of the bar, a couple of seats down from an attractive woman with long blond hair and a warm-looking smile. A tall, slim black guy was standing in front of her while she remained seated, and it looked as if he was making the moves on her. She was laughing as he talked. I ordered a beer and sat back to watch.

A few minutes later, another woman came in and sat down at my end of the bar. She had a heavy layer of makeup, long red nails, tight black pants, and a black mesh top. She also had a hardened, weathered edge that I found unappealing.

The sound guy came over and the two started to talk like they knew each other. Because there was music playing, I couldn't hear their entire conversation. When the man walked away, the black guy who'd been talking with the attractive blonde came over and started talking to the woman I decided to call "Mesh-top."

She interacted with him but also kept a distance. Her body was pulled back and her demeanor was distant. A few times, while the DJ was adjusting the music, I heard snatches of their conversation. The black guy was saying stuff like, "You're too hard on me—you've got me all wrong." I couldn't help but start laughing.

When the black guy noticed my laughter, he got a little self-conscious and said, "Hey, he's laughing at me."

His tone was friendly and I just shrugged my shoulders.

Suddenly, Mesh-top turned to me and pointedly asked, "What do you do for a living?"

"I'm a lawyer," I said.

Mesh-top turned back to the black guy and said, "See, he's a lawyer. Now that's a real job."

In the past, whenever my lesbian friends and I would sit down to share stories about our latest dates, there was a noticeable difference in our delivery. The first thing they inevitably shared was the profession of their partner. They would proudly say, "She's a doctor" or "I've snagged a successful filmmaker," or "I'm dating a hot young lawyer."

But I always found myself leading off with a physical description: "She's got those narrow dancer's shoulders" or "God, she's got this tiny, perfect ass that could fit in my hand" or "Her breasts are so perky—it's like they stand at attention."

One day, while having lunch with a lesbian acquaintance, I pointed out a waitress to her that had a hip, trendy, cute "dyke" look. I said, "Hey, isn't that your type?" She responded, "You know, at this point in my life, I'm just too old to date a waitress."

I looked around the bar and noticed the blonde had stepped outside for a cigarette. I slid off my bar stool and headed out the front door to join her. She kindly gave me a cigarette, and we chatted for a while.

The woman's name was Sandy, she worked as a tollbooth collector, and she had a boyfriend and two kids. When I heard that one of her kids was thirteen, I said, "No way, you look much too young to have a teenage kid."

"Aren't you sweet," she said, and gave me a peck on the cheek.

When we went back inside, I sat down next to Sandy and ordered a couple of drinks. She asked me to dance, and we headed to the floor and danced to some old seventies songs. After the music was over, I went in search of the bathroom.

The door to the men's room was a battered-looking wooden door that didn't have a lock. When I stepped inside, I was facing a toilet against the wall with a urinal right next to it. I instantly became nervous. I really didn't want anyone seeing me with my pants down and my prosthetic pinned to the inside of my underwear. I figured that I'd just better be quick.

I pulled down my pants and sat down on the toilet, facing the door, waiting for it to open. But it didn't. I managed to finish, pull up my pants, and get out of there before anyone came in.

When I got back to Sandy, there was a guy sitting in my seat. As soon as he saw me approach, he jumped off the stool, said "I'm sorry, man," and moved on.

A few years ago, Ashley and I were having dinner in a posh, outdoor restaurant with a view of the ocean. It was early in our dating, and we were at our most romantic, holding hands throughout the dinner and, at times, kissing.

At one point we noticed two guys openly staring at us. When I got up to use the bathroom, they approached her and asked if they could join us.

As I continued talking to Sandy, the bar filled up until there was a decent crowd of people. And so, when a couple of people who knew Sandy came up to talk with her, I grabbed my beer and set out to roam through the room.

As I moved around the tables, I noticed there were a lot of guys and women sitting together, so it was hard to tell who was taken and who was free. I noticed a couple of women who were really attractive and when the seat next to one of them opened up, I walked up and politely asked if I could sit there.

"Well, he might not like it," the woman said, pointing to a guy at the bar and then to her finger, which held a diamond ring.

My luck didn't get any better. Everyone I passed seemed either deep in conversation or totally disinterested. In fact, no one seemed to really notice me. And I couldn't help but think back to my days at chic lesbian bars where I approached the hottest-looking bisexual women and ended up with a pocket full of phone numbers.

I now wondered if the attitude of these women was different because women are used to having guys relentlessly pursuing them in bars, but in the lesbian community this kind of pursuit was much less common.

I headed back to the other side of the bar and saw Sandy was no longer there. I took my old seat back next to Mesh-top. She was talking to a big, tall guy with a broad, scruffy face. When she saw me, she leaned in and said something to him.

He looked at me and said, "Hey, don't indict me, bro."

Mesh-top leaned over and said, "He just got out of jail."

The man stepped up to me, stuck out his hand, and said, "Hey, man, I'm Nick."

"I'm Dhillon."

"Hey, like Dylan on that *Beverly Hills 90210* show . . . and you've got that cool hair, bro."

I laughed, then looked over his shoulder and noticed a guy had just come out of the bathroom and there was no one there for the moment. I walked into the men's room, shut the door, and quickly pulled down my pants. This time took a little longer because of the extra beers I'd had. I was just finishing and thinking, Almost done, I've almost made it, when a guy came barreling into the bathroom and headed straight for the urinal.

In one swift, motion, I jumped off the toilet and pulled my pants up, exclaiming, "Hey man, I'm trying to take a dump."

He said, "Take one, man," and started to piss at the urinal.

I realized then that he was not only drunk, he was totally unobservant.

I relaxed, flushed the toilet, and said, "No, man, I need my privacy for that." He laughed, turned his head to look at me while he was still pissing, and said, "Hey, are you Italian?"

"No."

He zipped up and turned to face me, "Are you Portuguese or somethin'?" He was slurring his words.

I said, "Nah, just a mix of other stuff." I then changed the subject. "How's the action out there for you?"

"Not good," he said. "But, hey, what are you gonna do, huh?" He laughed, put his arm around my shoulder, and walked out of the bathroom with me.

———

AS I WOUND MY WAY BACK THROUGH THE NOW CROWDED bar, I thought I heard my name. I looked around and saw Nick standing over by the pool table.

"Hey, Dhillon, come here, man. You gettin' any tonight?"

"Not really."

He put his arm around me and said, "I'm not gonna be happy until you leave here with some pussy tonight, man."

He then swept his arm across the sea of faces. "Come on. Who do you want in here?"

I pointed out an attractive blonde I'd noticed earlier. "I think she's good-looking."

At that point, the black guy whom I had seen earlier passed by, and Nick stopped him and said, "Hey, man. My buddy Dhillon here wants to meet that girl over there," and he pointed to the blonde.

All of a sudden, they both start gesturing wildly toward her, trying to flag her down like a waitress. She couldn't help but notice their gesturing and started to walk toward us.

Nick leaned over to her and said, "This is my buddy, Dhillon. We go back a long way, so I want you to be good to him because he's a really good guy."

I cut him off and said, "Listen, please ignore him. I just wanted to meet you because you looked like a really warm person."

"Well, thank you," she said, smiling. "I am a really warm person."

And then she asked what I did for a living. After I told her, she became really animated and said that she was studying to be a court reporter. As we continued talking, I found out she had a three-year-old daughter and had to go on welfare to qualify for aid to get through school. I found it really impressive that she was willing to tackle full-time studies while raising a young child.

The woman asked what had brought me out this way.

"I was just going for a drive and first landed in the town one exit over."

"You know," she said. "That town is known for its use of methamphetamines. In fact, this whole county is really into that. I used to do it, but I quit five years ago."

As she was finishing, a guy came over and said they were leaving. The woman turned to me and said, "I'll be back in a little while."

I walked to the bar to get another beer and ran into Nick again. Before he could recruit another target for me, I said, "So, how about you? How are you doing in here?"

"Hey, it's like a lottery, man. I'm just trying to decide who's gonna be the lucky one to get the prize."

"Well, good luck. I'm going to ask that girl over there"—I pointed to a tiny Latina woman—"to dance."

Nick slapped me on the shoulder, said, "Right on," and I set off in her direction.

The Latina woman was holding a drink and talking to a couple of friends. I asked her to dance; then, as she wasn't very enthusiastic on the dance floor, we ended up going outside for a cigarette.

While we were standing by the building, the woman said something about having to get up early the next morning to work out. When I responded that I, too, worked out, she said, "Really?" with a mixture of disinterest and skepticism. And then I heard her say something about my being a "small" man.

My immediate impulse was to go back inside that warm bar, walk up to the guys, and say, "Hey, man, that girl said I was small." I knew that without a moment's hesitation, they would put their arms around me and say, "Fuck her, man. Come on, we'll find you another."

But I didn't. Instead, I pulled out my car keys and headed home.

Nineteen

JANUARY 1999

I am talking with a man about how much I want a functional penis, and he starts telling me all about the hassles of having one, such as worrying about not being able to get hard at the right time, or getting a woman pregnant. I know he's trying to be nice and cheer me up, and for a brief moment it almost works. . . .

While brief trips to foreign places distracted me from my own state of incompletion, there was always one place that brought it home: the men's locker room.

On days I went to the office, I often stayed late to avoid the rush-hour traffic, taking the opportunity to use the courthouse gym. It was a small gym, consisting of a couple of Lifecycles, two Stairmasters, a rowing machine, and a basic set of weights. One of my coworkers dubbed the place the "rehab" gym, saying it reminded him of those sparsely equipped gyms you'd find in a rehabilitation center. But it was free and it got the job done.

And right down the hall and around the corner was the men's locker room. It wasn't much—just an extended bathroom with a few lockers crammed into the corner and a couple of shower stalls. But it served the same purpose as a locker room. And it was that purpose that separated me from the other men. For what was routine and uneventful for them was for me an exercise in contained frustration.

I could strip down to my briefs and the firm bulge that pressed against me. I could walk around in my bare torso—scars and all—and feel a sense of belonging. But I could not go further. I could not completely abandon my prosthesis, toss it into my locker, and make it into that shower. Even if I could easily get away with it by wearing a towel wrapped around my waist; even if no one stole a second glance in my direction; and even if the whole place were empty. I could not abandon that part of myself without feeling like I wanted to run home, lock the door, and not come out until this was all over. My prosthesis had become the glue that was temporarily holding me together.

And tonight was no exception. In fact, it was worse. I had just finished my workout and was sitting on the bench in the changing area, pulling my boots on over my sweaty socks, when a man named Sam came in.

Sam had been at the court for several years and was one of the people who had given me a really kind letter when my transition had been announced. That—along with the fact that he was a gay man—left me with no concern about whether he was uncomfortable with my presence in the locker room. But *his* presence made me uncomfortable.

You see, Sam was one of those tall, beefy guys who liked to strut around the locker room completely naked. And it was this very comfort he had with his own body that highlighted the discomfort I felt with mine. When he sauntered naked into the shower stall, I felt the sweaty weight of my damp clothes clinging to my body. And when he emerged and casually toweled himself dry, exposing his entire body to the air, I became sharply aware of the separation between my own flesh and the prosthesis that was pressed against the inside of my briefs. The silicone mold that had felt warm and comforting before now felt awkward and sticky. By the time I walked out of that room, the envy and the longing had eaten their way through me, leaving an empty, lonely void in the pit of my stomach.

As I trudged through the rainy night toward the nearby parking lot, carrying my work clothes in one hand and my gym bag in the other, I felt the envy turning into despair. It was one of those dark moments when I wondered if I would ever make it home.

When I spotted my car parked alone in the far corner of the lot, I felt a sense of hopelessness. The light drizzle was turning to rain, but I kept my slow and heavy pace. There was no one waiting for me at my place. But worse, I realized that even if there had been, I would not have picked up my pace.

When I arrived at my apartment, I peeled off my damp clothing and stepped into the shower. The water from the nozzle was a strong, forceful stream, and it quickly turned steaming hot. I picked up a bar of soap from the edge of the tub and began to lather my neck and my chest, letting the hot water seep into my sore muscles. As I ran the bar of soap across the flat hardness of my pectoral muscles, I felt that usual initial warmth. I continued down toward my stomach, soaping the area around my rib cage. In the last year, my torso had become thicker and denser, and it seemed that the muscles around my ribs had grown more prominent. As the soap reached my stomach, I glanced down and focused my eyes on the area where my pelvis joined my upper thigh. A few months earlier, I had noticed a line of muscle that had started jutting out.

Keeping my mind's eye focused on these images, I rubbed some soap on my hands, working up a lather, then quickly began to wash the area between my legs. As my hands made contact with my flesh, I could feel my jaw begin to clench. A dense cloud of polluted frustration began to form just below the surface. But instead of rinsing off and moving on, I did something that provoked me even further. Or, more accurately, a part of me did.

As I extended my pinkie finger and moved it toward the opening of my vagina, there was this cruel devil's advocate, saying, Come on, what's the fucking big deal? You've had this body part all your life. Why are you making such a fuss now? And like a fool, I took the bait. It was almost like a test. I needed to know.

I slowly pushed the tip of my pinkie into the opening. I felt a contraction. And then a tightness enveloped my finger. There was a pulling sensation. And then came the rage.

"FUUUUUCK YOU," I yelled, as the bar of soap smashed against the tiles. The bile of betrayal pierced through me, and I wanted to hurl my body through the glass doors, smashing my way out of there.

I pulled open the shower door, tearing down the towel that was hanging above me, and quickly grabbed a fresh pair of briefs. I savagely thrust my prosthesis into the crotch of the briefs and yanked them up fast and hard against my pelvis, trying to block out the rage—or at least put a lid on it.

I stormed into the kitchen, grabbed a glass from the cabinet, and lifted a half-empty bottle of wine from underneath the counter, cursing the fact that I had no hard liquor in the house. When my glass was full, I put down the bottle. It was then that I felt another surge of rage rising up. It snaked its way through me like a bitter poison. I wanted to get it out of me, to expel it.

The toaster was sitting on the counter, and I hurled it to the kitchen floor. It made a loud, resounding crash, and the metallic parts shook inside, spilling crumbs all over the linoleum. I grabbed my glass and moved to the living room, toward the sofa. But when I reached it, I did not sit down. Instead, I put down my glass and headed to the bathroom.

I opened the cabinet doors underneath the sink, reached into the far rear corner, and pulled out the bag with the prescription bottles. I ripped open the bag, found the vial marked diazepam, and opened it up. I poured a large pile of the little Valium pills into the palm of my hand. I then extracted one, put the rest back in the bottle, and walked out of the bathroom.

I was angry and I was overwhelmed. But I was not suicidal.

AN HOUR OR TWO LATER, WHEN THE VALIUM AND ALCOHOL had transported me a good distance from the immediacy of my emotions, I began to see things more clearly. With my nose no longer pressed up against the dirt, I could make out the lines and patterns. All was now becoming logical.

As my mastectomy had approached, my discomfort with my breasts had increased dramatically. I remember saying to Selena that I just wanted to tear the globs of flesh from my chest. I'd even resorted to binding them down with my boxing wraps during lovemaking. At the time, I was surprised by the strength of my reaction. I had thought that the knowledge that there was relief in sight would make it easier for me to let go of any discomfort. After all, it was all going to be over very soon.

But comparing that memory to my reaction this evening led me to a different conclusion: whatever it was that I had buried, whatever I had stuffed away and left for dead, was not only very much alive, it was aware of all that was happening. And each time I got closer to the light; each time it saw an opening, it came up for large, greedy, gulps of air. It was as if it knew exactly when it was safe to rear its head.

By the time the midnight hour had arrived and passed, I was exhausted. The adrenaline of frustration had completely run its course, and the aftertaste of Valium had left me feeling mellow and calm. That, in combination with the self-reflection, found me with a sense of nostalgia—a desire to connect with someone or something that knew my history.

The time difference between the United States and Germany was nine hours. My mother would be making her way through her morning routine just about now. I walked to the phone and punched in the fifteen digits that connected me to her. As I was waiting for her to answer, I went back to the sofa and lazily fell into the cushions, propping my feet up on the glass coffee table.

My mother answered on the third ring. "Hallo?"

"Hi, Mimsie. It's me."

"Ah, Dhillon, how are you, dah-ling?"

"Oh, well, I've just had a really rough night. I feel like this whole process is taking forever—and the waiting is killing me. It's just hard to be patient."

"You know, dah-ling, I think this is a time for tremendous growth for your soul. And maybe the pain you are feeling right now is also because you are carrying the pain of others who will follow in your path. You will make it easier for them to do this."

It felt comforting to have my mother acknowledge my own pain, to have her say, "Yes, this is very real." But the notion of my carrying the pain of others was not something I was prepared to embrace. I was barely making it myself. And given my current state of emotions, I was more inclined to get behind the "each man for himself" credo.

As we talked, my mother mentioned that my father had offered to pay for her to fly out during my April surgery. She said, "What do you think; do you want me to come?"

It had been almost five years since I had seen my mother. And the eager, naive boy in me who so desperately wanted his mommy quickly swept aside any potential doubts and said, "Yes, that would be great." With maternal visions dancing in my head I quelled the lingering concerns with a single all-encompassing explanation: whatever it was that caused me to keep a measure of distance from my mother, whatever it was that caused that need for separation, was simply owing to the fact that I was going through an unconscious battle with my gender identity—that I didn't really have all of myself.

It wasn't until the next morning—when I woke up with a slight sense of panic—that I questioned my decision.

When I was eight, I developed pneumonia. For three weeks I had a terribly high fever and was in and out of consciousness. I remember saying to my mother, "Mommy, I'm going to die, I'm going to die."

My mother stroked my hair and with teary eyes said, "No, darling, you're not."

Every time I called for her, she appeared by my side, feeding me small spoonfuls of sugar-sweetened yogurt so the antibiotics would not upset my stomach. The fever finally broke and I slowly regained my strength.

Life returned to normal. When my parents resumed their arguing, my brother stood off in the corner of the room. I, however, stepped in the middle, yelling at my father to leave my mother alone. When she later came to my room, crying, she brought a mattress with her to spend the night. And I let her in.

As she sobbed over my father's temper, I spoke to her in soothing tones, letting her know that I was on her side. It never occurred to me to do otherwise. I figured I owed it to her.

Twenty

FEBRUARY 1999

I am making a trek with a group of people up a tall mountain. Everyone is talking excitedly about an amazing house we are going to see when we reach our destination. When we finally get to the top, we meet up with a very old woman who leads us on our final stretch toward her home. As we get nearer, I see a house that looks completely unfinished; the foundation and basic frame are up, but there are no walls. The woman turns to us and says, "Isn't it amazing? Look at my huge windows. . . ."

Some people believe there is a benevolent force in the universe; that just when we have crossed our darkest hour, a moment of grace will arrive. If there was such a force operating in my life, then it had taken on a most feminine shape. For it was beginning to seem that whenever I was most consumed by my own misery—whenever I wanted to hole up and shut out the world—the gentle presence of a woman would arrive to lift me up.

So perhaps it was not just a coincidence that I should receive this message at this particular time.

"Hi, it's Virginia. I'm coming to San Francisco next week and I'd love to see you."

I met Virginia more than three years earlier, while attending a housewarming party with Ashley. I was standing in the corner of Virginia's living room when we were introduced. She was blond and blue-eyed, with the kind of pale, porcelain skin and soft oval face that reminded me of those women cast in films based on adaptations of Jane Austen novels. At the time, she was twenty-one or twenty-two, and she had a girlish innocence that revealed her age yet a refined social grace that belied it. I was instantly captivated.

But Virginia was Ashley's friend—not to mention the fact she was involved in a relationship of her own. So I quickly covered my attraction in my usual clumsy way—behind my obnoxious sense of humor. I don't even remember what I said, but Virginia giggled in a very flirtatious way that made me feel as if we were engaged in our own little game.

We didn't talk much more that afternoon. But I do remember her passing by a few times and glancing over her shoulder in my direction. It was the kind of glances that were less about her noticing me and more about her checking to see if I was noticing her. It was the kind of glance that pulled at that part of me that loved to pursue.

I stood in front of the bathroom mirror, dressed in a black suit and white shirt, and lightly splashed on cologne. I felt a surge of excitement and was trying to picture Virginia's face in my mind. I was trying to imagine how my face would look through her eyes. Would it seem strange? She had moved out of state before I started my transition, and although I had recently sent her some photographs, this would be the first time she would see me in person. As a man. And something about imagining my own face through fresh eyes allowed me to once again focus on what I'd accomplished, instead of what I had not.

As I drove over the Bay Bridge to pick up Virginia, I felt like a nervous schoolboy on his first date. This was even though I knew the woman who was waiting for me already had a lover. I felt this way because what I was looking for that night was not consummation—for which I was wholly unequipped in any event—but a sense of hope. And the fact that there was chemistry between Virginia and me; the fact that she referred to herself as bisexual—and had been with men—made me think that I just might get it.

After we initially met, I periodically ran into Virginia at parties and gatherings of mutual friends. Each time our interactions remained brief and we were surrounded by groups of people.

I do, however, remember one evening, where we had a few moments alone. We were standing outside a restaurant after a birthday celebration. When the meal was over, I had followed her outside so I could join her for a cigarette.

When she extended her silver cigarette case toward me, I noticed there was only one cigarette left. Normally, I would have said "Are you sure it's okay?" or "I don't want to take your last one." But instead, I brusquely said, "Hell, you probably have a whole carton of these stashed somewhere," and greedily reached out and grabbed the last cigarette, cockily tucking it into the corner of my mouth.

When I look back on that moment, I can't help but see a frustrated little boy pulling on a pretty girl's hair in an aggressive attempt to cover up his crush.

When I arrived at the address Virginia had given, I was facing a large Victorian house on the corner of a street. I found a parking spot, walked back to the house, and knocked on the front door.

When the door opened, Virginia's friend, Jennifer, greeted me. I recognized her from having spoken to her at some of our gatherings over the years, but she said, "Nice to meet you," and stuck out her hand.

"Good to see you again, Jennifer," I replied.

Behind her, I caught a glimpse of Virginia approaching the open doorway.

She had shoulder-length hair styled in a chic, wet look, and her makeup was subtle, with just enough lipstick to catch my eye. She was wearing a purple jacket that had a metallic sheen, and I could see the collar of her light blue blouse underneath.

Virginia smiled when she saw me. As she opened her arms to embrace me, she said, "You look great."

I hugged her back and whispered, "So do you."

I remember feeling self-conscious under the watchful eye of her friend. As soon as we separated from the embrace, I said, "Ready?" and began to steer her toward the door.

"Is it strange to see me for the first time since the changes?" I asked as we headed to the car.

"No, not really, because you sent pictures and we've talked on the phone. But while we were waiting for you, Jennifer was referring to you by your old name and saying, 'When is *she* going to get here?' I kept correcting her, and told her she would get it when she saw you." Virginia then asked, "Are there still people in your life who slip up with the pronouns or has that ended now that you look so clearly male?"

"I wish it were totally over, but there are still a few people who screw up at times."

As I backed out of the parking space, I said, "You know, I find there are so many gestures and expressions that now feel so natural. And yet, before, they didn't feel right. I know there are women who are comfortable expressing male traits, but for me it just felt jarring somehow—like they didn't go with my voice or face."

As I was saying this, I realized I had a strong desire to spill myself out to her, to confide in her. Something about our dynamic made me feel an intimacy with her.

The last time I saw Virginia, I was just months away from my first surgery, and she was on her way to graduate school in Iowa. I had attended her going-away party, and toward the end of the evening we decided to have dinner before she left town. It seemed strange that our first time alone together would take place just before we went our own separate ways.

At the dinner, I was so intensely focused on my transition, that my overactive libido was substantially overshadowed. In retrospect, I think it actually made me a better dinner date. For I was finally subdued enough to have a normal conversation with her. It was during this evening that I found out that Virginia was a creative writer and the graduate degree she was pursuing was a master's in fine arts. When I expressed an interest in seeing her work, she promised to dig up some short stories and send them to me.

When I eventually received the package in the mail, I set it aside until my weekend workshop at the meditation school. At the Saturday lunch break, I waited for the temple to clear out, then found a sunny spot at the end of a wooden bench under the windows. I slid my hand into the large manila envelope and pulled out two short stories.

One story described the interaction of guests at a wedding, while the other told about two people taking a trip across the country. But what was consistent throughout both stories was a sense that the central character felt invisible in a world where almost everyone communicated on the most outer surface.

The words Virginia had chosen revealed a delicate precision that conjured up images of fine brushwork across a canvas. And as my pages were illuminated by the sunlight that had warmed its way through the stained glass of the temple, I felt a sweet sense of connection.

We arrived at the restaurant and were led toward a large oval table that was surrounded by a plush, red, high-backed booth. It looked as if it were out of a *Godfather* movie. The lighting in the room was low and had a rich, muted tone.

When the waiter arrived, I selected a wine for the two of us, having first discussed the wine list with Virginia. And as I did so, I relaxed. I had spent the last few minutes trying to hold myself back, trying hard not to take over too much. It was something that hadn't concerned me in my former identity, but now seemed to periodically creep into my conscience, hovering around like a cloud of judgment.

As the waiter was placing our wineglasses on the table, I slipped off my jacket and put it at the end of the booth. When I brought my arms back toward the table, Virginia reached over, extended her index finger, and gingerly traced along one of the pinstripes in my shirtsleeve, remarking, "You are so dapper."

I could feel the coolness of her touch through the thin fabric of my shirt. It was a sensation that gave me the feeling I had been here, in this moment, many times before.

I asked Virginia about her recent trip home, and she began to tell me about her family. She came from an upper-class background with a mother she described as neurotic—and obsessively preoccupied with the rules of proper social etiquette. She said it was largely because of her mother's influence and emphasis on social rituals that she tended to use weddings as settings for her short stories.

I then asked Virginia if she'd ever had any personal desire to get married or fantasies about weddings.

"Oh, sure. In fact, when I was a little girl, I used to run around the house with an old shirt wrapped around my head, pretending it was a bridal train. I think it's my mother's preoccupation with the superficial social ritual that makes it all so complex. I guess you could say that I have kind of a love-hate relationship with weddings."

When I asked some follow-up questions about her family dynamics, she veered off into the story of a recent event that had taken place at her home. And as I listened, I felt more and more drawn to her. There was an open sincerity she had toward her own pain that was similar to the bond I felt with my closest friends. It was a common tendency to dig rather than to bury—a tendency that often left us feeling like outsiders in our families, but made us instant allies with one another.

Our appetizers arrived, and we realized we were not ready to order our main course. Instead of opening the menus, we sent the waiter off for some more wine and continued talking.

"I'd like to hear more about your transition," said Virginia. "I found the *New Yorker* article really interesting, but I kept wondering about the terms 'transgender' and 'transsexual.' Do they have different meanings?"

"Well, I know some people use the terms interchangeably, but to me and medically speaking they are totally distinct. One is a social issue and the other is a medical one. So, for example, transgendered people are not necessarily uncomfortable with their body; it's society that's uncomfortable with them because they look—and perhaps feel—neither distinctly male nor female. So there is a societal pressure for them to 'choose' a particular box, when they would just be fine if people left them alone. Transsexuals, on the other hand, have a biologically induced split between the chemistry of their brains and some aspect of their body. So even if all societal roles around gender were eradicated tomorrow, we would still feel a need to have surgery."

206

"I remember," Virginia said, "some of the transsexuals who were interviewed in the *New Yorker* saying while they were able to maneuver with some success in the lesbian community, they really didn't fit in."

"That's true," I said. "I definitely felt that."

"I remember when you and Ashley were going out, she used to talk about you all the time. She said that you had that 'boy energy.' She went on and on about how romantic you were, and I remember thinking at one point how we should really trade lovers."

I smiled at the compliment, and then asked, "So, do you find me more or less attractive now? You can be totally honest—I don't mind."

"Well . . ." she thought, "I've always found you attractive, and I still do. But to the extent you seem happier . . . this way, maybe more."

She then asked about my surgeries and I told her about my upcoming surgery with Dr. Laub, and my continuing and growing desire to be in a body that was completely male. As I was telling her about one of my most frustrating and painful moments, her eyes softened and started to glisten. It was an expression that held so much tenderness, that I felt an overwhelming desire to put my head in her lap.

The waiter reappeared, and we realized we had better make a dinner selection or we'd be talking for the rest of the night. We had already been in the place for almost two hours. We each picked up our menus, taking our task very seriously, and staying focused until we had chosen an entrée—salmon for her, ravioli for me.

After the waiter had set off toward the kitchen, I placed my menu back on the table, leaned in a little, and said, "I have to admit I've always been attracted to you, but I kept a distance for so long because I met you through Ashley. But I want you to know it's not just a physical attraction—it's a sense that there is a real potential. And that's a rare thing."

Virginia turned slightly red and started to smile. She looked down at the table and said, "All of sudden I feel really shy. I don't know what to say."

I remember wanting to lean over and gently turn her toward me for a kiss. I wanted to reach into that moment rather than pull away from it. But I also knew there was no way I could pull that off without crossing a line.

So I steered the conversation to a direction that removed her from the spot-light, without really changing the subject at all.

"One of the biggest loves in my life was a woman I met during my last year in law school. And I knew from the first time we went out that there was something real and substantial there."

"How could you tell?" Virginia asked.

"Well, there was a weird mix of nervous excitement and familiarity—things were new and intense, but effortless at the same time. . . . So, who was your big love?"

"I guess it would be this guy, Dean. He was my first serious boyfriend, and maybe it was so intense because we were really young. But he had a way of making me feel very beautiful and wanted."

She stopped for a moment, thinking, then turned to me and said, "In fact, you remind me of him. You, too, know how to make a woman feel that way."

Virginia was not the first bisexual or lesbian woman to compare me to a male ex-lover rather than a female one. But she was the first to do it since I had transitioned into manhood. And I immediately noticed a difference in my reaction.

My former self would have hungrily focused on the gender within the compliment, thinking, "See, I'm not crazy—you, too, see the boy in me." But that evening, living inside a face that everyone now saw as male, I found myself sitting back and just enjoying the compliment itself —all of it.

When our food arrived, we once again shifted topics, this time veering to Virginia's life in Iowa. It was at this point that she brought up her cur-rent lover—a writer she'd been seeing for the past six months. And as I lis-tened, I felt an irritation rising. It was as if this third person had suddenly shown up at our dinner table, breaking into the fantasy I had that Virginia and I were on a romantic dinner date.

As I continued to listen, trying hard to contain the possessive streak that had been ignited, she began to tell me about some of the problems she and her lover were having and the ways in which she was dissatisfied with the relationship.

Now, had this conversation taken place at the start of the evening, I might have been able to put on the friendship hat for a moment and be a supportive listener. But at this point, I was too far gone. I was thinking, "Man, this women gets to sleep with Virginia, to touch that body whenever she wants, and she's not even treating her well? It's not fair."

Containing my thoughts has never been my strong suit, so when Virginia mentioned yet another disappointing aspect of the relationship, I found myself blurting out, "Why stay when you could be with me?"

Virginia's face clouded over and she said, gently, "Dhillon, you're crossing the line. It feels like you're criticizing my relationship."

"I'm sorry," I said. "I don't know your lover. I was just reacting to the things you were saying."

It was our first awkward moment of the evening and the competitive perfectionist in me thought, Damn it. Things were going so perfectly. Why did I have to push it? I was sitting there, trying to figure out what to say next, when Virginia moved in a little closer.

"So, how's the ravioli?"

"Great," I said. "Do you want a taste?" And as she accepted a bite from my fork, I felt better.

I then asked her about dessert, and she agreed to share one with me. I picked up the menu and ordered something with chocolate. When it arrived, I moved in closer to her as we dipped our spoons in the same plate. By the time we had scraped the last remnants of chocolate off the dish, we were back to our flirtatious banter.

While our plates were being cleared away, Virginia set off for the restroom and I asked for the check. I glanced down at my watch and saw it was almost eleven o'clock. We had been at the restaurant for more than four hours.

But I was not yet ready to let her go—to return to my everyday reality without just a little more fuel for the fantasies that would carry me through. And so while Virginia was in the restroom, I plotted my next move.

When she returned, I said, "It's still early and my place is right over the bridge—less than ten minutes away. Why don't you come over for a bit? I'd love to show you a new song I just finished."

Virginia looked a little hesitant. "Really? Just ten minutes away?"

"Absolutely. I'm the first exit over the bridge."

WHEN WE ARRIVED AT MY PLACE, I PULLED SOME WHITE wine from the fridge while Virginia took a seat on the sofa in the corner of the living room. I poured us each a glass and brought one to her, setting it down on the glass coffee table. I then grabbed a stool from my breakfast bar, retrieved my guitar from its stand, and brought them both over to the center of the living room, across from Virginia.

"My voice is still settling in and I've just recently starting singing again, so bear with me."

I then softly strummed the first chord, and started the words to "No-Man's-Land," building in volume when I hit the chorus. It was a song that I had started writing during the early stages of my transition:

. . . Take my hand, I'll show you land
that cannot be defiled

Lose your feet
the path to beat
is well within your mind

in no-man's, no-man's-land,
No-Man's, No-Man's-Land.

When I finished, I slipped off the stool and put my guitar back on its stand.

"I love your voice," Virginia said. "It seems completely settled to me."

I was standing next to my keyboard and recording equipment, and on a whim I asked if she wanted to hear a piece of recording from my old voice to compare. She nodded, and I put in a tape of an old recording.

I was surprised by my own actions. Normally, I would be reluctant to play a recording of my former female voice for fear that someone would be even more likely to slip into the old pronouns. But the fact that I didn't feel any hesitation with Virginia told me just how secure I felt in the way she saw me.

"It's funny," she said after I had played a snippet of my former voice. "I know I'm supposed to be more familiar with your old voice, but it sounds strange to me now."

Virginia then asked if I would play another song, and as I sat down at my keyboard, I remember thinking if I can't touch her or say romantic things to her directly, this is the next best thing.

After the second verse, I stopped and said, "That's as far as I am. I haven't finished the rest yet."

"I feel calmness come over me when you play," said Virginia.

"Is it the music or the lyrics?"

"I don't know what it is specifically. I just know I feel peaceful and calm."

It was a response that, in its sincerity, once again drew me to her—for there was no attempt to shape her answer into something I was looking for.

WE SPENT THE REST OF THE EVENING DRINKING WINE AND talking about workshops we had each taken to develop our creative skills. And even though I had finished performing for her, I continued to sit in places where there was something stationed between us, such as the keyboard or the coffee table. It was extra insurance to keep me in line.

By the time we had drained our glasses, it was well after one o'clock and Virginia was fading fast. I picked up my car keys and we headed out the door.

On the way home, we were quiet, listening to the music from the car stereo. When we pulled up to the house where she was staying, the street was quiet and the parking spots were full. I double-parked and met Virginia at the curb by the back door of the house. I remember standing there, facing her, and hanging back a little; I still needed to be careful.

Virginia leaned in, kissed me on the cheek, and then briefly embraced me. As our cheeks grazed against each other, she said she liked the way I smelled. We separated and she said, "Thank you for a lovely dinner," and kissed me once again on the cheek. She then turned and walked to the house. I stood there watching her until she had unlocked the door and stepped inside.

As I was crossing back over the Bay Bridge, I reached over and turned off the radio, making my way home in silence.

A WEEK LATER, I RECEIVED A CARD FROM VIRGINIA, THANK-ing me for "the dinner, the music, and the charm." And at the end, she had added the following words:

> It really was wonderful to see you in your "new" incarnation. Wonderful, too, to rec-ognize it, not as something entirely new, but as something that was always there.

Twenty-one

MARCH 1999

I am in Australia, swimming down a long canal and wearing nothing but a long T-shirt. I feel terribly exposed without any shorts on. When I emerge from the canal, I hold my T-shirt over my lower body as I run through the backyards of houses, trying to stay hidden. I come upon the porch of a house and see swimming trunks hanging on the doorknob. I run to the porch, take the trunks, and race off before I'm caught. . . .

As I traveled south down Highway 101 to my pre-op appointment with Dr. Laub, I was thinking back to that July in 1997, when I was driving down this very same highway on my way to Los Angeles.

It was less than two years earlier that the thought of a male face was just a fantasy, tucked away in the farthest reaches of my mind. And now my own reflection in the mirror was as natural and familiar to me as the feeling of the seat belt across my flat chest.

I was thinking it was barely a year earlier that I had reacted with shock when my friend Jack spoke about the removal of his vagina. And now I was thinking that I couldn't wait to get rid of mine—and feeling as if some part of me had already let it go; that this was just the final, formal ritual.

When I arrived in Palo Alto, I first turned into the Stanford University campus, driving past medical buildings until I found the blood bank. Dr.

Laub's office had instructed me to donate a pint of my own blood for the surgery, just in case there was significant blood loss.

When I walked up to the reception desk and gave my name, the people there retrieved my registration form and the instructions from Dr. Laub's office. I was then handed the inevitable clipboard and told to fill out the information.

At the top of the form, my name had been printed and next to "sex" was the letter "M." I breathed a sigh of relief and began answering the questions. And then I came across one that stumped me.

Under the heading "Males Only" was the following question: Have you had sex with a male since 1977?

Well—yes, I had, but at the time I was female. So why were they asking the question? Was it because they were assuming that a man who was having sex with another man would be having anal sex and anal sex was risky? But if that were the issue, why not ask that question specifically? And if being on the receiving end of anal sex was the risk, why not ask the question of women, too? Or was it being implied that gay or bisexual men were carriers of the disease? And if so, wouldn't a woman who had sex with a bisexual man also be at the same level of risk?

Without knowing the assumptions behind the question, I was at a loss as to how to answer. But in the end, all of my musings were merely academic. After all, I was only donating the blood to myself. I finally checked "no."

AFTER DONATING MY PINT, I DROVE TO DR. LAUB'S OFFICE and was given a series of additional forms. I was told to hold on to the consent forms so the doctor could go over them with me.

As I was filling out the last of the requested information, the front door swung open and Dr. Laub entered. He walked up to me, and vigorously shook my hand.

"I should go and put on a tie for our appointment."

I laughed and said, "Why? I'm not wearing one."

But once again, I appreciated the fact he went out of his way to show respect.

We went to his office, and he immediately launched into a step-by-step explanation of the upcoming surgery. The procedure would last about seven hours and he would first remove the vagina, which would take up almost half the surgery time, as it had to be done very slowly and carefully. Dr. Laub told me the removal of the vagina had traditionally been accompanied by a great amount of blood loss, but since doctors had started using a new piece of equipment—called the argon beam coagulator—they'd had almost none. I also found that Dr. Laub did not personally do the removal of the vagina—that was done by an expert who specialized in that area. I didn't know this, but apparently there are women who develop cancer of the vagina and have to have it removed. For a moment my thoughts strayed to those women. For if there were women who were devastated by having to undergo a hysterectomy, what would the removal of a vagina do to them?

He also explained that while he would create the extension of my urethra through the tip of the penis, he would temporarily create a small hole as a backup exit from beneath my scrotum because the tissue forming the new urethra needed time to heal and urine would be too acidic for it. Dr. Laub said he would close up this hole during subsequent surgery when he would also place the permanent testicular implants.

A question nagged me about my new testicles, and I finally brought it up. "From what I understand, testicular implants are made of silicone. Are there risks there? I mean, do you believe that the illness women complain about with silicone breast implants is real?"

"Yes," he said. "It absolutely is real, which is why we had you fill out a form that identifies symptoms that predispose you to the disease. But you should also know that the kind of silicone used for testicles is much more solid than for breast implants, which have to be softer than testicles. The silicone used for testicular implants is so dense that even if you cut it over and over, it stays solid. So it's highly unlikely that it would leak into your system or be absorbed by it. On top of that, it is a much lower grade of silicone."

When I asked why they didn't use saline, he said it was because FDA approval costs millions of dollars, and there weren't enough patients to make a market for the product.

Dr. Laub then went over the consent forms with me, which required him to go over all possible risks—in great detail. As I heard him tell me that the removal of the vagina, because of its close proximity to the bladder and bowels, could result in problems with incontinence or basic functions, I felt a surge of fear. What if this happened to me? What if I'm incontinent? That led to the next thought, which was, I don't have to do this. I could back out. And as soon as that thought crossed my mind, I felt a different kind of terror. Another part of me felt terribly threatened and said, No way. That's not an option. All of these thoughts sped through me within seconds and culminated in my inwardly throwing up my hands as I thought there's nothing I can do—except pray that things will turn out well.

As Dr. Laub continued to go through the list of risks, I went through the same emotional thought cycle several more times until I finally just started tuning him out. After all, what was the point of letting all of these negative images pollute my psyche when there was nothing that was going to stop me from moving forward?

When I left his office, I stopped off to see the program coordinator, Judy Van Maasdam who informed me about my aftercare options. The surgery itself was done on the premises, which contained an outpatient surgery center but no overnight facilities. So within hours of the surgery, I would have to get up, go into a car, and proceed to some type of aftercare facility. Since it was such major surgery, I could not drive all the way home for at least two days.

Judy told me that my choices were to stay at a nearby motel or the local recovery center, which is an aftercare facility with a full nursing staff and twenty-four-hour care. Judy strongly suggested the aftercare facility.

"The vaginectomy is a very painful surgery, and people say they feel as if their insides have been ripped out—which they have been."

"Well, I'm not that concerned about pain, because I figure as long as I stay on the meds, I'll contain it. But I am worried about potential complications and making sure that I have some medical help right after surgery."

The cost for the Recovery Inn was five hundred dollars for the first night and three hundred fifty dollars for each night thereafter, while the motel would only cost me seventy a night. I was once again reminded of the constant tension between cost and comfort. But in this case "comfort" was not just about feeling cared for; it was about reducing my chance of postsurgical complications. It was about improving my chances of success. It was with this latter motivation in mind that I scheduled a few days at the Recovery Inn.

On the drive home, I found myself filled with a jumble of thoughts and emotions. I knew this surgery was not going to be like the others. I was not going to wake up, spend a few days in recovery, and be done. Rather, I was going to wake up with a swollen mess of tissue and pain, only to spend the next six months inflating my scrotum and urinating from a hole underneath my testicles. Then—maybe—I would end up with a permanent set of balls and a penis that could functionally urinate. But I would still be too small for intercourse. And the fact that I suddenly found my mind focused on the latter worried me.

As long as I was waiting for another surgery, I could hold on to the hope that better things were coming. As long as this transition was not officially over, I could soothe myself out of the dark moments with the knowledge that I was not going to stay like this forever. But now that I was heading toward the final stages, I couldn't help but wonder: What if it isn't enough? What if I'm not entirely happy with the results?

What if I still feel incomplete?

A WEEK BEFORE MY SURGERY I STOOD IN THE CUSTOMS AREA of the San Francisco airport waiting for my mother to emerge. I had moved to this section after seeing her flight number lit up on the board, focusing my attention on the doors that brought in the latest arrivals. I knew my mother would be one of the first to make it through the door. She was just not the type to sit back and wait.

My mother's hair was the first thing that caught my eye. It was a brighter red than I remembered from the days she first began using henna to turn her blond into a deep red. And it was now permed into a frizz of curls.

The next thing I noticed was how much older she appeared than I had pictured her in my mind. When she saw me waving and made her way toward me, smiling, I saw the lines creasing her face in a way that made me think of people I put in that "older" category. And while she was a year away from sixty, I had never imagined her that way. In my mind, my mother remained young and vital. In my mind, my mother remained powerful.

We embraced and after I picked up her largest bag, we walked arm in arm toward the car. On the way home, I asked if she was hungry.

"There's a place near my house where I always get dinner. We could pick up something."

"That would be nice," my mother said. "I couldn't eat that awful junk food they have on the plane."

When we went inside the restaurant, I ordered a chicken dish, rice, yogurt with cucumber, and a Greek salad. As the co-owner was putting together our takeout, I introduced my mother, and he said that I must look more like my father. It was the first time someone had suggested I did not look like my mother, and it made me wonder if my transition into manhood had diluted the resemblance between us.

When we arrived at my place, I pulled out some plates and cutlery as my mother looked around the loft.

"I love the tall ceilings and huge windows," she said. She then looked up at the open platform above the living room where I had placed my bed and asked, "Aren't you afraid you'll roll out of bed and fall over the edge?"

"Yes," I said, laughing, "a little. I've been meaning to put in a small railing."

As my mother stepped into the bathroom, I pulled out a bottle of wine and two wineglasses and set out some plates. Throughout dinner we sporadically engaged in small talk, but for the most part stayed subdued. My mother was tired from the flight, and I was trying to get accustomed to seeing her face after spending the last five years talking over the phone.

After we cleared away the plates, I went to pull out the sofa bed. As I was going to the closet to pull out some sheets and bedding, my mother followed me into the other room.

"Can I sleep in here?" she asked. "You could just put the mattress on the floor by the wall here."

"Are you sure? It's quite cramped."

We were standing in my office, and there was barely enough room to put the mattress in the space at the foot of my desk.

"Yah, I don't mind. It's quite cozy."

I went to get the mattress from the sofa, but I remember feeling surprised by her request. The notion of her being comfortable creating more space between us was not something I had expected. I was expecting the mother who had come into my room after a fight with my father and had slid her mattress right up next to my bed.

As I got into bed that night, I remember thinking that my mother's presence there felt almost surreal. Because I had not seen her since long before I had begun this transition, it seemed as if she represented another lifetime—a lifetime that now, in many ways, felt alien to me. Whenever I came across an old photo of myself, I found myself thinking, Who is that person? It was as if I were looking at a ghost, trying to find the substance inside.

And now, here she was—this powerful representative of my past. My mother. And, after having spent the last two years taking apart the most basic parts of my identity, I couldn't help but wonder, What else was not real? What else was I still holding on to?

I woke up the next morning to the sounds of my mother's making her away around the loft. When I leaned over and looked down, she had a bathrobe on and a towel wrapped around her neck. I lay my head back down and croaked out a greeting.

"Ah, there you are. Dahling, I hope you don't mind, but I was washing my hair this morning, and I just couldn't resist cleaning your bathroom. I started with the bathtub, but then I got going and did the basin and toilet as well."

Mind? Why would I mind?

"Are you kidding? I'm thrilled. Feel free to clean anything you want." I swung my legs over the edge of the bed, rubbed my eyes, and said, "I'll make us some coffee."

I climbed down the ladder and padded into the kitchen. As I was filling up the chamber of my espresso maker, I asked my mother if she wanted some fresh-squeezed orange juice. "I usually make some in the morning."

"Mmm, that sounds wonderful."

I picked some oranges from a nearby bowl and pulled a knife from the drawer. Over breakfast, we talked about the upcoming surgery.

"I just can't believe they expect you to get up after seven hours of surgery and leave to go to another place. I'm so glad you decided to stay at the recovery place with the nurses. I feel a lot better having some professional help those first few days."

When we had finished with breakfast, I put on my running gear while my mother donned her walking shoes, and we drove to a nearby beach. I wanted to get in a few more good runs before surgery. And I knew my mother liked to walk.

As we approached the seashore in Alameda, we both commented on the beautiful day. It was bright and sunny and unusually warm. And although it was still too early in the season for sunbathers or swimmers, there was a fair number of weekend strollers walking along the sidewalk that ran along the edge of the beach.

I drove along the shore, showing my mother the route I would take—how the sidewalk led to the nearby park, then ended with a path that opened to a set of homes lining the waterfront. We agreed to meet back at the entrance forty-five minutes later.

I began my run slowly, taking in the salty air and enjoying the slight breeze coming off the ocean. By the time I entered the park, I was in full stride, sweat pouring down the front and back of my sweatshirt. When I reached the gated entrance to the seashore homes, I turned around and made my way back.

I was passing a couple of isolated picnic tables near the entrance when I spotted my mother. She was doing some stretching exercises. My first impulse was to go over to her. But I held myself back. Something told me it was important to just continue with my run, to let this moment lie.

As I continued down the path, I watched my mother walk away from the picnic bench. And I remember thinking, despite all her proclamations of femininity, her energy and her body movements were actually more masculine than feminine. She had the forceful, brusque movements of so many German women I had known.

As I linked my observations to her German heritage, I found myself becoming more curious. I thought about the differences in masculinity and femininity among various cultures, such as the robust and hearty masculinity of the Irish versus the absence of that type of masculinity among most Asian men. And it made me wonder: if our cognitive structure—or brain "sex"—is affected by the hormonal environment of the womb during fetal development, are those hormonal levels also different among the various ethnic groups? Was it possible that the dietary differences among cultures—such as large amounts of soy in the Asian culture and the phytoestrogens they contain—could also affect the womb environment? Or was the difference passed on through the genetic material that set the stage for development of the brain?

And was it permissible to even ask these questions?

ON THE WAY HOME, MY MOTHER AND I STOPPED AT THE grocery store and picked up several bags of fresh ingredients for the evening's supper. I had invited a few friends to meet my mother, and she was planning to prepare her version of Indian chicken curry.

Back home, we ate a small lunch, going over our plans for visiting the wine country the next day. I showed my mother a map of some vineyards and made marks on the ones that looked most interesting. As we cleared away the dishes, she said she wanted to get started on dinner preparations. Curry takes awhile.

"Do you need me to help you with something?"

"No—why don't you play some of your music?"

Relieved, I happily trotted over to my keyboard and took my seat.

I started to play some chords to warm up, trying to decide which song to play first, but then stopped. I looked up at my mother and said, "Hey, I was just thinking. So many mothers make their daughters help them in the kitchen or have them learn basic cooking skills. But I don't remember your doing that. I mean, I remember spending a lot of time talking to you at the kitchen counter, but I don't remember cooking. How come you let me get away with that?"

"I just like to have the run of the whole kitchen when I'm cooking. I don't really like anyone interfering with my system."

Shortly after we moved from Europe to Connecticut, my mother became active in several groups, including the National Organization for Women and Amnesty International. However, when other women spoke of joining the workforce as the ultimate proof of emancipation, my mother would laugh and say loudly, "I don't need to work outside the home just to prove that I am emancipated."

A few hours later, the scent of spices wafted into the living room: turmeric, coriander, garlic. My mother was happily humming along to my music, and I felt a sense of security and comfort as I played.

When my mother had finished, I poured us each a glass of wine. As the chicken continued to simmer and marinate in its juices, we chatted away until the door buzzer sounded.

The first to arrive was a friend who had just returned from Bali where she had been studying new mask-making techniques. We had met a few years before, and I had invited her because I knew my mother would find her interesting. I had barely shown her inside and poured her wine when the buzzer rang again, leading me to Sue, who had returned early from the Peace Corps after struggling with a nasty staph infection. She had met my mother several times and would be waiting with her during my surgery. The other two who came were an old law school friend and a colleague from the courthouse.

Dinner went beautifully. Whenever I brought my friends together, they tended to get along well, carrying conversation with relative ease. And the friends I had introduced to my mother over the years always got a kick out of her strong, opinionated statements.

During a rare lull in conversation, one of my friends mentioned she was quitting her law-firm job to travel around the world for six months.

"That's wonderful," said my mother. "So many people live a life of just doing what they are supposed to do, instead of what is good for them." And then she put her arm around my shoulder and said, "That's why I am so proud of him—he does what he wants and doesn't give a damn what anyone thinks."

To hear my mother talk about how proud she was of me and this journey; to hear her using the pronoun "he" in reference to a child whom she had claimed and raised as a daughter filled me with gratitude. I remember watching my friends as they listened to her and thinking, Yes, this is my mother. Isn't she something? My mother was not the only one to feel pride that night.

The next morning, I was making coffee and my mother was in the shower when the phone rang. It was Virginia, calling to wish me well in my upcoming surgery.

She had recently sent a card in which she had tucked a poem she had copied by hand. It was a poem about rebirth and awakening.

As we were talking about the long follow-up procedures that would come after the surgery, I said, "I'm beginning to think that my main lesson in having to go through all of this may not be so much about gaining some special insight into gender. I think it may be more about learning patience and how to surrender control. I'm realizing that I've never been good at either of those."

At the time, I did not know the full significance of that statement.

CROSSING THE GOLDEN GATE BRIDGE, FLANKED BY ITS DEEP, red wings, and surrounded by a view of shimmering ocean and green hills, filled me with the same sentiment I have always felt when I cross the bridge on a sunny day: I live in the most beautiful part of the country.

As we got closer to the counties of Napa and Sonoma, the sun became stronger and hotter through the windshield. Without the ocean breezes, the temperature was ten to twenty degrees warmer in the wine country than it had been in San Francisco. As we entered Sonoma County, I remember pointing out areas to my mother and showing her a spot where I'd like to eventually settle down. We entered a stretch of road lined with vineyards and, yearning to get out of the hot car, drove into the first winery. I pulled on my shirt, and stepped out of the car.

We stepped into the main entrance and found ourselves standing in front of a gleaming wooden counter. A woman behind the counter greeted us in French, referring to us as *Monsieur* and *Madame,* and after we both responded in French, they continued the conversation that way, explaining the wine selection and asking for our order. I managed to make it through the first few sentences, but then started to get lost, so I let my mother take it from there. We picked up our glasses of wine and carried them into the other room, laughing. That was another aspect of my mother I liked very much—she loved to immerse herself in whatever language or culture was presented to her, rather than feeling the need to assert her own. Whenever I called and got her answering machine, I couldn't help but be impressed with the fact that her message was delivered in German, then English, then Italian.

After we had toured the hallway, looking at displays and reading the signs, we headed toward the woods and began traveling down the path of a marked walking trail. As we reached a clearing, we stopped to look at the vast expanse of open land and vineyards.

"So much of this area has a European flavor to it," said my mother. "I could live here."

On its face, it was an innocuous comment. But my reaction was sudden and swift. "But this is my area," I protested. I immediately regretted how much I had extolled the beauty of northern California.

"Just because you want this place to yourself doesn't mean I should stop myself from moving here if the opportunity should arise."

"What opportunity?" I thought. And then I wondered why she would so adamantly assert her right to come to the one corner of the world I had claimed as mine if I didn't want her here—wasn't that what therapists call passive-aggressive?

But as we continued on and my anger subsided, I found myself questioning my own reaction. Did I really need all this space to myself? And of what, exactly, was I afraid?

ON THE EVENING BEFORE MY SURGERY, MY MOTHER WAS making pasta when the phone rang. It was the anesthesiologist, calling to get some basic information. I remember being surprised; no other anesthesiologist had ever called me at home before surgery. But he was all business, and he had a quick way of talking—like a sergeant preparing for battle.

After I hung up, my father called, wishing me well. By the time we ended our conversation, it was after nine o'clock. Dr. Laub had prescribed some pills for me to take the evening before surgery and the way the label was worded, I somehow thought they were high-speed laxatives or designed to empty my stomach. Based on this assumption, I ate a hearty meal and polished off a fair amount of ice cream for dessert.

By midnight nothing had happened from the pills, so I prepared myself for bed with a very full stomach. I remember a nice sense of anticipation and excitement. I was now only seven hours away from surgery.

I walked to my mother to say good night. As I came toward her, I experienced a wave of nostalgia—and then—a twinge of guilt for my earlier statements at the vineyard. I reached out to embrace her and said, "Thank you for continuing to love me throughout all of this. I know I haven't always been easy."

My mother started to cry and said, "Thank you for choosing to live. So many people would have just given up in your situation."

And in that moment, I thought, "Maybe this is it now. Maybe everything will finally turn out all right."

Twenty-two

APRIL 1999

I am being wheeled in for surgery and everything is disorganized—no one seems to know what he is doing. A nurse comes over to put in my IV and it hurts, so I ask her to take it out and put it back in properly. I keep feeling a desire to stay awake so I can monitor the whole operation. I don't trust that things are going to go smoothly. . . .

The alarm sounded at 5:00 A.M., and it was dark outside as I slowly crawled out of bed. I still had a very full stomach and I was hoping I might get my system moving enough to use the bathroom. But without any coffee in me, it was a lost cause. And that standard presurgery instruction had now been etched into my mind like a repetitive mantra: no fluids after midnight.

As my mother and I quietly got our things together—and waited for Sue to arrive—my mind continued to stay on my stomach. I don't remember feeling any genuine fear or apprehension at the time. At that point, the idea of potential complications was just that: an idea. My surgeries had been so smooth and uneventful that there had been no opportunity for my mind to wrap itself around any concrete fears.

———

WHEN WE ARRIVED FOR THE SURGERY, THERE WAS NO ONE visible and we didn't hear any sounds in the place. It seemed deserted. Eventually a door opened and an older woman in surgical gear led me to a changing area. I put on a thin gown and carried my cap in my hand to where a gurney was waiting for me. Once I got in the bed, the nurse brought over a thick, warm blanket and placed it over me. All of her movements were quick and efficient; she had clearly been doing this a long time. She then set off to the waiting room and returned with Sue and my mother, who sat in some chairs by the gurney.

As we were all waiting, a tall, middle-aged guy came in and asked the nurse for a towel. She got it for him, then came back to me and said, "That's your anesthesiologist. He likes to ride his bicycle to the surgeries; he's in amazing shape."

When the anesthesiologist had finished drying off, he came over and began to go over the preparations. He used that same, rapid-fire speaking style I'd heard last night and it was hard to squeeze in a question. I would have preferred him to be a little more mellow, but he struck me as very competent so I just settled back and relaxed. Toward the end of our conversation, Dr. Laub appeared, and I introduced him to Sue and my mother.

It was at that point that I began to feel there were too many people around. I knew I was about to go under soon and I wanted to get into a quiet place. So I turned to my mother, and to Sue, and told them I'd like to be alone. They each came over and kissed my cheek. And then they were gone.

As soon as they left, I felt calmer—and more focused. While they were wheeling me into the operating room, I remember thinking that I hadn't seen Dr. Cholon—the pretty woman I had met during my first appointment with Dr. Laub. I'd thought she was assisting him.

When I asked for her, the nurse looked at my expression and said in a teasing tone, "I think someone has a crush."

Then the anesthesiologist piped up, "Don't worry, I'll keep an eye on her for you. It's my job to do the dirty work."

I started to laugh, then felt a strange sensation in my hand. When I looked down, my entire hand was filled with blood. Somehow the IV had backed up or come loose . . . or something. One of the nurses grabbed my hand, adjusted the IV, then taped it back down. Another nurse replaced my bedsheet, which had become stained with blood.

When everything was back to normal, the anesthesiologist came back and said, "You're going to feel a slight burning sensation as the drugs go in, but it will go away after a few seconds."

I remember thinking that was weird; none of my other surgeries had been accompanied by such a sensation. But there it was—a slight stinging and then a coldness as I felt the substance make its way through my veins. I wondered if each anesthesiologist used different combinations of drugs. And then somewhere toward the end of this thought, my mind became hazy. Distorted. And then I was out.

I AWOKE TO A HUGE WAVE OF NAUSEA. I REMEMBER SAYING, "I'm going to be sick" and then a nurse was holding my head and a basin as my whole body was wracked with violent heaves. But nothing came out. I then felt a wet cloth on my forehead. And I knew that things were not right.

Then Dr. Cholon was hovering over me. Her surgical mask was pulled down around her neck and her hair was tucked under the surgical cap, highlighting her flawless face as she gently said, "I've been here the whole time."

I heard concern in her voice. I saw my own hand reaching out through the bed rail as I wrapped my fingers around her thumb. And then I was out.

When I opened my eyes again, Dr. Laub was hovering over me saying, ". . . So you lost over a liter and a half of blood—three pints. We had to stop the surgery. We had to transfuse you with other blood. Your donated pint was not enough and. . . ."

The only thing that caught my attention were those six words: "We had to stop the surgery." I felt a terrible panic. No. No. This can't be!

I was frantic as I asked, "How far did you get? How much did you do?"

I had to know—now. But then I was out. Again.

The next time I awoke, a nurse was adjusting my IV. As soon as Dr. Laub's words came back to me, the panic started again.

"Where's Dr. Laub?" I asked the nurse. "Please bring him here. I have to ask him something. Please."

And then Dr. Laub was there again.

"So how far did you get?" I asked. "What happened?"

"I've told you several times now, but you don't remember because of the anesthesia. We should talk later when you've had more rest."

And I said, "No. Now. I need to know. Please tell me again."

And he said, "We finished removing the vagina and I started building the extension to your urethra, but by that time you had lost too much blood. It wasn't safe to continue."

So they'd barely done the first part. I had no scrotum. No little penis. Nothing. And I immediately wanted to fix that. To change it. To skip to the future.

"When can we go back in? When can we finish?"

"I'm reconfiguring as we speak. We'll make a plan."

I fell back on my pillow and said, "Goddamn it. Fuck."

Suddenly, my mind flashed to the *New Yorker* article and I remembered it had described Dr. Laub as a devout Catholic. I turned to him and apologized for swearing in his presence.

I heard him say, "It's okay to swear; I'll swear, too—goddamn it."

And then I was back, trying to assert control again. "Can we do the next part all at once? Can you put in the testicles then, too?"

"We'll see," he said. "It's possible. We'll just have to see."

I felt a little better. Maybe we could make up lost ground in the next surgery. Maybe not all was lost. Then I was out again.

WHEN I NEXT AWOKE, I WAS IN A DIFFERENT ROOM. IT WAS quiet and there was just one other person in the room—a nurse. I figured I must be in a recovery area.

The nurse came over and began to adjust something on the side of my bed. When I looked up at her, I noticed that she was not one of the nurses from the operating room and I found my attention resting upon the features of her face. Her blond hair was swept back with one of those headbands women wear in commercials for facial cleanser, accentuating her soft, delicate features in a way that reminded me of Dr. Cholon. And then, for some reason, I found myself focused on her eyebrows. They were these high-arched, perfect eyebrows that look like they've been shaped by a professional makeup artist. Thinking aloud, I said, "Wow, you really have some cool eyebrows."

The nurse said, "Well, thank you," in a casual, friendly tone that completely belied the fact that we were in a hospital and I was speaking to her with tubes out of everywhere.

Some tubes were coming from my crotch and when the nurse pulled up the blanket, I saw two tubes leading out from under my briefs. They looked like the same kind of drainage tubes they had put in after my chest reconstruction. Then there was the catheter—the tube that was between my legs, draining urine from my bladder into a bag hanging from the side of the bed.

Other than tubes, there was not much else to see. My crotch was covered with a tight bulge of bandages beneath a pair of mesh briefs. And as I was watching the attractive nurse work near my bandaged crotch, I remember feeling a sense of relief. For that thick bulge of bandages between my hairy, muscular legs made me look like a normal guy who'd had some type of genital surgery. There was nothing to reveal the full truth of what lay beneath. And I was grateful for the reprieve.

"Where is everybody?" I asked. "Where is Dr. Laub?"

"He's talking with the Recovery Inn. He's filling them in on the surgery before you go over there."

What she didn't say—and what I found out later—was that Dr. Laub was arguing with them because they didn't want to take me. I had lost so much blood, they thought I was too unstable.

As I became more coherent, I began to notice more. I saw that I had an IV coming out of each arm, and both of my forearms were crusted with blood and bruised. I lifted my head to look around some more, but quickly felt a wave of nausea. I said, "I feel sick" and dropped my head back onto the bed. A few moments later, the nurse came and gently placed a warm, wet towel on my forehead. I closed my eyes to let the wave pass.

When I opened them again, the nurse was standing a few feet away from me. I remember feeling a lot better. The nausea was gone, and I felt a light haze around me—like a pleasant coating. It made me wonder if she'd given me more medication.

I turned to the nurse and said, "What's your name?"

She replied, "Mary."

I then asked, "How long have you been working here?"

"Just two weeks."

I lay my head back down and started giddily babbling something about how nurses were like guardian angels to me. I remember her saying, "It's really nice to be thought of that way." She had a really sweet, affirming tone that reminded me of one of my childhood kindergarten teachers.

She then took a few steps toward my bed and said, "Can I ask you— how is your family with all of this?"

I sleepily waved my hand in the air and said, "Aww—they're fine."

The nurse responded, "That's great—really great." And then she busied herself by checking my tubes again.

I continued rambling for a while about unrelated topics and then slowly started to drift off. At one point I opened my eyes and saw Mary sitting on a stool a few feet from the foot of the bed. She had a curious expression on her face—as if she was studying me. And when she saw me looking at her, she quickly turned away, like she was embarrassed.

I drifted off again, waking occasionally to find Mary with the same expression. At one point, the thought occurred to me that if she'd only been here two weeks, she might not yet have met anyone with my condition. Perhaps she was looking for some female features within my face or wondering how the transformation took place. Whatever it was, I didn't mind it at all, for I sensed nothing but kindness and tenderness in her.

It seemed as if I'd been in the recovery area for several hours when Dr. Laub appeared again and said that the Recovery Inn was ready to take me. He said they'd retested my blood levels while I was asleep and the hemoglobin levels were showing up as normal now; my body seemed to be recuperating from the blood loss rather quickly. He also told me he had spoken to my mother and that she and Sue were on their way. As he was walking away, I heard him tell Mary that my mother had said it was a full moon that day and one should never operate on a full moon. I felt a sense of irritation upon hearing that.

As soon as Dr. Laub was out of the room, I was relieved. It was just Mary and I again. Things were peaceful with her. Quiet and still. I continued to drift in and out of consciousness as Mary gently made her way around the room, staying close by. During the times she approached the bed to check on things or make adjustments, my pattern of drifting in and out remained the same. Her presence was so amazingly subtle, it seemed to have taken on the natural shape of the air around me.

I was still in a quiet, peaceful state when Sue and my mother finally arrived. As they entered the room, my mother walked in first, while Sue hung back.

"My, your cheeks look so pink and healthy!" cried my mother.

Her tone struck me as loud, and I immediately felt conflicted because I was not glad to see her. And I didn't want to feel that way.

"I told Dr. Laub they should not have operated on a full moon," she said. "I remember noticing it this morning, but I didn't say anything. I should have thought about it before—we could have rescheduled the surgery."

I said, "Whatever—it's done now."

Mary suggested my mother and Sue drive the car around while I got dressed and my mother volunteered to get it. As she headed out, I felt sad—like reality was now coming in and I was leaving behind the hazy, suspended limbo I had shared with Mary. Mary brought over my clothes and started to help me get dressed. I remember going really slowly, delaying things. I wanted to stay a few more minutes with her. Everything about her was so soft and tender and spacious.

Getting off the bed was difficult. With the tubes sticking into my crotch, I couldn't actually sit up without their digging into me—I had to sort of roll off the bed sideways. The nurse helped me into a wheelchair and wheeled me down a ramp to the car. I slowly climbed into the passenger seat, and lay back as far as I could to avoid sitting on those damn tubes. My mother got into the backseat and Sue took over the wheel. I then said good-bye to Mary and she gently shut the car door, waiting in the drive-way as we pulled away.

THE DRIVE TO THE RECOVERY INN WAS AWFUL. WITH EVERY bump, I felt the tubes dig in. They had stopped the pain medications toward the end of my stay, and I was starting to feel a dull ache in my crotch. I glanced at Sue and noticed how nervous she looked as she drove over each bump, slowing down to a crawl and checking my expression along the way.

When we finally arrived, I expected the staff to be waiting to transport me to my room. But no one was there. At this point, my mother took charge and ran inside to get someone while I sat in the car, cursing. My mood was going from bad to worse as I realized the hard part was just beginning.

A few minutes later, someone came with a gurney. When we arrived in my room, it struck me as a reflection of my ever-descending mood. The room was small and had very little natural light. My mother's pullout bed was at the foot of mine, with just inches between us.

It took a while for the nurses to get me into bed and even longer to figure out how to hook the IV again to the bag. By the time the nurses were finished, my dull ache had turned to a sharp pain. But all of that was overshadowed by a depression that was starting to settle in like a cold, dark winter evening.

I was given some morphine, which ended up making me nauseated again, which led to more antinausea medication. At one point I requested juice; my lips were dry and cracked, and my mouth felt as if it were full of cotton. But the nurses told me I couldn't have any juice or food. I gave up and eventually passed out.

When I woke up, Dr. Laub was talking to my mother. Noticing I was awake, he told me he had just gotten back a pathology report. Apparently, when they removed the vagina, the tissue had bumps all over it that looked like cancer. But it wasn't—the report showed it was benign. Dr. Laub said it was just a virus—warts—probably caused by the testosterone. It was another dramatic turn of events, and I was just glad they had not told me their fears before the report came back.

I was quickly losing confidence. And faith. In a last-ditch effort at some sort of hope, I asked Dr. Laub about the next surgery and what we could do. But he was vague and just said he was working on a plan. At that point, I turned away and closed my eyes. As he was walking out, I heard him talking to my mother in a low voice. And I heard him say, "He's okay physically, but he's about sixty percent mentally."

I instantly felt a surge of rage. I wanted to yell, "I'm not some goddamn mental patient."

But I didn't. For as quickly as my anger rose, it fell right back down again. At that point, even my own anger felt impotent. Deflated. Pointless.

THE NEXT FEW DAYS PASSED IN A HAZE OF DEPRESSION AND pain. I pressed the call button every time I woke up and requested more drugs so that I could fall back into unconsciousness. There was a brief visit from the doctor who had removed my vagina. He was a young, tall Asian man who had filled in for the older surgeon Dr. Laub normally used. I couldn't help but think his youth or lack of experience might have been the culprit in this disaster. When he lifted the blanket and checked under the bandages, I felt another surge of rage. Here he was, exposing my female genitalia, groping me, reminding me of what I lacked. What I was missing. And I couldn't help but hate him. I wanted him out of there. I refused to acknowledge him or speak to him. He left quickly, saying things looked "fine." And I couldn't help but think that he was just there to cover his ass. He didn't give a shit.

As I was drifting back into my drug-induced haze, my mother walked into the room.

"Hi, Dhillon," she said loudly.

It was the third or fourth time she had done that—addressed me loudly while I was drifting off. I remember asking her not to do that—not to talk to me when I was trying to sleep.

"But you always have your eyes closed. How am I supposed to know when you want to talk?"

"When I start talking."

I remember wishing that I could just be alone.

By the second day I was starving, but no one would let me eat. That evening, my mother was talking to a nurse about her dinner, asking whether the place had vegetarian food. I remember hearing her rattle off a list of specific requests, including an order for a bottle of Perrier. Where does she think she is, I thought—some goddamn spa?

LATER, ONE OF THE NURSES CAME TO GET ME UP FOR A SHORT walk. She said it was important that I start my system moving. I slowly and carefully dragged myself up, then mustered my strength so I could hop out of bed without impaling myself on the drainage tubes. As I stood there, holding on to my IV pole, feeling weak and shaky, my mother started to laugh.

"Oh, my God," she laughed. "You look like Jesus Christ in your gown."

I clenched my jaw and slowly made my way out of the room. I walked down the length of the hallway. And then I came back. As soon as I got into bed, I asked for more pain medication.

The next day, Sue came but I didn't feel like seeing anyone so she went for a short walk with my mother. With my mother out of the room, I felt more space around me. And whatever had been feeling cramped or dampened in me started to expand a little. There was a sense of sadness. And I felt very alone. I found myself thinking back to Mary and wishing she were here. No one here made me feel the way she had.

As I continued to lie there alone, I wondered if I had been too hard on

235

my mother. I wondered why I hadn't reached out to her. She'd come all this way to take care of me. Why wasn't I letting her do that? I started to feel a little sliver of childlike hope as I thought, Maybe I can change that. Maybe I just need to show her what I need.

WHEN MY MOTHER CAME BACK TO THE ROOM, I SAID, "HI. Will you come over here and hold my hand while I just quietly lie here?"

My mother seemed surprised but pulled up a chair by my bed. She reached over, took my hand, and clasped it in hers. Her touch felt warm and rough. And she had somehow pinned my thumb under hers in a way that felt confining rather than soothing. But I wasn't ready to give up. I slowly moved my thumb out from under hers until it was free and just lightly resting on top.

My mother pulled her thumb out from under mine and immediately reasserted her grip over mine. I pulled mine out again. But she put hers on top again. I started to feel like I was caught in a bizarre game of thumb wrestling. And my mind could not quite grasp how this could be. It was so contrary to what I needed. After a few more minutes of this, I said, "Okay, thanks. I'm going to sleep now." As I turned away, I felt more alone than ever.

The next day was Easter, and in the morning a nurse brought over a three-page fax from Dr. Laub explaining the possible methods he could use to finish everything during the next surgery. On top of the fax he had written that he would stop by in the afternoon for a "nice Easter discussion."

As I went through his notes, it became clear to me that if we did this all at once, we would be making medical history. There were various points at which he had question marks after his notes, which listed specific risks if he did everything during the same procedure. Seeing those question marks made me more than a little apprehensive. It was not what I'd been hoping for.

"It looks as if it might be risky to try to finish this all at once," I said when he arrived. "What do you think?"

"We'll just have to see how good the blood supply is to the tissue. If it's pink and healthy, then I'll move on."

His tone then changed from clinical to serious as he said, "We need to talk about the emotional aspect of failure. It's important for me to know that a patient is prepared for that and has good support. Unlike the legal profession where lawyers are generally in adversarial positions, in the medical profession we all work as a team toward a common goal."

I understood what he was getting at and I said, "I'm going to be all right. But I need some time to let myself be upset. I can't just bounce right back. If I did, it would just hit me later."

"When things go wrong, I feel bad and guilty, too. When you're upset, I'm upset."

"Well, when I'm feeling crappy, I can't make you feel better about me feeling crappy. You can't expect that from me."

Dr. Laub suddenly burst into laughter, "That's true."

He then reached out his hand toward me and as I went to shake it, he unexpectedly leaned over and pulled me into a quick, awkward embrace. It wasn't just the physical move that caught me off guard; it was the emotion behind it. There was this huge sense of relief and joy emanating from him that felt like the kind of emotion a father expresses after almost losing a son. It was the strength of that emotion that closed the distance I had created between us in the past few days. For until that moment, it had never occurred to me that my surgery would impact him beyond the professional level.

After Dr. Laub left, I did not feel more confident that I would get everything done in a single surgery. But I did feel a deeper sense of confidence in him—not only as a doctor but also as a person.

UNFORTUNATELY, MY BREAKTHROUGH WITH DR. LAUB DID not carry over to my mother. In fact, things got worse. That evening, I was finally allowed to have my first meal. But after four days of not eating and of taking large doses of pain medication—including morphine and Demerol—I had pretty much lost my appetite.

The nurse brought several pills along with the meal. As she was making some adjustments to my bed, my mother started to give advice. It was something that she had done throughout the past few days and each time it had seemed unnecessary to me. Intrusive. And it reminded me of times in my past when I would call my parents and while I was talking to one of them, the other would repeatedly pipe up in the background, interrupting the flow of conversation. They were like children competing for center stage.

After I had eaten as much as I could, I took the pills and swallowed them. As I lay there, waiting for the drugs to take me away, it occurred to me that my mother's presence in this facility was not just emotionally disruptive, it was actually unnecessary. For the things that she was best at—such as preparing meals and making concrete plans and arrangements—were already being done by the medical staff.

I was continuing to ponder this as my thoughts began to lose focus, and I heard myself saying to my mother, "I don't need you here."

My mother repeated what I said in a mocking tone and then laughed at me, and I began to feel I was in the middle of a cruel nightmare. Things became more unfocused after that, and I drifted off.

When I next opened my eyes, the room was dark. I assumed I was awake and I lay there for a moment, trying to focus my eyes. My heart was racing rapidly. And then in the darkness, I saw a nurse enter the room.

As the outline of her form came up to me, she doubled over and fell onto my bed. And then—in a sudden, disjointed moment—I saw myself fall forward and land at the foot of my mother's bed. As soon as I landed, her leg came out from under the covers and kicked me in the head.

It was at that point that I thought, "This must be a dream. This can't be real. Wake up. Focus." And then suddenly I was back in my bed, and everything seemed normal. I sighed in relief and tried to stay awake, afraid of being hurled back into the nightmare.

But within moments, I was tossed back into another series of images, this time more violent and intense. When I snapped out of it, I thought, "That wasn't like a regular dream. I don't think I even fell asleep." Panicked, I rang the nurse's bell.

"I saw these weird images," I said when she came. "It was like a nightmare, but I think I was awake. My heart's racing."

"Don't worry," the nurse responded quickly. "You were just hallucinating from the meds. I've seen it happen before. Here, just come out of bed and we'll walk it off."

I struggled out of bed and followed the nurse, rolling my IV tower with me.

"My grandmother hallucinates just taking half a tablet of that pain pill," she said as we were walking down the hall. "And you had much more."

The nurse then continued to chatter away in a cheery, friendly voice. Normally I would have been irritated by this bubbly, "chatty Kathy" personality. But she was perfect in that moment. Anything light and busy to keep my mind from falling back into those dark images.

The nurse brought me to a small library and said she'd be right back. When she returned, she had a blanket in one arm, and toast and juice in another. She wrapped me in the blanket and I sat down in one of the chairs. Dr. Laub had removed my tubes during his last visit, and I was now able to sit upright without feeling anything digging into me. As the nurse put the toast and juice in front of me, she inquired if it was all right if she sat with me and kept me company. I immediately liked her for asking.

The nurse sat down and started talking away. "People always ask me what it's like to work with transsexuals and I explain to them that it is not some rash or sudden decision that you make, but rather something that you've known forever—at least on some level."

I smiled as she said that, but at this point I would have smiled at pretty much anything she was saying. I was just happy to be surrounded by something pleasant and warm. As she continued to talk, I munched away on my toast and took sips of the juice.

After about an hour had passed, the nurse said, "I think you'll be safe now. I think you'll be able to sleep."

She walked me back to my room and tucked me into bed. And she was right. I fell asleep shortly after she left and didn't wake up until the following morning, when Sue arrived to drive me and my mother home.

Just before checking out of the center, the nurses gave me medication to avoid nausea, so I spent most of the hour-long drive drifting in and out of sleep. When we arrived home, I walked through the door to my living room and was immediately enveloped with another level of depression. For standing in the midst of these familiar surroundings meant facing the hopes and fantasies that I had deposited here—the image of my walking through the doorway one large step closer to being a complete man. And the contrast between those images and my harsh reality left a pit of emptiness lying in its wake. I went straight to the sofa bed, which had been pulled out, and lay down.

THE NEXT MORNING, I WOKE UP KNOWING I NEEDED TO have a bowel movement. It had now been a week since surgery and I was afraid there might be something wrong, since they had operated very close to that area during the removal of the vagina. I was afraid that any amount of pushing or straining would pull at the stitches in my crotch.

I got out of bed and began to shuffle my way to the bathroom, dragging my catheter bag behind me along the floor. Once inside, I reeled in the catheter tubes and shut the door behind me. I stood there for a few moments, wondering how to approach this.

I turned around until I was standing with my back to the toilet. Gradually, I bent down and began to remove the mesh briefs. I slowly sat on the toilet, making sure the catheter had enough give so it was not being pulled as I squatted. I pushed. And then I relaxed. I pushed again. And then I stopped. I felt something wanting to come out. But it was hard as a rock. I suddenly had an image of myself bleeding into the toilet. And I was terrified.

My whole lower body felt cramped and clogged. Whatever was there was now weighing upon me like a big, heavy stone. I stood up and pulled my briefs back up. My legs were shaky as I made my way out of the bathroom.

I found my mother reading on her mattress. As I walked over to her, I felt weak and clammy. And scared. I said, "Could you please go to the drugstore and get me some stool softener? I've got this bowel movement coming, but I'm really scared I'm going to tear open the stitches."

"I was going to do my hair and then some shopping," my mother said. "I might have gone, but since you say you don't really need me, why should I rush for you?"

And that was it. The final straw. And I snapped.

"You fucking bitch. I'm fucking falling apart here, and you're playing this manipulative shit. Fuck you. I don't goddamn need you. Get the fuck out of here."

In that moment, I despised her. I felt as if everything had been a sham—her flattery, her show of support, all of it. And now her true colors were coming out. The ones that always seemed to show when she felt rejected.

I pulled on my boots, grabbed my car keys, and left. I barely remember the drive to the pharmacy or purchasing the stool softener. Everything had been overtaken by rage. And it gave me a surge of energy.

When I got home, my mother was in the shower. I poured a glass of water, ripped open the top of the stool softener, and swallowed a couple of the red gel capsules. I then restlessly paced, continuing to mentally curse at my mother until my adrenaline finally ran out. I walked to the sofa bed and lay down.

The last time I saw my mother in person was after I had just graduated from law school. My father was working with a company in Germany at the time, and my mother was staying at his place there. One night while I was visiting them in Munich, we were having dinner at a restaurant and got into an argument. I don't even remember what it was about. I just remember both parents' criticizing me for something. As we were walking back from the pub, my father, who had a tendency to get nasty sometimes when he drank too much, continued to berate me. My mother switched sides and began defending me, acting as though she had been on my side all along.

When we arrived at my father's apartment, I went into the living room where they had set up a cot for me and got into bed. My mother came in, but I didn't want to talk to her. I was angry with her for having initially been on my father's side. She left, upset.

A few minutes later, my father came in, wondering why I wouldn't speak to my mother. Then my mother returned, wanting to talk again. I became frustrated but kept an even tone as I said, "Please, I just want to be alone—I just need some space."

My father returned again and said, "Your mother is sitting in the hallway, crying."

My mother was sobbing in the hallway because I would not let her come in to comfort me.

I awoke to the sound of the telephone ringing. My mother picked up the receiver.

"Hallo?" She turned to me and said, "It's Virginia. Do you want to talk to her?"

She brought over the receiver and I held it in my hand, waiting for my mother to leave the room. When she did, I quietly said, "Hi."

Virginia's voice was filled with cheer and anticipation as she asked how I was doing. While I was at the Recovery Inn, she had sent me another card. On the front was a picture of two empty beach chairs perched at the edge of an ocean.

"Not good. Things didn't go as planned. They had to stop partway through, so I'm not done."

I explained about the blood loss and the transfusions and heard Virginia take in several breaths as she listened. And then she said, "I'm just shocked. I didn't know there was this much risk."

"I don't care about the risk, I just wanted to be done—or at least close to it. And I'm just not. That's the hardest part of it all."

"I am so sorry."

Virginia's tone was soothing and tender in my ears. And I found myself saying the next few words in the voice of a little boy. "I just wish you were here. I just wish I could hold your hand."

Virginia's voice caught, as she said, "Oh—I would hold your hand." I remembered her glistening eyes in the restaurant. And the way her touch had felt when she ran her finger along the stripes in my shirt at the restaurant. And that's when I began to cry. It was the first time I had let myself cry since the surgery.

Virginia continued to stay quietly with me. After some time had passed, I said, "Thank you. Thank you for listening."

"I'm here for you unconditionally. Anytime."

I thanked her again and as we were saying good-bye, she said, "I love you."

For a fleeting moment, another part of me kicked in—the part that is always assessing my chances. What does this mean? Is she saying it as a friend? But I quickly let it go. For in circumstances like these, all bets are off. There are no rules. It's just pure human connection.

"I love you, too."

And then I clicked off. As I lay there, absorbing her words, I could feel everything thawing inside. The hardness, the rage—it all seemed to be dissolving under the warmth of something new. And it was she—Virginia—who had unlocked it all. And it was through her that I finally got it—that I saw everything.

This warmth and openness was the real me. It was my natural state. And the rage—that murderous, overwhelming rage—was not. It was simply a reaction to my circumstances. It was the desperate frustration of not getting what I so needed: tenderness, spaciousness, a gentle holding. And getting what I needed from Virginia so closely on the heels of my rage and desperation with my mother, allowed me—for the first time in my life—to break through a murky, cloudy, haze. And I saw my mother for real.

My mother was the kind of mother who could physically move mountains for me. She could aggressively take on anyone who wasn't behind me, and she could—when needed—flatter me with words of conviction and motivation. But she could not hold my pain with a gentle grace; she could not tenderly receive my grief without clutching it or trying to shape it. And I had spent the better part of my life resenting her and punishing her—on one level or another—for that. For as long as I remained engaged in this battle with her, I didn't have to face the hardest truth of all—that she would never fulfill these needs. It was simply not within her.

As I got out of bed, I had a sense of sorrow. Sorrow for myself and sorrow for my mother. I walked around the corner to where she was sitting on the mattress.

"I'm sorry I said those things to you. I was just hurt and I needed something that you can't give to me. It's not your fault."

My mother started crying and said, "You're just cruel to me because I'm your mother. You're nicer to your friends."

I felt a rise of anger returning. And I realized that hope is a most tenacious lover. For some part of me had hoped my epiphany would reach her and we would both move into the light—together.

I sighed. "Look. If you're hurt or angry by what I said, then tell me. Tell me about your own feelings, but don't tell me about mine."

"I used to get hurt by all of you in the family and the cruel things you say," my mother said, tears still streaming down her face. "But now it just rolls off me."

It was the trait that I least respected in her: stoicism. False strength.

I felt a sense of calmness as I said, "I really need for you to leave. I need to be alone here."

I remember being very aware in that moment that my request came from simple necessity. I was taking care of myself.

"Well, I'm not going to pay to change my flight."

I sighed again. "I'll pay whatever it costs. Just do it. Please."

MY MOTHER ENDED UP FINDING A FLIGHT OUT THE NEXT morning, and a friend from work came by to drive her to the airport. I went along, quietly sitting in the back with my leg bag tucked under my sweatpants. When we reached the airport, I got out of the car to say good-bye.

"I made some food last night and put it in packages in the fridge for you," my mother said.

"Thanks. I appreciate that. Call me when you get in so I know you arrived safely."

I reached over and we briefly embraced. But neither of us said, "I love you."

WHEN I ARRIVED HOME, I IMMEDIATELY NOTICED THE EMPTIness inside. But it was not a lonely kind of emptiness. It was spacious and light. And I remember feeling as if I had just liberated myself from some very old, dark place.

Part Three

RAISING

THE SPIRIT

Twenty-three

MAY 1999

I am in a car with my mother, and she pulls over to let me out at the base of a huge staircase. As I am leaving, she says, "I love you." I respond, "You love me the way you want to love me, not the way I need to be loved— that's not love." I jump out of the car and run to the top of the stairs. I travel through a long hallway and find myself in the office of my spiritual teacher. I start to spill out all my feelings and as I am talking, I feel the teacher's sympathy enveloping me. . . .

In May I went back to the office with a body far less than I had imagined, but at least free of any serious complications. After an excruciatingly painful office visit, I was urinating the same as before. My bowel functions were also back to normal.

Upon returning, I found out I had received a large promotion for which I had applied. I was now the new head of the criminal division of the court. It was not only a vote of confidence from my superiors but a strong show of support from my colleagues who had contributed to the selection process. I was going to have to give up some of my telecommuting privileges and be in the office more often, but I had applied for the job on the assumption that I was into the final stretch of my surgeries. And by accepting this promotion, I was keeping that assumption alive. I was moving out of my hibernation.

My mother knew I had applied for the position and when I told her I'd been selected, she responded to my e-mail with a detailed message of how I deserved it and why she knew I was perfect for the job. As I read her words, I once again realized that when it came to my career or concrete matters of the outside world, my mother had my number. It was with the inner landscape that we so often parted ways.

As I found myself trying again to reconcile the vastly different sides of my mother, I remembered the words spoken by the head of my spiritual school, delivered in his thick Middle Eastern accent: "The issues with the father—those can be resolved in this lifetime. But those with the mother, those are never truly finished; those we take with us to the grave."

LATER IN THE MONTH, I RETURNED TO MY SPIRITUAL SCHOOL after having taken several months off—a hiatus motivated by the fact that with each passing month that I entered the temple, I was more apprehensive and guarded than the previous one. For unlike my workplace where slipped pronouns had now dwindled down to the very occasional exception, they were still the rule here. And unlike my workplace where any mistake was immediately followed by an apology, slips that occurred here often went unnoticed by anyone other than myself.

The spiritual teachers had been supportive of my need to take a break, but they had also made it clear that it was my problem and not that of the students. For in their view, it was just another opportunity for me to grow—a harmless little pronoun that meant so much to me because it was my gender identity that had been wounded, not anyone else's. And I wanted to believe them—not just because they were wise teachers but because there was so much important work that I had done here. And so much of it was about more than just my gender.

I chose a Tuesday evening to make my return, easing back into the program during a small biweekly group meeting. This particular night, the people gathered had begun an exercise referred to as the development of the "group pearl." Each student would have an opportunity to go around the room, look all the others directly in the eye, and tell them how he or she perceived them, thereby clearing the air of projections or assumptions. The person receiving the information was not allowed to respond, but was simply to listen. The ultimate purpose behind the exercise was to allow the group to obtain a greater intimacy and cohesiveness.

It took quite a long time for each person to go through the entire circle, so only a small handful of people went that night. But the ones who did left an indelible mark on me.

The first was the gay man with whom I'd had the unpleasant encounter the previous year when he referred to me as "lady." We had since spent a pleasant afternoon together shopping for the group lunch. So as he made his way around the circle and came closer to me, I was not particularly concerned. For in my mind, we had reached a silent truce that afternoon.

The first thing he said was, "You remind me of the bullies who used to call me a sissy and beat me up on the playground as a kid."

I remember first smiling at the word "bully," and thinking back to my competitive antics on the playground. But when he reached the part about people beating him up, I felt a twinge. I would never attack someone unless I was under attack. As he continued, he veered into a direction that I had not expected.

I had assumed that after he made this comparison, he would take some responsibility for the fact that his history and past wounds had prevented him from seeing mine. But that's not what took place. What he actually said was: "I hate the kind of masculinity you have come to embrace. And I stay away from what I hate."

As he continued around the circle, saying kind things to some people and relatively benign things to others, I felt myself pulling away from the group. And once again I felt like an outsider.

The next man who spoke was one of those very sweet guys who are always trying to make everyone feel okay. When he reached me, he said, "I love that rambunctious, mischievous boy—the kind of boy who says, 'Yeah, I hate that girly shit.' " He smiled at me, as though he were giving me a great compliment. But I just felt even more invisible. For underneath his statement was the same implication as that of his predecessor: my own masculinity was somehow dependent upon a rejection of someone else.

The next person was a woman with whom I'd always felt a special connection because so many of our struggles were similar. And I relaxed, for I knew she would be kind.

When she reached me, she began to cry as she said, "I really don't want you to leave this group. I've learned so much about myself through you. And I think of you as so much more than just a man or a woman."

I felt a lump in my throat as the emotion behind her words touched me. But the words themselves left a sad aftertaste that lingered with me as she continued to move through the circle. And as I followed that trail, my mind reached back and called forth an old piece of information.

When I was in undergraduate school, I studied the work of a cognitive psychologist named Abraham Maslow. Maslow had developed what he called the "Hierarchy of Needs." It was a pyramid-style model where the bottom of the pyramid represented basic human needs such as food and shelter, while the peak stood for more highly developed concepts such as autonomy and self-actualization. Under Maslow's theory, if one of those basic needs remained unmet, one could not climb the higher levels toward the pinnacle of self-actualization.

Tonight, as I sat in this temple, I applied Maslow's theory to myself. And what I found out was this. Until this most primary—physical—aspect of my identity was on solid ground, I could not fully and freely embrace what lay beyond. In other words, until I was accepted as a man, I couldn't be "more than just" a man. It was like trying to climb a ladder and reaching the third rung, only to have someone constantly come along and kick it out from under me.

THE LAST PERSON TO HAVE A TURN THAT NIGHT WAS A physician who had always struck me as very tightly contained. Even during the most intense work, as he spoke of deeply painful experiences, it seemed excruciatingly difficult for him to let out his emotions. Shortly before my break from the group, he had shared with us his growing awareness of how a rigid, judgmental force within kept him in line at all times.

And as I took in his cramped form, the little kid in me wanted to grab him and shake him and say, "Hey, man—come on. Let's have some fun!"

That night, as he made his way around the circle, I was curious as to what was coming my way and—admittedly—apprehensive. I was thinking that someone with emotions as big and messy as mine would not be easy for someone like him.

So I cannot say I was totally surprised at the first words out of his mouth: "You are at the top of my list of people who bring out a reaction in me. And I find myself having all of these conversations with you in my head." But then, just as with the other members, came the inevitable part two: "I have spent so much of life struggling with my own masculinity and learning to embrace my femininity, I have a hard time with your rejection of the female in yourself and others. I'm just . . . I just have concern for you."

Had he just stayed with the comments about his own experience, I would have felt a kinship with him. But his assumption that the particular balance he was seeking in himself was somehow truer or more genuine than mine quickly destroyed any of that potential. But it was his final comment that truly sealed the deal. The statement was delivered in a paternalistic tone that I imagined him using with patients in his medical practice. And that tone triggered my anger. For it reminded me how medical professionals had the power to pathologize people like myself.

I followed the rules of the group and did not respond to any of the comments I heard that night. But by the time I left the temple, I felt as if I had been strung up in the middle of the room and used as a punching bag. I was bruised and angry and hurt. And tired. So very tired.

I felt as if I had spent the last year and a half there fighting. Fighting to be recognized, fighting to be respected—hell, just fighting to hear the proper pronoun. And I had gotten nowhere. That night I gained some painful insight as to why. If this is what people were thinking, why would they expend any effort to use the proper pronoun? Why would they recognize something they didn't believe was real or valid or—for that matter—good?

When I got home, I continued to confront the fallout. My moods were like a roller coaster, surging from peaks of rage down to valleys of despair, and then back to the tiredness—the tiredness of going nowhere. The tiredness of paying hundreds of dollars a month to go to a place where I left more damaged and distrustful than when I came in. That just couldn't be right, could it? How could this be good for me?

When I got into bed, I lay awake for hours, my mind still. At some point, my thoughts strayed back to the beginning of the evening, when the purpose of that particular exercise had been announced. The "group pearl." The cohesiveness.

It was at that point that I realized I already had everything they described. Just not with them.

Every time I entered my workplace and walked toward my office, I felt an immediate sense of warmth. Even when I was in a lousy mood and didn't want to deal with anyone, I still felt that warmth. It was borne from a deep sense of trust that had developed over the past two years through many interactions, that told me those who knew me were with me.

Whether it was a small comment about how my newly emerging sideburns framed my face, or a deeply apologetic e-mail quietly sent to me after a slipped pronoun, or the delight in someone's voice when he or she told me one of the newly arrived interns had referred to me as the "cool, alpha male," I could sense their support was not just politically correct behavior, it was pure and genuine affection. And during this time, while I was still fighting the frustrations of my physical incompletion, I really, really needed that.

And I did not need this.

This was the comparison that triggered the same shift in perspective that occurred during my mother's visit. And I saw that everything I'd done with her, I had been doing with my spiritual group.

I had been battling them and punishing them and resenting them. And I had been doing all of this in an attempt to assert control over them. But I could not turn my spiritual group into the kind of group that I needed it to be any more than I could change my mother. And recognizing this, I could finally free myself.

———

I NEVER RETURNED TO MY SPIRITUAL GROUP AFTER THAT NIGHT. And despite having spent so much time struggling to stick it out and fearing that I would lose my way without the guidance of the teachers, I never experienced a moment of regret. And what I know now is that the night I walked away from that temple is the night that I added another crucial piece to my own.

Twenty-four

JUNE 1999

> I have just emerged from surgery and look up to find a sea of relaxed and reassuring faces hovering above me. I reach down and feel bandages covering my crotch and have a vague sense that there are testicles beneath the bandages, but I am not entirely sure. . . .

In June I found myself back on the familiar stretch of highway toward the town of Palo Alto and the offices of Dr. Laub. But while the route was familiar, the sense of apprehension I felt was not. It was a new kind of apprehension—the kind borne out of specific past experience as opposed to pure speculation.

When I arrived at Dr. Laub's office, he was standing in the hallway, talking to the receptionist. He greeted me and ushered me into an examination room, saying, "Let's have a look at the tissue and see how everything's doing."

As he was examining me, he told me that since my last surgery, he had done another urethral extension in my type of penis surgery and this one had been completely complication free. I was extremely happy to hear this and told him, "You know, I thought about giving up on the urethral extension and going for the simpler version, but in the end I just couldn't bring myself to compromise."

Dr. Laub said, "I understand completely. I've received two-page letters from patients describing their first time urinating while standing up."

We then discussed the post-op protocol. I would remain in Palo Alto for two days, but this time I could stay at a motel. I would wake up with testicular implants and two catheters. After twelve days, the doctor would remove the catheters. Once he had verified the newly formed urethra through the penis was healed and operational, he would close up the backup hole in the scrotum in a second surgery. At that surgery, he would also, if necessary, position the testicles more precisely.

As I listened to him, I became very excited. I said, "The thought of waking up with balls—that's what keeps me going each day."

He laughed heartily at my choice of words, but his reaction held no surprise, telling me that I was not the first to express such strong emotion over a couple of testicles.

As I began pulling up my pants and the doctor prepared to leave, I remembered another matter I wanted to discuss. I said, "Dr. Laub—there's one more thing I need to talk to you about. It's . . . more of a business issue. And I need your advice."

"Sure. Why don't we meet in my office after you get dressed."

The doctor left, and I finished buckling my belt and gathering up my belongings.

When I got to his office door, it was slightly ajar. I knocked and Dr. Laub beckoned me inside, saying, "Please, have a seat." He shut the door and sat down at his oval desk, facing me, as he said, "So, what's going on?"

I reached into my briefcase and pulled out a folded sheet of paper and handed it to him.

"That's a bill I got for over a thousand dollars for the extra blood work and transfusions I needed in the last surgery because of complications. I was really angry when I got this bill, because I can't help but feel that if you'd had the older, more experienced surgeon, none of this would have happened. You never had this complication before me. And I'm inclined to go after the surgeon for this bill, because I don't think I should have to pay for his mistakes. But I came here to talk with you first, because I respect you and if you think my pursuit will negatively affect your relationship with these surgeons or cause problems, I'll reconsider."

"Well," said Dr. Laub, "I've been working very hard with this group of surgeons at forming a broader relationship for future surgeries. So, yes, if you pursue it, they might get the impression that gender patients are more likely to sue and it could damage things in the long term."

"Tell me," I asked, "do you think my bleeding would have occurred with a more experienced surgeon?"

"I can't say, because there is always a risk of excessive blood loss. But a part of me suspects it would not have occurred. But I can also say the guy you had is excellent, and there was nothing egregious I saw about his technique."

I slowly let out a long breath. "I appreciate your honesty. And I don't want to damage things for future patients—that's why I'm here, talking with you first."

"I think of you as a friend, Dhillon, and I ask you, as a favor, to not pursue it."

I agreed that I wouldn't, and he looked extremely relieved. As I rose to leave, Dr. Laub came over, shook my hand vigorously, and said, "You are a really, really good guy."

I stopped at the reception desk to pay for the next surgery. When I looked at the list of charges, I saw the anesthesiologist's fee, the surgery center fee, and the charge for the testicular implants. But there was no surgeon's fee listed at all. Dr. Laub was not charging me for his services.

As I was walking toward the car, another thought struck me. If things had gone right during the last surgery, they would have placed balloon-type expanders in my scrotum to inflate it over the next six months and to make room for the testicular implants. But now, because they noticed my scrotal tissue was stretched enough without the placement of the expanders, I was not only going to get the implants sooner but I was saving the more than $3,000 that the expanders would have cost.

But it wasn't just this financial balancing act of tabulating losses and gains that boosted my spirits. Something about having spoken to Dr. Laub about it all, instead of going off on my own in my usual half-cocked way, left me with the sense that the bond of trust that had formed between us during the Easter conversation at the Recovery Inn had just been deepened and made stronger.

THE NIGHT BEFORE MY SURGERY, I SPENT MOST OF THE TIME in the bathroom, alternating between bouts of vomiting and diarrhea. As I sat there, hugging the toilet bowl, I kept praying, "Please, God, let me be all right by morning."

I was still in the bathroom when the morning light came in through my apartment windows, but I was finally down to a few isolated dry heaves.

When Jared—my friend from the FTM meetings—arrived to pick me up, I felt stable enough to get into a moving car and spent the drive to the surgery center figuring out what I was going to say to the medical staff. I didn't like the idea of lying outright, but I also didn't want to say anything that would jeopardize my surgery.

When I arrived at the center, I didn't have to wait long before I was ushered into the changing room, then placed on a gurney and wrapped in a warm blanket. While we were all waiting for Dr. Laub and the anesthesiologist, a nurse asked if I'd experienced any problems in the last twenty-four hours, such as a fever or nausea or pain.

I hesitated, and then said, "Well, I had a little bit of diarrhea last night."

"Maybe you had a touch of the stomach flu that's going around," she said. And then to my relief, she added, "I think we can go ahead with the surgery and it will just heal itself."

After the nurse left, I lay down and closed my eyes. I felt drained and tired and dehydrated from the long night. Since I wasn't allowed to drink anything after midnight, I hadn't been able to replace any of the fluids I'd lost.

I was started to drift off to sleep, when I heard my name, "Dhillon?"

I looked up and saw a short, middle-aged woman with a warm, tan face standing next to me.

"Hi. I'm Terri Homer, your anesthesiologist."

During my pre-op appointment, I had requested a different anesthesiologist. The IV-backing-up incident that had occurred with the last guy, along with his abrupt military-style manner, was something I just didn't want to repeat.

"Are you sure?" Dr. Laub had asked. "Because that guy actually saved your life. It was only because he was so fast at putting in a second IV line to transfuse you that we were able to replace enough of the lost blood in time."

Dr. Homer began my IV and said, "Okay, you're going to feel very relaxed in a minute. This is a good mix I have for you." The anesthesiologist spoke as if she had just fixed me a really good cocktail.

And she had. The first thing I noticed was that there was no burning sensation as the substance entered my veins. I then felt a slow, warm glow, and a very smooth relaxation took over my body.

"Man," I thought, "this really is an art—this whole sensation feels better than any of the other times I've been about to go under. . . . She's really . . . really great . . . woooow."

And then I was out.

WHEN I WOKE UP, I FELT UNBELIEVABLY GOOD. THE NAUSEA was gone, and I felt no pain. I remember thinking that the antinausea drugs they use during anesthesia must have cleared up my stomach problems.

I reached between my legs and felt a mass of bandages and some tubes. When a nurse came in, I asked, "Do I have balls? Did they put them in?"

She nodded, and handed me a note from Dr. Laub.

"He's going to see you tomorrow for a follow-up, but he wanted to give you this in the meantime."

I picked up the paper and began to read the doctor's handwritten words: "The surgery could best be described as beautiful—in fact, you have the best metoidioplasty on earth. All goals were accomplished."

I first felt a small burst of joy, followed quickly by some doubt. Even if things had gone great during surgery, we wouldn't know until later whether the new urethra—urinary chanel—was complication free. Plus, there was still another surgery to go.

But the other reason my joy was somewhat muted was because of the one additional piece of information that was always tugging at the corners of my mind: even if everything turned out perfectly, I would still only have a very, very small penis.

JARED ARRIVED TO TAKE ME TO A NEARBY HOTEL. THE RE-covery nurse came to help me get dressed. As I put my arms through the shirtsleeves, I asked her, "Where's Mary? She was my nurse the last time."

"Mary's been helping at her husband's practice. He's an ophthalmolo-gist and does eye surgeries to correct vision. He's gotten really busy."

It took me a moment to digest the news that Mary was married. But then I found myself thinking, Of course she's married. She's exactly the kind of woman men dream about—flawlessly beautiful, tender, giving, kind. The kind of goodness that makes you want to be a better person.

And so by the time I was fully dressed, I found myself accepting the fact that Mr. Eye Doctor had won over my Mary. But there was one thing that I couldn't fully get behind: the use of Mary's talents for patients in an eye doctor's office. I felt it was a waste. She had such an amazing effect on me during the most traumatic surgery. What she had was not just a skill or a talent. It was a gift. And I couldn't help but feel that it was being wasted when there were so many others lying in hospital beds at their darkest hour, waiting to be touched by an angel. An angel I knew as Mary.

I slowly made my way to Jared's car, and then he drove a quarter mile down the road and turned into the motel. I got out and retrieved the key from the desk clerk who held my reservation. I remember trying to look alert, keeping my catheter bag tucked in my pants and hidden under my bulky sweater. I didn't want them to reject me because of fears of liability or the like.

Jared drove me to the base of a staircase, and I began the slow climb to my second-floor room. When I opened the door, I was relieved. The room was clean and reasonably spacious. Across from my bed was a small alcove that led to another small room with a bed. I had arranged for that room so that whoever was staying with me would have a place to sleep. My friends had agreed to take shifts based on their work schedules.

I undressed down to my mesh hospital briefs and then slid under the covers, pulling out the sheet and carefully arranging my catheter tube so that it hung over the edge and drained into a bag on the floor. Jared came in with some cranberry juice and crackers, and I took some of both to go along with a couple of pain pills, in an effort to stay ahead of any post-surgical pain. And then I lay back and drifted off to sleep.

I AWOKE TO THE SOUND OF THE PHONE RINGING NEXT TO MY bed. There must have been an extension in the other room, because I heard Jared quickly grab the receiver.

"Hello? Just a second. I'll see if he's awake."

"Who is it?" I asked sleepily.

When he said it was Virginia, I immediately reached over and picked up the phone.

"Hi," she said cheerfully. "How are you?"

"Things went really well." I then lifted up the covers and looked at the bulge of bandages on my crotch and spoke in a dramatic tone used by announcers, "I have mass. I now have some mass there."

She laughed and said, "Oh, I'm so happy things turned out well."

I felt my mood creeping higher as I said, "So I'm gonna see you next month, right?"

"Of course. I've been looking forward to our dinner."

Virginia was coming to town to visit friends, and I told her I wanted to take her out for an extravagant dinner to celebrate my surgery.

"I've already picked out a great dress for our evening," she said, smiling through the phone.

There was a soothing, sweet quality to her voice, and I knew she was not just telling me about the dress for her own sake—she was doing it to give me a specific image to hold on to during my recovery.

"So—any idea as to what jewelry you might wear?"

"Oh, I thought I might wear this gorgeous diamond bracelet I got as a gift."

"Really?" I asked. "Someone must have been generous."

She laughed. "Oh, yes. Very."

A few weeks ago Virginia and I were talking on the phone when I did the one thing I was always warning myself not to do: I veered the conversation toward sex and our potential as a couple. I knew she was still grappling with her relationship, and although it was in a bad enough state so that she was coming to San Francisco alone, she was still not officially single.

I began my usual routine of asking questions about sex and relationships in a general sense, referring to past lovers, and then as Virginia answered, adroitly shifting to the more specific dynamic of "us."

Before I could stop myself, I heard myself asking, "Have you ever imagined us doing it?"

". . . Yes . . . and that's all I'm going to say." I could feel her blushing over the phone.

After we hung up, I found myself vacillating between wanting to push harder, to win her over, and feeling guilty for putting her in this position while she was still struggling with another relationship. It was these conflicting feelings that led to my next step—an act that would allow me the selfish pleasure of romancing her without making her feel angry or threatened. And the way I accomplished this most difficult feat? Humor. I figured it's really hard to be mad at someone when they've got you laughing.

I located a diamond dealer and picked out a diamond bracelet. I had it gift-wrapped, and inside the package I included a card on which I wrote, "Please accept this gift as my apology for being an incorrigible flirt."

The next morning, before heading home, I stopped by Dr. Laub's office for a brief checkup. As I sat in the examination chair, he slowly unraveled the bandages and proudly handed me a mirror so I could see the results.

But while the surgeon was used to seeing his surgical results in the early stages, I was not. The tissue looked like a swollen mess at this point. The scrotum consisted of two separate masses of tissue, one riding up a bit high toward my penis, the other a little lower. I said, "Why are the testicles separated?"

"I'll fuse them together in the next surgery after I pull it all down more squarely between your legs."

The one area to benefit from the swelling was my penis. The head was surrounded by tissue that made a very natural-looking foreskin and was three or four times the diameter it had been before surgery. It was also positioned up and out in a way that made it look like a natural penis with the shaft about one inch longer than before.

Other than the large diameter of my penis head, there wasn't that much to impress me, but I held myself back from forming any strong conclusions. It was far too early for that.

I SPENT THE NEXT TEN DAYS HEALING AT HOME. EACH TIME I moved, the catheter pulled at the inside of my bladder and scraped at the lining, causing it to itch and be irritated. I tried to lie as still as I could at night while simultaneously keeping my legs elevated on pillows and positioned frog-legged so that my scrotum didn't have too much pressure on it.

Days later, Sue drove me to Dr. Laub's office to have my catheter removed. Suffice it to say, it was a miserably painful process. When I pulled my pants back up, Dr. Laub and I discussed the timing of the final surgery. We agreed on the end of October. As I turned to go, I said, "I'm going to use your bathroom before I leave. I want to be sure all is okay."

I locked the bathroom door behind me and sat on the toilet. There was not much in my bladder, so I wasn't expecting a forceful stream. I just wanted to make sure that the small, temporary, backup hole the doctor had hidden behind the scrotum was working.

I tried to take a few breaths and as I did so, I looked down at my testicles. They were much less swollen now and were looking like normal balls, instead of a mass of tissue. And while one of them was definitely riding high, I found the sight of both comforting.

After I finished in the bathroom, successfully I might add, the relief was immense. All the tension from the many moments of fear had literally drained away.

When I got home, I went straight to bed. It was the best sleep I had in two weeks. With the tube out of my penis and the catheter gone, every part of my body was able to relax. Of course, the Demerol helped.

When I awoke, it was late afternoon and the sun was streaming into my living room, spilling into my bedroom loft. I felt a delicious, lazy, afternoon warmth envelop me.

I reached down underneath the covers and, without really thinking, began to gently rub my genitals. The warmth intensified and localized between my legs. And so I continued, intensifying the pressure on the head of my penis.

I came quickly and easily. And though there had not been much risk that I would lose my ability to orgasm, I still felt a sense of relief and—in that moment—gratitude. Even though my orgasm was still accomplished more by rubbing than by pulling. Even though there wasn't enough of a shaft for me to close my hand around.

It was not until I returned to work that I first felt the deeper impact of this particular stage of surgery.

As I walked through the hallways of the courthouse, I became aware of a shift in my center of gravity. With my prosthesis now gone, there was less of a noticeable bulge on the outside. But on the inside was the knowledge that what I did have was now connected to me. And somehow that knowledge fed back into my psyche and resulted with my feeling more anchored and confident and centered within myself. So much so that I began to use the shower in the men's locker room.

I still remember the sensation of standing in that hot, steamy shower for the first time—the reassuring comfort as I cupped my round, firm testicles in the palm of my hand, rinsing off the soap that had matted down the hair on the skin. Prior to my surgery, they had shaved my genitalia, but it had quickly regrown on the skin surrounding my balls, giving them an even more natural, integrated appearance.

When I stepped out of the shower and took off my towel, the reflection that I saw in the mirror, although perhaps more fitting in size to a younger boy, brought a measure of peace that, in this moment, was just enough to quiet the demons. For while there was still a measurable distance between what I saw in the mirror and what I imagined in my fantasies, it could not compare to the monumental distance I had already covered. What I saw now was vastly different from the place where I had started—a place that had evoked a most primitive rage and sense of core betrayal.

Toward the end of the month, Sue invited me to a small gathering held at a French restaurant in downtown San Francisco. I readily accepted, feeling more than ready to shed my recovery-induced hibernation and toast in this new level of completion.

On the way, I realized that there would be people there whom I had not seen since I had begun this journey. But when I felt excitement rather than hesitation at the thought of such exposure, I again realized just how much this recent surgery had given me.

At the restaurant, Sue saw me approaching and quickly ran over to hug me. She was in full party mode, eyes sparkling and filled with energy. She had saved a seat next to herself and as I went to claim it, I heard my name. When I looked up, I saw a balding, round-faced man—one of Sue's former roommates.

The man held out his hand and as I reached to shake it, he looked directly into my eyes. And he said, "Dhillon, you look great. You really do."

To this day, I have not forgotten that look. It was a look that held nothing but pure joy and excitement. It was a look that said, "I am so, so happy for you." And it was a look that made me feel deeply ashamed.

When Sue first moved to San Francisco, we got together once a week for dinner and bad television. We alternated between her place and mine, so during the times I went to her house, I frequently ran into some of her roommates. I was always friendly to the females, often flirting with one I found attractive. But when it came to her one male roommate, I found myself feeling irritated and standoffish—as if he had somehow stepped into our space.

But beneath that was another, deeper judgment. Something about his meek, passive personality brought out a lack of respect in me. I would always think, "Christ, where's your backbone?"

Looking back now, I know that my behavior was largely fueled by a cramped, competitive resentment. Some deeper part of me was thinking, "It's not fair. I'm more masculine than him—and yet he's got the pecs, the dick, and the male recognition."

As I interacted with him throughout the rest of the evening, I kept thinking, "How could I have been so cruel to someone so kind?" I was incredulous. It almost felt like I must have been in some sort of drug-induced blackout or haze. As if I had not been myself. For I felt nothing but warmth that night. Clear and simple.

As I drove home later in the evening, I thought about how many times I must have hurled hateful and demeaning comments at other men because of my own cramped situation. I even thought about my political work and the marches and angry speeches. And I wondered how much of my contribution was truly about a specific cause and how much was about using the cause as a vehicle for my own personal, repressed, or unresolved rage.

I thought about so much that night.

Twenty-five

JULY and
AUGUST 1999

I am in the dormitory of a college campus in the late afternoon, and a group of people invite me to go see a movie. As we are walking to the theater, I notice a really pretty, sweet-looking blond girl. We get a bit closer, and she falls into step beside me. All of a sudden I realize that I have my guitar with me; somehow I have left my room carrying it. I need to drop it off at the dorm but I don't want to lose the girl, so I run back as fast as I can and leave the guitar with the person at the front desk. The desk clerk wants me to wait for a receipt, but I am already halfway toward the door and say, "Just write 'guitar' on your slip and my initials."

When I get back to the theater, I notice that the girl I liked has stayed behind to wait for me while the group has gone on ahead. I ask her why, and she simply says, "I just wanted to." I lean over and kiss her on the cheek to thank her. As we walk toward the theater, I feel a warmth and innocence envelop me—as if we are in high school and this is my first date. . . .

The night before I was scheduled to pick Virginia up at the airport, I stayed very late at the office, working at a feverish pace to get ahead in my caseload so I could have a relaxed breakfast with her the following day. Every so often, between making revisions and scribbling long notations in the margins, I would picture Virginia's face, her tender eyes, and I would feel a quick rush in my gut. And as I sat there under the fluorescent lights, surrounded by empty, dark offices, I let myself imagine just how good it would feel to have someone to come home to after a late night like this. Someone like Virginia."

WHEN I SAW VIRGINIA WALK THROUGH THE ARRIVAL GATE, I noticed that her lipstick was freshly applied. I hoped it was for my sake.

We shared a quick kiss, and a warm embrace. When we separated, Virginia tugged lightly on my tie.

"Look at you—you look so professional." I wasn't really required to wear a tie when the judges weren't around at the courthouse, but I had put on my best suit and tie in an effort to impress Virginia. The male equivalent of lipstick.

When we arrived in the city and crossed the street toward a coffee shop, I put my arm around her. She stayed close to me, and I felt as if I had just scored a point in my imaginary game book. It was only through these moments that I had any concrete proof of how I was doing.

We ordered coffee and pastries and sat down at a small table against the wall.

"It feels kind of strange to be here," Virginia said. "I feel like I've lost contact with so many people. Right now you're the person I feel closest to here."

I reached over and took her hand and said, "I'm really happy to see you."

She let my hand stay there as we continued talking, and my mood rose. I didn't ask about her lover, but there were moments when I caught glimpses of emotional weariness in her, as though she was drained. It was during those moments that I wanted to ask, but I held back because I knew even if my motives started out pure, they would quickly change and I would find myself silently rooting for their breakup. I just didn't want there to be any insincerity between us.

When it approached late morning, Virginia said, "Don't you have to get to work?"

"Soon—you're more important right now."

She smiled, and we each got another cup of coffee and continued chatting away.

I did finally get going sometime after noon, figuring it wouldn't look too impressive to wear my power suit, then blow off work altogether. I dropped Virginia at her friend's house and we agreed to talk the following week. She was going to be a part of a friend's wedding and was spending the next few days doing wedding-related things with guests who'd flown into town.

As I drove to the office, I came down from my euphoria. I had just barely gotten reacquainted with her, and now I was going to have to wait again. She must have read my mind, because I had been at the office less than an hour, when she called.

"I just want to tell you how much I enjoyed the breakfast, and I look forward to spending more time together."

I spent the next few days thinking about her constantly. And while I had experienced this feeling as anticipation and excitement before, it was now turning into a form of torture. Fantasizing about Virginia while she was thousands of miles away was one thing—but while she was in the same town? It pained me to imagine her looking gorgeous at the wedding and not being able to see her. Or dance with her. And it hurt to know I hadn't been invited to any social gatherings with her friends. I started to feel like I was being compartmentalized. Or like I was some sort of secret.

I found myself engaged in imaginary debates as I punted around various arguments. "Even if she's got a lover, can't I be invited as a friend?" was one. And then: "Maybe she's not inviting me because she doesn't see me as just a friend. It's not like I'm 'one of the girls.' Maybe that's a good sign." On and on I went.

IT WAS DURING THE SAME WEEK THAT I HAD ANOTHER follow-up appointment with Dr. Laub during which time he removed the stitches in my scrotum. Certain areas were extremely sensitive, and I yelped in pain several times. When I was finished, I drove home. Alone. I had been through so much on my own that I wished that for once I could have had someone with me. Someone with whom I was intimate enough to let inside that exam room. Someone who was tender and gentle. Someone like Virginia.

BY THE TIME VIRGINIA AND I SPOKE AGAIN, I HAD GONE THROUGH several more rounds of emotions, ending with cranky and frustrated. I tried to cover my feelings, but the more we spoke, the harder it got. After briefly mentioning the wedding, she talked about things she'd done with her friends during the week. It was then that my mood slipped even lower.

Virginia told me she'd gone to a bar with her friends and entered a trivia competition. As soon I heard her talk about how one woman's boyfriend had racked up points, I felt as if a knife had been stuck in my heart. Just hearing that a guy was there, that he'd gotten to be with them, killed me. It nailed everything right on the head. Everything that I wanted.

Virginia picked up on my mood. "What's wrong? You suddenly got quiet."

Hearing her ask made it worse. For it was her sensitivity and intuition that made me so attracted to her. And once again I felt torn. The rational part of me could see all she was doing was celebrating with her friends, and I didn't want to make her feel guilty for that. At the same time, I didn't want to be fake or put on a happy face when that was not how I felt.

"I was just thinking that if your girlfriend was here, she'd be at all of these events with you. But because I don't have that status with you, I'm not. And that makes me sad."

"But we'll have our own special time this week," Virginia said. "We've got the dinner this weekend."

"I know," I said halfheartedly. I was having a hard time bouncing back.

We made plans to see each other the next night for dinner. As we were ending the conversation, Virginia said, "I just get this feeling—like something has shifted between us."

I didn't know what to say, so I just said I'd see her the next day. When I got off the phone, I found myself returning to the conversation. What was my rush with a relationship? Virginia was not truly available. And I wasn't either. I still had another surgery to go. And then who knows what else? But perhaps that was why my feelings for Virginia had taken on a new sense of desperation. Maybe I just needed to know there was one thing that was going to turn out perfectly—one thing I could count on.

In the end, nothing solved my most immediate problem: How could I possibly get through the next few days without sabotaging my chances with Virginia?

WHEN I PICKED HER UP, VIRGINIA WAS WEARING A LONG, pale blue cotton dress, and as she climbed into the passenger seat, she reached down and gathered up the loose material before closing the door.

"I really need to talk to you about something," I said. "Is it all right if we first stop by my place? I don't want to worry about being interrupted or overheard."

As we crossed the Bay Bridge, the radio was playing quietly in the background, but we remained silent. At one point Virginia let out a small, nervous laugh and said, "It feels serious in here. Almost ominous, "But I continued to stay quiet, all of my attention on the upcoming moment.

When we walked into my apartment, I gave Virginia a seat on the sofa as I poured two glasses of wine. I went into the living room, set the wine on the coffee table, and sat next to her. She looked at me with an expectant expression, waiting.

"I just need to get this out—however it comes." I took a deep breath and then began: "When I saw you six months ago and we had dinner, I walked away with very strong feelings for you. I've always found you physically attractive, but I was really struck by how natural and right it felt to be with you. And it's been a long time since I've met someone who I feel I could fall for—head over heels.

"After that dinner, I bought a rose and put it next to my bed because my mother told me that according to the Chinese tradition of feng shui you should place something live in the corner of your bedroom if you want a particular relationship to flourish. When the rose began dying a few days later, I bought another one and put it there. And then, finally, I went out and got a small plant.

"Now, I've never taken care of a living thing—not an animal, not even a plant—but I wanted to do something to bring us luck, to nurture the potential. So I've been faithfully watering that plant. When you sent me pictures of yourself, I put one in that corner. And now when I wake up, I see your face and say hello. And when I go to sleep at night, I say good night to you. Just knowing there is some potential has kept me going through the tough times. But lately I have started feeling like I'm the only one carrying this hope. And it's been taking a toll. These last few days have been really, really hard—having you here in town and not being able to see you. And when I heard how your friends were bringing their boyfriends, I just felt some part of me snap. I wanted that for myself. I want to be your boyfriend.

"I know on a practical level that wouldn't work right now. You're still in a relationship and there's the long distance and my own unfinished stuff. But what I'm afraid of is that even when you are free, even when time has passed, that you will not end up giving me a chance—that I am just some sort of flattering flirtation for you. And that scares me."

I let out a long breath and leaned back into the sofa.

"So are you giving me some sort of ultimatum?" Virginia asked.

"I wish I could, but what would that serve? I can't force my heart into going somewhere else. But I do need to know where I stand and what I mean to you."

It was Virginia's turn to take a deep breath.

"Well, I was afraid that tonight you were going to tell me one of two things: either bad news about your health or you were going to give me some sort of ultimatum. And I was equally afraid of both.

"Yes, I feel a strong pull toward you. I felt it after our dinner and I've thought about it a lot. In fact, I was surprised how much I thought about it. But then Mona arrived back in town, and I got back into that relationship.

"I do feel that you really see me—the core of me. I do sometimes won-der if perhaps you have misperceptions about me, though—like thinking I'm five-foot-four when I'm five-seven. But on a core level, you see me. The past few days, I have been thinking and grieving about a lot of things in my life. One is that I need to address my relationship with Mona when I get back.

"But, Dhillon, even if that breaks up, would I call you immediately and say, 'Let's go?' No, because there are still other considerations. For one thing, I am totally without direction right now and need to decide where I am going to live and what I am going to do.

"And for another . . . you're . . . you're a man."

I couldn't believe it. Not this. Not her. The one who proclaimed her-self to be bisexual—who told me she still fantasized about men. Not the one person I felt so understood by in this transition—the one person who had never once slipped up or used the wrong pronoun.

"Wait a minute," I said when I finally got my bearings back. "If you feel strongly toward me, how can gender be relevant to you?"

"But it is relevant—if gender wasn't relevant, you wouldn't have done what you did."

"I did what I did so I can feel at home in my body. That's why it mat-ters to me. Why does it matter to you? Is it that you are physically less at-tracted to a male body? Or are you worried what your lesbian friends might think? Or is your lesbianism a part of your identity in a political sense, and you feel that by dating a man you are buying into the main-stream?"

"I guess a little of the last two."

"To the extent it's about what your friends think—how can you let that stop something really strong? And if it is about not wanting to buy into mainstream society, to the extent that I'm out about myself, I challenge the mainstream more than any lesbian. Hell—it's still okay to make transsex-ual jokes."

"You're saying I'm shallow, Dhillon. I'm feeling judged."

"I don't want to judge you, but—well . . . hell, yes, I am. You're the one who told me you would not have been a lesbian but for the fact you had some lesbian friends in college, so to me that is letting an identity that got created by default rule you."

"But a lot of who we are is created by default. I might not have been a writer but for a certain environment in which I was raised."

I felt myself getting more exasperated, "But at some point we look at what has been created and see if it is who we really are—if it really fits us—and then we throw out what is not real. "Doesn't it even remotely scare you to lose this potential with me?"

"Yes, of course it does."

"And you really have strong feelings for me?"

"Yes, you must know that."

"No, you are so careful and private. I'm always the one talking about how I feel about you."

She laughed and said, "So, you're the woman in the relationship."

My own laughter was laced with anger as I said, "Yes—so what's the fucking holdup?"

Virginia became more serious and sat up a little, "Do you think you have to trust yourself to know what you want? I mean, I went to a psychic a while back, and he told me that I love myself but I don't trust my intuition. And that is accurate. I doubt every decision I make." She then looked at me directly and said, "I'm being as clear and honest as I know how. I can't give you an easy answer."

I felt her sincerity, and for a moment I forgot my anger. And as soon as I did, I felt drained, tired. When I felt my head growing heavy, I dropped it into her lap. And as she started stroking my hair, I started muttering, venting in a stream of consciousness. My tone was more petulant little boy than adult:

"Fuck lesbians. Fuck all of you. When I was in a different body, you all wanted me—drooled over me. And now it's different? Well, you're all hypocrites because I'm the same person."

Virginia didn't say anything; she just continued to stroke my hair as I vented my frustration. But as I ran out of words, I found my attention shifting. I became aware of the soft, sweet-smelling cotton of her skirt against my cheek. And I felt her fingernails lightly grazing my scalp and combing through my hair. And the inevitable happened.

I started to want her. A series of images flashed into my mind. My lips on the palm of her hand. My mouth on her mouth.

My reaction to those images was to push them out of my mind—to be the good, considerate boy, so I wouldn't ruin my chances.

But then I thought, what chances? She just shot me down, so what incentive did I have to hold back? What's the worst that could happen? She could reject me, but since that already seemed to have happened, I had nothing to lose. But if she responded, it might make her more aware of our chemistry. And it might prove I was right—that she was denying something strong for reasons that were weak.

I sat up. I knew she was wondering what I was going to do—or say—next. I moved closer until my face was a few inches from hers and said, "I've waited years to kiss you; can't I at least have one kiss?"

"You haven't waited years."

"Yes, I have."

When my lips touched hers, I felt a tiny taste of her tongue as she extended it between her slightly parted lips. It was a tender, gentle kiss and when I pulled back to gauge her reaction, I did not hear any protest. I heard a sigh. The good kind.

It was all I needed. I used my lips to part hers and opened her mouth and mine, as our tongues entwined for a hungry, passionate kiss. I then slid my mouth up her neck, to her ear, and then down again, first grazing my teeth and then biting her. She responded by arching her head back to expose more neck. And I continued to bite, breathing hot air against her skin.

She finally pulled away. "That's some mouth you've got there."

"That's not all."

"I bet." She then regained her composure and asked, "Can we go to dinner now?"

Virginia got up and I ran my hand across my face. In my mind, I had just scored another imaginary point and gained a temporary reprieve from the awful sting of rejection.

———

AS WE WERE WALKING FROM THE CAR TO THE RESTAURANT, we held hands. Several people smiled at us and I let myself pretend we were the young, charming couple they thought us to be.

The restaurant was a casual Italian place, and our waiter was a friendly guy who was a little too chatty and intrusive. When he brought our food and asked if we needed anything else, I said, "Yes—to be left alone for a while."

To his credit, the waiter graciously bowed out, and Virginia said, "I was hoping you'd say something."

The dinner was great. Not so much the food—or even the wine—which were both average, but the time we shared. We laughed and talked the night away, getting louder and sillier as we drank more wine. Our talk had definitely released something in each of us. And while I knew the sadness and frustration over her rejection or, perhaps more accurately, her unwillingness to commit to any future would probably return, I just wasn't there right now. I was busy milking every moment I had with her.

After our second bottle of wine was gone, so, too, had the other patrons in the place. We were the last who were left and thanks to our friendly waiter, who encouraged us to stay as long as we liked, had even outlasted most of the staff. By the time I paid the check, it was after midnight. I had my arm around Virginia as we made our way back to the car and on to a gourmet ice-cream shop down the street. I got us each a cup of vanilla ice cream and two café lattes, which we took back to my house.

As we kissed again, between bites of ice cream and sips of coffee, it occurred to me that she might regret this in the morning. I knew her well enough to realize that she liked to keep things organized and controlled—that this hedonistic behavior, characteristic of myself, was an aberration for her. And if she did wake up with a sense of regret, she might cancel our special black-tie dinner—the one I had been looking forward to for so long.

I stopped eating, moved back a little, and said, "So are we still going to have our black-tie dinner?"

"Yes—although I might be a little nervous."

I breathed a sigh of relief. I still had one night left. One night where I could pretend we were exactly what everyone who encountered us thought we were: a young couple in love.

It was close to 2:00 A.M. by the time I dropped Virginia off at her friend's house. On my way home, I found myself reviewing the events of the evening, particularly our earlier conversation. Something about her words tugged at my mind.

About eight years ago, while in undergraduate school, I developed an overwhelming crush on a beautiful blonde in my creative writing class. After becoming friends, we ended up sleeping together. It was romantic and passionate. We continued the affair, but when I started to pursue a relationship, she said she couldn't do that. Although she had very strong feelings for me, she just couldn't deal with the societal implications of the relationship—the societal implications of being with a woman.

It was the irony of all ironies. Eight years ago I was rejected for being a woman. And now I was being rejected for being a man. It suddenly struck me as hilarious, and I started to laugh. I laughed all the way home.

I laughed so hard there were tears in my eyes.

THE NEXT FEW DAYS PASSED RELATIVELY QUICKLY. VIRGINIA came by the office for lunch, and while at a nearby Vietnamese restaurant, we hit a tense spot when I probed her for more clarity about her own sexuality and feelings for me.

"My lesbianism is not just some false cloak I put on every day," Virginia said. "After all these years of being with women, they have become more familiar and men have become less familiar."

I knew then it was time to stop the interrogation. I was not going to win her by beating her down like an opponent. This was not a chess game. After a change of subject and some lighthearted banter, we made it past that spot. And once we had, we expressed our excitement over the upcoming dinner. It was now just a day away.

———

THE RESTAURANT I HAD SELECTED WAS CALLED JARDINIÈRE. It was located near the San Francisco Opera House and it was the perfect place for an elegant dinner: opulent but not ostentatious. The restaurant was divided into two floors, the lower of which was occupied by cocktail tables and a large, black oval bar.

A modern spiral staircase led up to the second floor and while most of the tables were spread around the room, there were a few, coveted, two-party tables. These were spaced evenly around a metal railing embracing a circular opening that looked down on the bar below. At the head of the circle, there was generally a live jazz band playing quietly in the background.

Shortly before I was scheduled to pick up Virginia, I was at the host stand of Jardinière, wearing my Italian, black wool tuxedo and a white tuxedo shirt, open at the neck. My shoes? Black construction boots, mostly hidden under the trouser legs. I just couldn't get behind the shiny dress shoe.

"I'm Dhillon Khosla. I have a reservation for seven-thirty and I just wanted to stop by to request one of the small tables upstairs that overlooks the lower floor."

"Yes," the hostess confirmed. "We already have a notation about that here."

"Great. And if I were sure it was appropriate, I would bribe you for the table. This is a really special night."

"That's not necessary," the hostess laughed. "We'll make sure you have a special evening."

I thanked her and went outside to retrieve my car, tipping the valet who had allowed me to leave it out front. Actually, it was not my car. I had rented it for the evening after concluding that my old Toyota Tercel with vinyl seats was just not up to snuff for a black-tie night.

A few minutes later, I found a parking spot a block from the place where Virginia was staying. When I knocked on the door, an unfamiliar face appeared. I was beginning to think I had the wrong house, but when

I asked for Virginia, she answered, "Oh, yeah, she's here," and opened the door wide enough to let me in.

I entered the house and encountered more unfamiliar faces in the living room, along with a friend of Virginia's whom I'd met once before. This woman greeted me kindly and told me that Virginia would be out shortly. She had barely finished her statement, when I heard the sound of heels. I looked up, and there she was.

Virginia was wearing a black dress that ended just above her knees and had narrow shoulder straps. The dress was made of a thin, filmy material that hugged her curves. On her wrist was the diamond bracelet I had bought her, and she had added a pair of matching diamond earrings. I looked at her face and noticed a subtle shade of lipstick and eye shadow—just enough to give her a hint of shimmer. The whole effect was one of flawless elegance.

I became aware of the watchful gaze of her friends, so after briefly embracing Virginia and telling her she looked beautiful, I made some movements toward the front door.

As I held the car door open for her, Virginia made an appreciative comment about the car and as I watched her settle comfortably into the spacious front seat, I was glad I'd gone the extra mile. When I climbed into my side, she also complimented me on my tuxedo.

"Yeah—but what about the construction boots? I mean, if you and I were a couple, would you have tried to talk me out of wearing these boots?"

Virginia laughed. "Probably . . . yes."

We arrived at the restaurant early, so we checked in with the hostess and stepped off at the lounge for a cocktail.

"How about we start with a glass of champagne?"

Virginia's eyes lit up, and she exclaimed, "Yes—let's!"

We found a small table at the edge of the lounge and I headed to the bar. The cost was appropriately outrageous and was a fitting start for the rest of this most extravagant evening.

When I came back, Virginia was looking around the place. Although it was early, the place was buzzing with conversation from the pre-opera crowd.

"This is really beautiful," she said as we toasted.

I looked down at her bracelet, and she held it up and said, "Isn't it gorgeous?"

"It looks much better on you than it did in the store. By the way, were you surprised when you got it?"

"I was stunned."

"I figured you couldn't get mad if I did it in a joking way."

Virginia laughed and said, "You just reminded me of a card that I've been wanting to give you. It has this quote that basically says, 'In those I don't like I can find no common denominator, but in those that I do, it's that they make me laugh.'"

The hostess chose this moment to arrive—our table was ready. She led us up the curving stairs, and then placed our menus on top of one of the select tables along the railing. It was the perfect spot—away from the traffic of the staircase and close enough to hear the band, but not so close that we couldn't hear each other.

I turned to the hostess and said, "Thank you for accommodating us," and she responded, "You were so diplomatic in the way you asked that we wanted to do this for you."

As the hostess walked away, Virginia smiled at me and said, "Well, someone made quite an impression." I couldn't have asked for a better start to our dinner.

I TOOK OFF MY JACKET AND HELD OUT MY ARMS TO VIRginia, pointing out the gold cuff links.

"I like the look of these, but it feels so constricting to keep my shirtsleeves closed at the wrist. I just want to roll up my sleeves."

Virginia admired the cuff links, then said, "Well, if you're really uncomfortable, you can take the cuff links off, but can you make it through dinner first?"

"I can try."

"Yes—please try."

I laughed. "Okay—now we really do sound like an old married couple."

"You're right—we do."

The waitress arrived, took our order for a bottle of merlot, and quietly disappeared. As we returned to our conversation, we ended up veering into childhood stories. Virginia told me that once, when she was a young girl, she was sitting at the dinner table and as everyone went around the table, thanking God for something, she piped up, "You're welcome."

We were both laughing as she said, "I was just so used to being polite and responding when someone said thank you."

"I might have done the same thing as a kid, but not so much out of politeness as grandiosity. When my parents told me that the next Messiah could be anybody, including me, I took them seriously."

Our wine arrived and as we started sipping, I noticed that Virginia slightly extended her tongue each time she took a sip. It made me think back to our night of kissing, and I wondered if that slight extension of her tongue during that first kiss was simply an automatic gesture. Whatever it was, it was damn sexy.

As we were scanning the menu, I asked her to give me her foot under the table.

"No." It was a halfhearted protest.

"Come on."

Virginia put it in my lap, but the heel and the straps dug into my legs. So I asked her to take off her shoe. She complied and put her foot back in my lap.

I started caressing the underside of her foot with my palm and then her ankle with both hands. Her foot stayed there throughout the entire meal and I kept one hand on it while I ate my food and drank my wine with the other.

At one point Virginia looked around and said, "I wonder if anyone can see. This feels really illicit."

I waved my free arm in a grand gesture at the crowd and said, "Look, all of these people are here spending a lot of money for their own special evening—the last thing they care about is what we are up to."

"You're probably right," Virginia said, and picked up her wine.

Halfway through dinner, we both got up to use the restroom. As we walked down the spiral staircase, I said, "Selena once told me that she looked forward to my transition so we could go to separate bathrooms. She wanted to have that privacy."

"It is kind of nice to have that separation."

When we returned to our seats, we finished our dinner and then watched the busboy clear away our plates, referring to us as "sir and ma'am."

"Is it strange for you to hear someone call me sir after all those years of hearing people refer to me as something different?" I asked Virginia.

"Actually, no. I don't feel any surprise—not one bit. I don't know why, but I just adjusted instantly—there was no effort involved."

Virginia looked down at my hands. "Did they change from the hormones?"

"No—why?"

"They look masculine to me. But maybe that's just because they're yours."

My heart ached. I felt so seen by her that I just couldn't imagine our not working out. I didn't understand how she could appreciate my masculinity so much and at the same time let it be the barrier that kept us apart. We began to talk about masculine and feminine personality traits.

"I think it is not about one side being superior to the other, but what brings out the best for each person," I said. "I can be really aggressive, and if I'm with someone who's also aggressive, it makes me more defensive in an argument. But what I like about you is that you point out when I've crossed the line without attacking me. And that makes me much more likely to back away. Like when I was mad at you for rejecting me for gender reasons and I started poking at your lesbianism, you didn't jump back at me but just said you felt judged—I really admire that."

"Really? I was afraid I was a total pushover."

"Not at all. It takes more strength to name your own feelings than it does to attack. Or maybe it's different styles. I don't know. I just know I wouldn't want to date someone like me."

We fell into a few moments of silence, just looking at each other. Virginia was the first to speak.

"Your eyes are so intense right now—sometimes when you look at me, the gaze is so intense I have to look away. It's almost too . . ." Virginia seemed to be searching for the right word.

"Exposing?"

"Yes . . . but it's also the way you focus in on a person sometimes. I bet a lot of people—men or women—think you are hitting on them when you give them direct eye contact."

"I just like to look people in the eye."

"I know. I imagine that a lot of people respond to you."

I smiled. "So, do you think I'm a flirt?"

"I think you appreciate beauty, but when you are really into something, you are in it all the way." Virginia's words evoked another tug at my heart.

I sighed and said, "But the one I want is breaking my heart."

And to my surprise Virginia said, "Right—that's why I have my foot in your lap."

The surprise continued as Virginia said, "I'm meeting tomorrow with some friends who live in the Bay Area to see if I can do the kind of work they're doing. I know you and I talked about going to the wine country, but I figure you wouldn't mind if it had to do with me maybe moving here." Virginia then laughed as she added, "I mean, I know how you pout when I don't do what you want."

"Come on—men don't pout."

"Yes, they do. You definitely pout."

I laughed—but in agreement rather than protest.

When the coffee and dessert arrived, I continued massaging Virginia's foot as we fed each other from the plate of assorted chocolates. By the time we had finished, we had matched our four-hour dinner record. But the night was not yet over. I still had one more trick up my sleeve—a sleeve that was about to be released from its cuff link and rolled up for comfort.

———

DESPITE THE LENGTH OF TIME THAT HAD PASSED SINCE WE had begun our dinner, I had not fully processed all of the wine we had consumed. As we pulled away toward our next destination, Virginia asked me if I was all right to drive.

"I'm probably legally past the limit, but I'm lucid enough to drive—carefully."

"Maybe we should get a cab."

"No—but let me pull over for just a second."

A few seconds was not going to sober me up. But that's not why I turned off. As soon as I was safely off the road, I reached over and pulled her toward me. When we stopped for air, Virginia said, "I hadn't planned on kissing you again. I was just going to give you a peck tonight."

"Yeah, right."

I grabbed her again and we continued to make out. I remember losing myself in the passion of the moment, letting my guard down. And as my mouth traveled to her ear, I whispered, "I just don't want to be without you."

"Dhillon, it scares me when you say that because I still have a relationship, and I don't want you to put your life on hold for me."

It was as if she'd thrown cold water on me. I started the car and pulled away, feeling angry and defensive, as I said, "I will not be less vulnerable just so you can feel more comfortable."

"I'm sorry."

Virginia's voice took on a more lighthearted tone. "Someone's buttons got pushed."

She moved toward me, trying to soothe me with her body language.

It wasn't until we approached our destination—a row of the finest San Francisco hotels—that I felt myself bounce back. As we walked arm in arm toward the Mark Hopkins hotel, I felt as if we had already been through an entire relationship, broken up, and reconciled—all in a few days.

The top floor of the Mark Hopkins Hotel, known as the "Top of the Mark," was a nightclub that offered breathtaking views of the downtown area and, on a clear night, of the whole city. We shared the elevator with another young couple, cracking jokes with them on the way up, and by the time we reached our floor, we were almost back to normal. Virginia headed off to the restroom while I walked into the lounge and secured a table by the window.

When Virginia returned, she ordered a cosmopolitan while I asked for a glass of wine. I figured if I was going to be irresponsible enough to drink and drive, I should at least stick to the same type of alcohol. After silently patting myself on the back for my wise decision, I turned my attention back to Virginia.

There was a live band, and a vocalist was singing an old slow ballad. I grabbed Virginia's hand and stood up.

"Come on—let's dance."

I held her close, admitting I wasn't much of a slow dancer. There were only two other couples on the floor, and as we slowly made our way around one of them, I said to Virginia, "Check them out. We've got to be better than they are."

Virginia giggled. "Shh—they'll hear us," but as we continued to move past the couple, awkwardly circling around the small dance floor, we both cracked up even more.

The band suddenly veered into an old disco song, and the dance floor immediately filled, limbs flying all over the place. I felt infinitely more comfortable, finding it easier to move my hips to a faster, funkier groove. Virginia and I were going full force when I put my arms around her waist and she put hers around my shoulders, letting me grind my pelvis against hers. I moved my arms lower and cupped my hands around her, feeling the slick, filmy material slither against her round, firm, voluptuous cheeks. Virginia felt incredible in my hands.

When the band took a break, we returned to our table to find our drinks waiting for us. I was still in overdrive from having Virginia in my hands when she made the next move.

She leaned toward me until our legs were almost touching and said, "You are so used to getting what you want that you can't stand it when you don't."

As if to punctuate her point, she put her hand on my thigh. My inner thigh.

It was classic tease. I knew that as surely as I knew it was my duty to call her bluff.

I leaned in close, looked her dead in the eyes, and with a smug expression, said, "You want me to want you; you need me to want you. You couldn't stand to have it any other way."

"Oh, you are so cocky, I love that."

We spent the rest of the night alternating between kissing and dancing until the last call for alcohol had long passed and the band had packed its gear.

THE STREETS WERE RELATIVELY EMPTY WHEN VIRGINIA AND I made our departure, so the drive home was a short one.

"This was a really fun evening, Dhillon—and an interesting one. We processed, we ate, we danced, we . . ."

"What is this?" I interrupted her, laughing. "Some polite wrap-up they taught you in finishing school? Aren't we way past that?"

It struck me as hilarious that Virginia was still applying good old-fashioned manners to a situation that had completely lost all etiquette hours before. As I walked her to the front door of her friend's house, she began to repeat her polite wrap-up. I let it go on for a while, then leaned in, and cut her off with a final kiss. I remember feeling a bit rude as I did so, but there was something about her attitude that had begun to bother me. I was now getting the sense that she wasn't just trying to be polite, she was attempting to inject a level of distance that left her feeling safe. But I couldn't snap back that quickly—I was starting to get whiplash.

I said a quick good-bye and jumped into the car, waiting for Virginia to step inside the house before I pulled away. I spent most of the ride home concentrating on the road, keeping both hands on the wheel and one eye on the speedometer.

———

I SLEPT LATE INTO THE NEXT DAY AND WHEN I GOT UP, I remember being grateful for the hangover that left me too brain-dead for my usual inner chatter and endless self-analysis. There was no manic debate over what I should or shouldn't have done. All that was there was a slight throbbing that made me incapable of focusing on anything more complex than pouring water into my coffeemaker. And after the last few days, it was exactly what I needed.

Twenty-six

SEPTEMBER 1999

> I am walking alone in the woods when I come upon a row of houses. As I pass by one of them, I glance into its large front window and see some men dressing as women. I stop to watch, and as I notice how much fun they are having, I start to laugh along with them. It suddenly begins to rain so I go to the front door and, after knocking, ask them to let me inside. The men refuse, angrily saying they heard me laughing at them. I try to explain that my laughter was in appreciation, but they refuse to listen. I finally turn away, making my way alone in the rain. . . .

I was working at home on a Friday afternoon when my computer monitor short-circuited and went black. I wasn't totally shocked; my entire setup had been purchased at a low-end computer store in San Francisco, which puts together systems, using parts from various manufacturers. The monitor was still under warranty, so I figured I would just take it in and trade it for another one.

The computer store was located toward the outskirts of San Francisco, in a neighborhood called the Richmond District. Going into the city had been easy traffic-wise, but a quick look across the highway divide told me that the return trip was going to be a nightmare. Every Friday, the rush hour would begin an hour or two earlier as people left their offices in droves in an effort to get a head start on the weekend.

As I made my way out of the store with a new monitor sitting by my side, I drove down Geary Street toward the highway. I had gone several blocks when I began to feel that familiar irritation kick in as I anticipated the thick, slow traffic that was waiting for me at the entrance ramp to the Bay Bridge. As I looked out my window and passed by a row of bars and restaurants, one familiar sign caught my eye. It was for an Irish pub called the Pig and Whistle that served both drinks and food.

It wasn't a tough decision: I could sit in traffic and suck in fumes for more than an hour or relax in a bar and enjoy a burger and beer while I waited out the worst of it. I made a quick turn into a side street adjacent to the bar and found an open spot half a block up. When I opened the heavy, wooden door that led into the bar, I was immediately greeted with the sounds of a jam-packed happy hour: laughter and loud chatter, clinking glasses, and billiard balls striking one another. I went up to the bar, sat down, and ordered a beer, burger, and fries.

As I drank my beer and waited for the food, I looked around me. Sitting to my right was a woman in a jean jacket, wearing shoulder-length brown hair and glasses. Her overall look was one of bookish androgyny. With her were two other women: one a pretty, vivacious blonde with long, curly hair and another with short brown hair and average looks.

I turned to the bookish-looking woman next to me, smiled, and said, "You and your friends should order some food so that I don't have to eat alone."

"Well, they like to watch their weight, but I like to eat. Heck, I like to have just the meat and the bun."

The women had a strong southern accent and when I asked where she was from, she said, "Arkansas."

As we continued talking, I had the sense that I was talking with more of a male buddy than a woman. There was something clearly masculine in her energy, and she spoke to me in a "man-to-man" kind of way. I began to wonder if one of the other women was actually her girlfriend. This thought then led me to wonder how the two of them would be treated in a conservative, southern state. Like many who had never been to the South, I had this stereotypic image of the place as a racist, homophobic, bible-thumping group of people who sat and drank mint juleps on the stoop of their *Gone with the Wind*–style homes.

I began to veer the conversation in a direction that would allow the woman to reveal herself more.

I said, "You know, I grew up on the East Coast and I've always had these stereotypes about the South."

"Like what?"

"Oh, that it's racist and homophobic and stuff like that. I mean, I like it out here, because everybody can be free to be themselves."

The woman said, "Well, that's not completely true about the South. I mean, I'm a lesbian and it's all right. It's harder on gay men, though."

"When you say 'all right,' what do you mean? Can you walk hand in hand with a lover down the street?"

"Well, I don't really do it, 'cause it would get a lot of stares and people would yell 'dyke' and stuff, but we wouldn't get beat up."

I was struck by her notion of what was 'all right.' And I suddenly felt this strong urge to shake her and say, "What do you mean that's okay? Don't you know you deserve better?" I was surprised by my own reaction.

When the attractive blonde came over, the woman I'd been talking with introduced her as her "ex-girlfriend." She filled her in on our conversation, and I leaned toward the blonde and said, "Hey, tell me this. I bet you and she couldn't have a romantic dinner without some guy interrupting your space, right?"

The blonde became animated and said, "Yeah, we've had guys come up to us and say, 'Thank you,' like we'd put on a show for them, or something."

The southern woman next to me said, "Yeah, but what can you do? I just try to live my life." The blonde, however, continued to cite examples and struck me as more bothered—or with a greater sense or entitlement.

When I had finished with my food, we all moved toward the back of the bar and played a game of pool. Between taking turns at the game, I continued to talk with my former bar-stool neighbor. She told me about her dream of being able to marry a woman and "provide" for her, and I again felt like I was talking to a buddy. And the more I treated her like one, the more she revealed to me.

At one point, the woman said, "I could never be with a bisexual woman. I mean I couldn't compete with that."

I said, "But why? If she's truly bisexual, then she'd be as capable of falling in love with you as with a guy."

I expected the woman's response to be something about the societal approval of heterosexual relationships and the way a bisexual woman in the South might choose a guy for that reason. But instead she responded, "Well, it's more like if she really is into dicks, then I can't compete with that—I can't give her that."

On the surface it was an odd comment. But I personally understood it well. I had spent much of my life feeling inadequate while dating straight and bisexual women, placing far more emphasis on the penis than they did.

The more I spoke with the southern woman, the more I found myself wondering if she was somewhere along that transsexual continuum. Would she be happier as a man? Or was she simply a masculine lesbian who wanted to express some of the traditionally male cultural attributes? But then what about her penis comment?

Were body image and cultural roles inextricably linked? Or where they entirely separate?

My conversation with the woman left me with many questions. But mostly it left me with a sense that I had turned an important corner. For it was the first time since my transition that I had been in the company of a group of lesbians and not felt the need to push away or separate myself. And I knew that it had everything to do with the fact that I was both seen and warmly accepted as a man.

And that difference brought out a different side of me.

IT WAS NOT UNTIL THE END OF SEPTEMBER THAT I PICKED UP the phone and called Virginia. I had spent the previous few weeks digesting the events of her visit and trying hard to reach some sense of clarity. But each passing day seemed to further distort my memory of what had happened between us. By the time I finally picked up the phone, I felt like a detective in search of some clue to a great puzzle. I had no idea what I would find on the other end of the line.

The first thing Virginia said was, "I'm surprised to hear from you."

"Why?"

"Well—I figured you'd struck me from your list."

My list? What list? "No—not at all. I mean, things didn't go exactly as I'd planned, but that didn't change my feelings for you. What about you— did you have a good time at the dinner? I still find myself laughing at that whole polite wrap-up thing you did at the end."

"Well, I was just doing that out of anxiousness."

"Anxiousness? What do you mean? Were you mad at me, or something?"

"Well, a little toward the end. I felt pressured. And then in the morning I woke up feeling . . . I woke up feeling slightly violated."

"*Violated?*" I felt the color drain out of my face.

"I don't mean in some sort of permanent way or irreparable way."

But there was no retreating from a word like "violated." I instantly felt like all those points I had earned on my imaginary scoreboard had been erased in one swift motion. They'd all been stolen, not earned.

My immediate response was a selfish one: I wanted to try to salvage some of those points—to somehow regain my advantage. To feel better.

I said, "Weren't there at least parts of the evening where you were into it?"

Virginia's voice took on a firmer edge as she said, "Dhillon, there you go again. I am saying something was not okay, and you are asking me to say that it was."

I sighed. "I'm sorry. I'm just trying to understand when the evening turned from mutual to pressured."

"Well, the whole dinner was fun. It was more later on."

"Why didn't you say something?"

"I should have, but I didn't want to ruin the evening. Then I was going to write you a letter, but I didn't know how to say it."

"Well, how can we prevent this from happening again in the future?"

"We probably can't, but I can just tell you how I feel and maybe you can check in periodically."

"So, if we ever have sex—which will probably never happen now—you want me to stop and check in along the way?" I don't know what compelled me to say this other than sheer stupidity.

"No, not like that."

I continued with a few more stupid questions until I finally snapped out of it. It was about then I realized that I was not going to get what I so desperately wanted—a complete recantation, the saving of my bruised ego.

"In the movies it always works," I said wistfully. "One person grabs the other in a passionate kiss and breaks through her barriers. I guess I saw the exchange in a different way than you did. Even when we were arguing, I was having fun—I was engaged."

"It's hard for me," Virginia said as her tone softened. "I mean, you must have been told this before, but you have amazing verbal skills—it's hard to keep up."

I remembered how Virginia had once said her biggest complaint with ex-lovers was that they had poor communication skills. And so I said, jokingly, "Isn't it ironic that the one thing you've been waiting for in another person comes along and now you can't handle it?" My tone was light-hearted, not confrontational.

Her laugh was the first truly relaxed laughter I had heard since we had begun the conversation. I joined in the laughter and said, "I guess I just went from prince to pig in one night, huh?"

She laughed again and said, "It sounds like a fairy tale."

After we made some unrelated small talk, we ended up back at our dinner, this time in a lighter tone, reviewing the food from the restaurant and the view from the hotel bar. Before I could catch myself, I found myself automatically steering the conversation into the sexual realm, telling her how much I'd wanted her that night and how hot she looked. By the time I caught myself, I felt like a hopeless addict. Even when I was going down, I was still reaching for the bottle.

"You should just stay with women." I sighed. "I just can't keep myself in line."

"So, you don't think I'm up to the challenge, huh?"

"No—I'm not sure that I am."

And that's how I felt—it was so hard to get it right, to have to watch myself constantly, to reign myself in.

I tried to think back to the years before my transition. It seemed I had gotten away with so much more before. Was it because my aggressive behavior was less threatening in a female guise? Whatever it was, I now felt like I was a young teenage boy starting the game all over again.

If ever there was a time when I thought I had some special insight into the minds of women, that time was now past.

Twenty-seven

OCTOBER 1999

> I am holding my penis in my hand and first feel surprised by its length because it is more than I had expected, but my initial surprise turns to sadness as I realize that it is still no more than a young boy might have as opposed to a full-grown man. . . .

In mid–October I was once again in Dr. Laub's office, preparing for what was to be my final surgery. But every time I heard myself say the words "last" or "final," I felt a sense of hesitation. It just didn't sound real. And as I waited for Dr. Laub to arrive, I found myself wishing that he would say something that would kick me into high gear—something that would give me a stronger sense of closure. Well, I got exactly half of what I wished for.

When Dr. Laub arrived, he gave me a quick greeting and immediately launched into a brief overview of the upcoming surgery: he was going to lower the scrotum and position my testicles more squarely between my legs. After that, he would fuse the two testicular sacs together, resulting in a scar line that would eventually fade to a barely visible pink—the same line that genetic men have on their scrotal sacs when they become fused in the womb.

Insofar as the new urethra was concerned, Dr. Laub was going to connect my old one to the new one he had already built through the penis, by bridging the gap between the two. He would also create another temporary bypass hole behind the scrotum so that a catheter could be inserted for two weeks while the tissue healed. Once again, the acidity of urine would be too harsh on newly healing tissue. But unlike the hole he had created previously, this one would be self-healing and would close by itself within days of the catheter being removed, thus allowing me to urinate exclusively through the penis.

When Dr. Laub had finished briefing me, he took a quick look at my genitals, remarking how well the tissue had healed. The swelling was now completely gone, and everything looked totally healthy. But what was most amazing to me was how there were no obvious scars. Anyone looking at me would never know I had had surgery.

Despite the impressive job the doctor had done, I couldn't help but comment on my penis size and ask him, "Can't you make it any bigger?"

Dr. Laub laughed and said, "About twenty percent of genetic men look exactly as you do when they first step out of the shower."

"Really? They're that small? I can't believe it."

"Sure." But on seeing my expression, Dr. Laub sat down next to me and said, "There is a doctor in Los Angeles who I've started working with—he's had tremendous success with penis-enlargement surgeries and is one of the only reputable surgeons in the business. In fact, he runs an entire clinic devoted to just that."

"So, I could do this, too? I could get bigger?"

"Sure—we've sent some of our patients to him. Judy can give you the information once you're fully healed."

And that is how I ended up getting my wish of leaving Dr. Laub's office with a greater sense of excitement, but without fulfilling the other desire—the need for total closure. For now that he had told me about the new doctor, now that I knew it was possible to get more, I instantly had visions of a perfect penis—visions of my pulling and grabbing my dick, rather than rubbing it during masturbation, visions of my entering my future wife and having normal intercourse.

But much as I was thrilled with this new window of hope, another part of me couldn't help but groan inwardly as I thought, "Man, will this quest ever be over? Will I ever be able to rest?" For as long as my mind knew that I wasn't finished yet, as long as there was more distance to travel, some part of me just couldn't let go and fully engage in life. I was afraid that if I stopped to rest for just a second, I would never get moving again—that I would become complacent. One day I would find myself among the ranks of those who sleepwalked their way through life and justified their compromised existence with dull-eyed clichés like, "Hey, as you get older, you learn to set your sights a little lower."

AS I CLIMBED OUT OF MY LOFT BED AND DOWN THE LADDER before daybreak, I began to wonder if I would forever associate dark mornings with surgeries. For these occasions seemed to be the only times that I began my day without any natural light to keep me company.

By now I had my presurgery routine down to a science: a quick use of the bathroom, a change of clothing, and then a final run-through of the contents of my overnight bag. By the time Sue arrived, I was waiting, anxious to get going.

As we headed down the foggy highway, I couldn't help but once again wonder how anyone could do this every day: leave the house while it was still dark and return home to that same darkness.

When we entered Palo Alto, I asked Sue to first stop at the motel, hoping I could check in early. I was hesitant to reveal that I was coming directly from major surgery, and yet it was my best chance of convincing the management to bend the rules a little. I ended up telling the clerk that I was having routine knee surgery, figuring that would make him less nervous. As it turned out, it was a slow day at the motel, and he handed over the keys to my room, wishing me good luck.

When I arrived at the surgery center, I encountered the same anesthesiologist as the previous time—the one who had given me the smooth cocktail mix that gently put me out. As soon as she arrived, she flipped through my chart until she found her notes from the earlier surgery. She quickly read through the recipe of drugs, muttering under her breath and nodding her head enthusiastically. When she had finished, she snapped the folder shut and exclaimed, "Brilliant!"

I couldn't help but laugh. There is nothing like someone who is passionate about her work—especially when you benefit from that passion.

As the anesthesiologist began my IV drip, Sue came over to me, kissed me on the cheek, and said she'd see me "on the other side." That's the last thing I remember. It was that smooth.

WHEN I AWOKE, I WAS IN THE RECOVERY AREA AND I WAS IN-stantly aware of an overwhelming, mind-numbing pain in my scrotum. The pain was so bad that tears started to stream down my face.

When a nurse arrived by my bed, I was barely able to speak, my voice a hoarse whisper: "Please, pain." The nurse gave me shot of Demerol, and I waited for the pain to subside.

The next thing I remember was seeing Dr. Laub by my side. He was smiling as he said, "Everything went beautifully. In fact, this is the best positioning I have ever done with testicles—they're sitting exactly where they should. You'll see."

As soon as I heard his words, I relaxed; but the awful, searing, throbbing pain remained. As I continued to wait for the Demerol to kick in, the pain throbbing in my crotch, Sue arrived. I was grateful to see her; I was dying to get a hold of some of the pills I had waiting at the hotel—the ones that had always blocked my pain before.

As Sue helped me get dressed, I slowly headed out the door and made the trek to Sue's car, my legs bent wide, like I'd just come back from a long horseback ride. It felt as if I had two basketballs between my legs and, as I shuffled along, I muttered, "How can it hurt this badly? What the hell did he do?"

It wasn't until I had arrived at the motel and had settled into bed that I finally felt the pain subside. When I later looked back upon this day—as well as on my overall surgical history—it struck me as odd that the most potent drugs, such as Demerol and morphine, were far less effective at controlling my pain than something as comparatively mild as Vicodin. With the stabbing pangs gone, I was able to fall into a deep sleep. For the rest of the night, pain was like an invisible alarm clock, pulling me out of sleep every three hours when the medication wore off and dropping me back into snooze mode as soon as the next dose hit my system.

By the next morning, Sue had left for work and Jared had arrived to take over. As grateful as I was to have friends who were willing to care for me, it was one of those moments when I found myself wishing I had a steady lover. After two years of different people and different shifts, I yearned for continuity. But while my wish had felt within reach during my last surgery, it now seemed farther away than ever.

I had not spoken to Virginia since our last phone conversation. She had left a message wishing me well for the surgery, but I hadn't returned the call. I didn't know how to do so without crossing that invisible line. The one that kept moving.

BEFORE CHECKING OUT OF THE MOTEL, I MADE SURE THAT I took a dose of pain medication to cover myself for my appointment with Dr. Laub and the long ride home.

While I lay back in the exam chair, Dr. Laub slowly unraveled my bandages and removed one tube, but left the other two in place. He then took out a mirror and held it close to my crotch, proudly exclaiming, "Take a look."

The first thing I noticed was how huge my balls were. Positioning both testicles squarely between my legs had turned my scrotum into one large mass. The swelling from the surgery basically doubled everything in size, which explained why I had so much trouble walking—and so much pain.

While Jared drove the forty-five miles to my place, I lay in the backseat with my legs again in a frog-legged position, trying to keep the pressure off my scrotum. Upon arrival, I slowly shuffled to my front door, then made my way to the sofa bed I had pulled out and prepared before my surgery. I didn't think it wise to climb the ladder to my loft bedroom with those tubes and fragile stitches.

———

IT WAS AN AWFUL RECOVERY PERIOD, PERMEATED BY INTENSE PAIN and discomfort. It wasn't until the middle of the second week that I finally started to feel like a human being again. As I became more mobile, I found myself counting the hours until my next appointment with Dr. Laub. I couldn't wait to get those damn tubes out of me, for while the scrotum was becoming more and more comfortable, the tubes were causing greater discomfort.

With each passing day, the catheter lodged in my bladder wore away at the lining, at times causing painful bladder spasms that convulsed my abdomen. Meanwhile, the tube in my penis felt as if it was becoming attached to my skin, causing the interior of my penis to itch, as well as the place where the tube emerged from below my testicles. Most of all, I was anxious for the suspense to be over. Would I have complications? Would I need more surgery? Would I be able to pee?

DR. LAUB WAS IN A CHEERFUL MOOD WHEN I ARRIVED, HAVing just returned from a trip to Cuba where he and his surgical team had operated on disfigured children. The trip seemed to have invigorated him. His energy level was in sharp contrast to my own. I was weak and tired. And nervous. Terribly nervous.

The surgeon ushered me into an examination room, and I immediately pulled down my pants, saying, "Please just get this tube out. It's been itching like crazy."

After much tinkering and tugging, the doctor finally was able to pull the tube free. It looked nasty—covered in greenish, slimy gunk.

"No wonder this was irritating you," he commented drily.

Dr. Laub then turned his attention to the catheter as I prepared myself for another tug. Because the catheter removal had never really hurt in the past, I was comparatively relaxed. Big mistake.

"Okay. Just take a deep breath and I'll slip it out."

I took a breath and Dr. Laub said, "Okay—now exhale." And as I let it out, Dr. Laub quickly pulled.

And I screamed. I had my hand between my legs and I couldn't stop writhing. I couldn't stop the wave of pain.

"I'm sorry," said Dr. Laub. "It will go away soon." He explained that because it was a temporary hole, the skin had already started closing around the catheter.

The doctor sat with me for a few moments until I said, "Okay. I'm okay. I'll be okay." Then got up and said, "Just relax here until you feel better. And when you're ready to try and pee, come and get me."

As I continued to lie there, feeling the burning subside, I mumbled to myself, "I'm so tired of being poked and prodded." I couldn't help but think that I was on my way to developing some sort of stress disorder. Any slight movement toward my genitals, and I would flinch in terror. I just wanted to crawl home and pass out.

But several minutes later, after the last wave of pain had dissolved, my old anxiety returned—the anxiety of wondering if I would be able to pee. As soon as I felt the anxiety, I found myself unable to stay still. I carefully pulled up my pants, climbed off the exam chair, and went in search of Dr. Laub.

We then went to the bathroom, where I had a very successful and much less painful outcome. It would be a little while before the temporary hole Dr. Laub had made would fully close, but I would soon be peeing like any genetic male and I was more than ready.

Dr. Laub said, "Don't push too hard or strain the next few days. Just let it come out at its own pace, okay? It will start slow and get better over time."

I agreed, and I pulled up my pants as the doctor backed away to give me more room. We headed out the bathroom together and when we reached the hallway, Dr. Laub slapped me on the shoulder and said, "All right, sir. I'll see you in a few weeks." And then he was gone.

WHEN I ARRIVED HOME, IT WAS PAST NINE O'CLOCK. THE first thing I did was pull the sheets off my sofa bed and fold it away, turning it back into a conventional couch. After that, I grabbed a beer from the fridge, lit a cigarette from the pack I had saved, and sat down to watch some television. After spending the past two weeks like a ninety-year-old incontinent man, I needed to feel young and normal again.

As I put my feet up on the coffee table, I found myself hesitating for a moment, automatically stopping to check on the positioning of my catheter bag. When I realized it wasn't there anymore, I let out a loud, celebratory "Yeah!" and emphatically dropped my legs straight out onto the table, crossing them at the ankles with my newfound freedom.

Twenty-eight

NOVEMBER 1999

I am sitting in a room filled with people playing various instruments. Although I don't know any of them, I start to sing to the music, making up lyrics as I go along. As I do so, several people start to join in, picking up on my words, and singing backup harmonies. . . .

I awoke to the sound of my alarm clock buzzer and reached out blindly to shut it off. I rubbed my sleepy eyes and slipped out of bed, climbed down the ladder, and padded barefoot across the living room carpet toward the bathroom.

My eyes were still half closed when I turned on the light, but the brightness made me squint until my eyes were small slits. As I turned toward the toilet, I muttered to myself, "I've got to put a weaker bulb in there." I lifted up the toilet seat and dropped my boxers to the floor.

As I started to urinate, my stream arcing into the toilet, I caught a sidelong glance of myself in the mirror above the sink. I saw a weary face filled with stubble. I reached up and comfortably scratched the underside of my jaw, feeling the sandpaper roughness against my fingers.

When I looked down, I saw my boxers bunched on the floor beneath my very male and hairy legs. And as I stood there, I felt a strong powerful solidity throughout my body. It was almost primal. Base.

When I came out of the bathroom, I brewed a pot of coffee, and after finishing my first cup, put on some slippers and walked out into the parking lot to check on my car tires. I had emerged from the grocery store the night before to find a flat tire and had used some temporary sealant to make it home but now the tire was completely flat.

I slowly shuffled back inside and changed into a pair of old jeans, a worn-out T-shirt, and construction boots. I went into the kitchen, refilled my coffee cup, and headed back out to the parking lot.

After setting my cup on the ground, I opened the trunk and pulled out the pouch with the tire iron and half spare tire. As I did so, I couldn't help but laugh. It looked so puny—like a kid's toy. The male counterpart to an Easy-Bake Oven. That, along with the mini-tire, made me think that the Toyota manufacturers were really out to save a dime on this one.

I slipped the tire iron around one of the nuts on the flat tire and pulled down with both of my hands. I pulled until the inside of my palms were covered with deep red gouges. But the nut didn't budge. I decided to switch strategies, and after making sure that the tire iron was still securely around the nut, I picked up my right boot and kicked down hard on the edge of the lever. Several times.

I heard a rusty squeak and then felt the nut start to give. I kept going until the nut was loose enough to unscrew with my hands. I followed the same technique with the other nuts until they were all loose enough to unscrew with my fingers. I then cranked up the car and began to remove nuts and bolts by hand, placing them on the ground next to my coffee.

I was sitting on the concrete pavement and working on the last bolt when I saw a neighbor come through the front door and into the parking lot. He was new to the building, having just bought the unit down the hall several months before.

As his six-foot-five frame approached, I nodded to him.

My neighbor looked at the tire, looked at me, and said, "Well, I hope you weren't in a rush this morning."

I shrugged my shoulders, "Nah, I knew about it last night, but just figured I'd wait until daylight to deal with it." The neighbor walked on to his car and I turned back to my tire.

For a moment, I found myself trying to imagine what would have

happened if it had been just two years earlier. It wasn't a difficult scenario.

The man probably would have offered to help me, seeing me as a
woman struggling with a flat tire. And as soon as he'd made the offer,
my shoulders would have tensed up. And I would have tasted rage. Felt
invisible.

As I reached to lift off the tire, I shook the scenario from my mind, returning my focus to the present. As soon as I had, all that remained was
the simple feeling of the sun seeping through my T-shirt and warming the
back of my shoulders.

I MADE IT INTO SAN FRANCISCO A LITTLE OVER AN HOUR
later, but instead of turning into the public parking lot next to the courthouse, I pulled into the tire shop across from it. I had been there several
months ago for a brake job.

When I got out of the car, the head mechanic came over and said, "Hey,
Dhillon. What's up?" I was surprised he remembered my name—and grateful that his was sewn on his shirt pocket.

"Hey, Mike. I just need to get a new tire." I pointed to the half spare
and added, "Something cheap."

Mike looked at the tire and said, "We've got a couple of specials. Let
me show you." He walked me toward the back of the shop and pulled out
a tire, going into its specs in great detail. Beyond the basics, I understood
very little. But the price was right—less than thirty dollars.

I then thought of something else. If I could leave my car at the shop
the entire day, I wouldn't have to pay for parking.

"Hey, Mike. Can I leave the car here and pick it up after work?"

"Yeah, sure."

"I was going to work till around eight. How late are you guys open?"

"We close the shop at eight." Mike then put his hand on my shoulder
and added, "but don't rush. I'll be here. I won't close the shop without you."

He quickly wrote up a work order, tore off a copy, and handed it over
to me. I tucked it in my suit pocket and gave him my keys.

As I came out of the dark garage and stepped into the sunlight, waiting to cross the street toward the courthouse, I once again felt the warmth. All around me.

IT WAS WELL PAST NINE O'CLOCK BY THE TIME I MADE IT home from work that evening. I unlocked my mailbox, pulled out the contents, and immediately recognized the thick gray newsletter. It was the current month's issue of the newsletter for female-to-male transsexuals.

My first impulse was to throw it back and lock the door of the mailbox. For as soon as I saw it, I felt a sense of anxiety. The same feeling I always felt when it arrived. The one I tried to dismiss because I had no explanation for it. Until tonight.

I left it sitting on my counter as I ate dinner. Finally, after exercising every delay tactic I knew, I picked it up with all of the enthusiasm of someone facing a dreaded homework assignment.

The issue was a special-theme edition. The theme: stories of people who had brushes with the law and were harassed or mistreated because of their gender. There were people who were partway through their transition who were placed in female prison cells as cops used their original female names, ignoring their current identity. On and on the stories went. And with each one, I felt my blood pressure rise. I got angrier and angrier. And I remember thinking, "Is this necessary?"

At the last FTM meeting there was a man sitting a few seats away from me who caught my attention. He was in his late fifties, had a gray beard, glasses, and a warm, square face etched with deep lines and creases. He caught my attention because he had an unusually contented air. During the introductions, he said he'd transitioned more than twenty years ago and was now living an hour north of San Francisco with his wife and kids.

As the meeting got going, a young guy started talking about how he had an FTM Web site and had been receiving hate mail. When someone suggested he stop reading the comments, he said, "Well, I feel I need to check it to watch my back. To know who's out there."

307

Several members nodded in agreement, and within moments the room was filled with angry responses and hostile accusations at the invisible enemies who lurked on the Web. As the tension mounted, I caught the expression on the new people's faces—the people who were just starting hormones or contemplating transition. They looked lost and afraid.

I then looked back at the older guy. He had a knowing smile on his face. When he saw me looking at him, he winked. When things had begun to quiet down, he spoke:

"You've all reminded me of an anecdote about Albert Einstein. During his time, there were many who thought he was odd and they gossiped behind his back, referring to him as unkempt and dirty and eccentric. One day, one of his colleagues came up to him and said, 'The things that people are saying—doesn't it ever bother you?'

"And Einstein responded, 'No—I don't live there.' "

That night, I sat down at my computer and typed out a letter to the FTM home office. It simply read, "Please remove me from all of your mailing lists."

As soon as I sealed the envelope, I got into my car and drove to the nearest public mailbox. I deposited the letter.

And then I headed home.

Twenty-nine

THE PRESENT

In my dream it is a year later, and I am just waking up on a peaceful, lazy morning. Golden sunlight is streaming into the room through window blinds as I slowly reach down and gently take my full-sized penis into my hand. As I'm holding it, a thought suddenly enters my mind: "It's time to go to the doctor. Time to get an EKG for my penis." The scene jumps, and now I am at the doctor's office, getting electrodes placed on my penis—to measure my heart rate.

Several months after my last surgery in 1999, things began to unravel. My testicular implants became infected and one was removed, and my urethra became blocked from scar tissue. In early 2000, I had emergency surgery to remove the other infected implant and to create a urinary diversion behind the scrotal tissue. After, I was left with nothing but a small stub of a penis through which I could no longer urinate and small, shrunken pockets—my former testicles. I was devastated.

As I lay curled up in a fetal position on my bed, pillows bunched up between my legs to try to avoid the emptiness that now remained, I wondered what God would be so cruel as to take away my hard-earned progress. Had I been too ungrateful? Had I wanted too much?

But as it turns out, it was quite the opposite. . . .

———————

I HAD TO WAIT SIX MONTHS TO MAKE SURE NO BACTERIA was left before I could do any new surgery. During that time, I began to do some research to see who might be best suited to fix my urethra, and I stumbled on several Canadian surgeons who were constructing full-sized penises, using blood vessels, nerves, and skin from the arm. Their results were fully functional—full sensation, normal urination, and erection—and looked aesthetically amazing. And, according to the Web site, "To date, no one has lost orgasm." I was captivated. And I began to think that maybe my complications were a sign—a sign that I was meant to go for more, not less.

I spent the next few months diligently researching all surgeons in the world who were constructing full-sized phalluses and even spoke to some of their patients. I found out that the last few years had been filled with huge advances in the technique and that the most successful surgeons were in Germany, Belgium, and Canada. There were some American doctors who also did the surgery, but they charged huge, exorbitant fees and had terrible track records involving serious complications and sometimes death of the phallic tissue.

The German surgeon, Dr. Paul J. Daverio, also practiced in Switzerland and had done the greatest number of phalloplasties: 140. He also had the lowest rate of urinary complications and no incident of tissue necrosis (death). Because of this, I was leaning toward going with him and even went so far as to set up a consultation with him in Geneva.

However, as my appointment was approaching, I received a brochure from Canada. Inside were postsurgery photographs of constructed phalluses. And once again, they looked amazing. So good, in fact, that you could pass them in a locker room and not think twice. But there was another piece of important information that began to shift my attention away from Europe and toward Canada.

Both the Belgian and the German surgeons kept portions of the former clitoris/micropenis tucked behind the base of the new phallus, while the Canadian surgeons stripped everything down to the base, leaving only the nerves. Because the constructed penis contained transplanted nerves from the forearm, the old nerves would have the opportunity to grow slowly into the new ones and make the penis completely sensitive from base to tip. Once the phallus reached full sensitivity, an implant for erection would be inserted—the same popular implant used by thousands of American men each year for erectile dysfunction. The implant consisted of a hidden capsule inside the penis which would fill with saline when an area near the base was pressed, causing a full erection on demand and subsequent return to a flaccid state.

The cost for the first major stage was around $24,000, while the subsequent implant would total close to $10,000. However, unlike the expense of my previous surgeries, the charges would include a one-week stay in the hospital, followed by two weeks in a beautiful, spalike resort with a full staff and daily meals.

As far as the nerve connection issue was concerned, I didn't understand the mixed strategy by the European surgeons. If they had success with some of the nerves, why not with all? And through corresponding with both the European and Canadian patients I saw a huge difference in response.

The European patients said that the sensation in their penises was a subtle feeling—like a feather tickling the skin—while the Canadian patients said that their phallus was fully erotic. I saw e-mail messages from patients who'd gone to Europe and admitted that they were not totally happy with the sensation and found orgasm difficult. But I saw no complaints from any Canadian patients. In fact, one of them sent the following e-mail in response to my detailed questions: "I can jerk off with my cock in my fist and have mind-blowing orgasms from blow jobs and intercourse."

It was all I needed to hear.

I booked my surgery in Canada for April 17, 2001. It was the earliest opening they had.

IT WAS AFTER MAKING MY DECISION THAT I HAD THE DREAM about having to get an EKG for my penis. I mentioned the dream to a close friend, saying, "Isn't that ridiculous—I mean, an EKG? For my penis?" I was laughing.

But my friend wasn't laughing. Her eyes were wide open as they looked into mine.

"It's not ridiculous. It's a symbol.. . . . You're getting your heart."

IN APRIL 2001, SHORTLY BEFORE MY THIRTY-SECOND BIRTHDAY— I flew to Canada and underwent a nine-hour operation and multiple blood transfusions. Afterward, I woke up to find nurses placing a handheld sono- gram device against my penis. One of them put the attached stethoscope into my ears and let me listen to the strong pulse of blood flowing within. It echoed the rhythm of my heart.

The next day, while my dressings were being changed, I lifted my head up and caught a glimpse of the results. The skin was pale and there were stitches at the base, but it already looked like a normal penis. When I reached down and gently wrapped my right hand around it, there was so much warmth radiating from the skin that I felt as if I were holding a hot water bottle. The blood flow was that strong.

I was in the hospital for a week. And every day, one of my surgeons— Dr. Pierre Brassard—came to visit. He was a good-looking guy with a French-Canadian accent and a penchant for well-tailored black suits with blue shirts. He also had an extremely gentle, respectful demeanor, always asking before he touched my bandages and gauging my mood before he engaged in casual conversation.

On the second day of my hospital stay, after they had given me another blood transfusion, I sat up when Dr. Brassard arrived. He commented that I looked much better, then said, "You've just made it through one of the hardest surgeries in the world. I have done many other types of complicated surgeries, but this is the most challenging surgery I've ever done."

When I asked him why, he said, "It's creating the blood supply to the new penis. I have to sew the vein in the penis to one in your body—usually one that I have rerouted from the thigh—and the first twenty-four hours are crucial. If the new connection doesn't take, I have four hours to make it back here before the phallus dies. That's why the nurses were checking the blood flow of your penis every hour."

When I asked him if he'd ever had a failure, he said, "Once—but I made it back in time and reconnected the phallus to another vein. Then it was okay."

Dr. Brassard added, "You know, you really are a bleeder. It's as if you have arteries coming from out of nowhere. After we were finished, the bleeding continued and we had to go back in to stop it." As soon as he said that, I thought back to my surgery with Dr. Laub and the new younger surgeon. Maybe all that blood loss wasn't his fault, after all.

Dr. Brassard continued: "The good part is that you have really thick, juicy veins. It was a pleasure to stitch them together. Some people have such thin, wispy veins that it feels as if one little breath"—he pursed his lips and pushed out a breath toward the imaginary vein he was holding between his fingers—"and they will turn to dust."

Dr. Brassard was the younger of the two surgeons, but from what I had heard, he was also the most talented one. He had been handpicked and brought into the practice just a few years before so they could start to do the penis constructions that required two surgeons.

When I mentioned to Dr. Brassard how I had heard that many of the male-to-female patients requested him for their surgeries, he humbly replied, "Ahh—it is just a phase. It will pass." And then he added, "If it weren't for Yvon [the older surgeon, Yvon Ménard], and his stubbornness, I would not be here today. Now when we go to medical conferences, other surgeons come up to us and shake our hands, amazed at what we can do, but in the seventies when he started this practice, no one supported him— they just ridiculed him. He was an outcast. All alone. And when something didn't go well, they would all rush to say, 'See—you shouldn't be operating on these people.'"

Dr. Brassard stopped when he saw my eyes filling with tears and quickly said, "Oh, I'm sorry. I don't want to get you upset."

I replied, "No, you didn't."

I wasn't crying because I was upset but because I was grateful—grateful that someone who didn't personally share my pain would nevertheless fight so hard—and risk so much—to take it away.

ON THE OTHER SIDE OF THE HOSPITAL, THREE PATIENTS WERE undergoing their final surgery to become complete women. I met them on the day we left the hospital and got to know them during the next two weeks spent at a beautiful aftercare home called the Residence. It was leased by the surgeons and located on a small island outside Montreal.

Since this was their final surgery, the three had all been on hormones for years. But what struck me as most extraordinary was just how ordinary they actually were. And I came to understand why they hated the term "drag queen" or "transvestite." For those who fit under such terms were typically an exaggeration or caricature. But these were women. Ordinary women.

And despite the fact that they were middle-aged, there was a youthful glow in their faces—faces that said they were just coming into their own. As I got to know the three women more, I found myself assigning them each a nickname: "PTA Mom" for the tall blonde who always tried to mother everyone and was organized and responsible; "Jackie-O" for the gorgeous, shy southern girl who always had a smile on her face; and "Rasta Mama" for the earth-goddess revolutionary who tended to her own organic garden, and loved to tell stories of the wild sixties and seventies, including one about a very well-hung Rastafarian.

Something about the timing of our encounter, the space we were in, the fact that we were all just beginning our life as complete men and women, allowed us to connect in an immediate way. There was no polite getting-to-know-you banter; we were too raw for that.

And so we just started in the middle.

One day, over breakfast, I remember one of the women saying, "Because of where we've come from, and all of the things we've experienced, our repertoire for humor is unending."

I said, "Hey, we could have our own sitcom."

"Yeah, but what would we call it?"

"I know—*A New Breed of Friends.*"

ONE OF THE HAPPIEST DAYS FOR THE WOMEN WAS THE morning that Dr. Bassard arrived to remove their dressings. I remember waking up to the sound of commotion: chatter and giggles from the room next door. When I looked at my clock it was 5:00 A.M. I normally would have grumbled a little and gone right back to sleep.

But I didn't. I felt a little surge of excitement. As if there was this celebration happening.

When I heard footsteps outside my door, I called out, 'Hey, hey, in here.'"

My door opened and a nurse stuck in her head, "Are you okay?"

"Yes. Is Dr. Brassard here?"

"Yes—he's with the girls."

"And he's removing the bandages now?"

"Yes."

As I lay back, I remember feeling a flood of emotion: joy, excitement. And a strange sense of pride.

Later that morning, while sitting at the breakfast table, I watched the women arrive. One by one. I watched the way they pulled out their chairs. The way they sat down.

Their faces were radiant. And that radiance infused their movements. As they reached across the table for what they needed, I saw it: a grace. The same as when you turn around and suddenly discover that your teenage girl has lost her clumsy awkwardness and turned into a full-grown woman. Right before your very eyes.

On the night before the women's departure, I was surprised to find my eyes constantly filling with tears. I lay awake in bed for hours; then, around 2:00 A.M., I lunged out of bed, grabbed a notepad, and wrote this letter for them to take home:

My dear Jackie-O, PTA Mom, and Rasta Mama,

For much of my life, I thought that the ultimate proof of my love of women was to embrace my female form, write love poetry to my breasts, and put my body into a beautiful, feminine-appearing package.

But during this trip, I remembered the real, true place for that love:

The excitement that propelled me out of bed at 5:00 a.m. on the morning it was time to have your bandages removed and to start your dilations was similar to an expectant father putting his ear to his wife's belly and hearing that first heartbeat. And the pride that I later felt when I saw you arrive at the breakfast table was similar to that of a father watching his teenage daughter develop into a woman.

I guess what I am trying to say is that you've all made me see that my truest and deepest connection to women and womanhood was not the time I spent inside that body, but the time I watched you all do it with an inner grace and radiant beauty that is in everything that you are. . . .

Love, d.

It has been several years since that trip to Canada, and yet I still look upon it as a most profound experience. Since my return, I have barely made it through a single day without being moved to tears. And each time I am in this state, I go through the same cycle of emotion:

I remember how long and hard and difficult this battle has been. And yet—somehow—I never once gave up or turned away. I kept my promise to that little boy—a promise that I now know was nothing less than an ancient, sacred pact. And I am awed and humbled by the overwhelming amount of love it must have taken to fulfill it.

AS FOR MY RELATIONSHIP WITH MY MOTHER, THERE AREN'T any neat conclusions. While I was able to let go of the expectation that she become someone I would like her to be, I remain unsure how to proceed with a relationship that is inherently limited.

I became acutely aware of this dilemma during a recent telephone conversation. Throughout the conversation, my mother repeatedly used the word "soul" and "God" and "spiritual." As she did so, I found myself becoming irritated. By the time we said good-bye, I was angry, and I did not understand my reaction. But I was curious about it—so much so that I spent the next three days in virtual hibernation as I waited for the answer.

On the fourth day, I awakened to find a particular biblical passage running through my mind: *"Thou shalt not use the Lord's name in vain."* And as I let the words sink in, I got the sense that the true meaning behind this passage was not that we should refrain from the use of religious profanity, but rather that we should not use a spiritual word without having personally experienced the meaning behind that word. In other words, to say "God" out loud, without having truly felt His presence—or to use the word "soul" without knowing your own—is to engage in a form of blasphemy. And some part of me recognized that this was what was happening during that conversation with my mother.

VIRGINIA HAS REMAINED A PART OF MY LIFE, ALTHOUGH WE never did become lovers. I pursued my surgeries and complications while she went through her breakup and began a new relationship—a relationship with a woman so sweet and kind and loving that I couldn't be jealous or bitter if I tried. A woman who, when I call, always goes out of her way to make sure that Virginia gets the message. When I once asked how she could be so gracious, she said, "I know you will always have a special place in her heart, and I would never want to deprive her of that."

After I got over my sense of awe, I let out a laugh and threw up my hands in mock defeat, saying, "Okay, that's it. You win. There's no way I could ever be *this* good."

But I know it wasn't just seeing who Virginia's lover was that influenced my reactions. It was also seeing who *I* have become—someone who has experienced severe pain and disappointment, and multiple surgical complications, only to end up with something even better than expected, something I didn't think was even possible.

And because of this, if something doesn't work out as I planned, I am much more likely to have faith that there is something greater, something even more right, just waiting around the corner. I may still kick and scream at first—old habits die hard—but there is a part of me that is slowly starting to recognize that what I experience today may very well be a form of preparation for that which will happen tomorrow.

In this vein, I have had quite a few dates and a couple of sweet and intimate affairs that have graced the hours between my legal work and songwriting—songs for a new album I began recording once my voice settled into its new register.

The album is called *The Temple* and is filled with material I have written throughout these past eight years—songs about my own struggle, songs about people who've touched me, and songs about that particular place in which I now reside.

And finally there are the songs written during those moments when I was sitting at my keyboard, imagining it was a grand piano in the living room of my future home, imagining my future wife sitting in a chair next to me, shoes off, sipping wine. And I am singing to her. Singing my heart out.

I'm still saving that seat for her.

ABOUT THE AUTHOR

Dhillon Khosla was born in Brussels, Belgium, to an East Indian father and a German mother. After spending his childhood in Europe, he completed his education in the United States, earning degrees in both psychology and law. For the past ten years, Dhillon has served as a staff attorney to state and federal judges and lectured on complex areas of criminal law.

Also an accomplished singer/songwriter, Dhillon recently completed an album of original songs called *The Temple*. His work has been described by critics as "alternative rock with a sophisticated edge" and selected by music supervisors for film and television. For more information on the book and his music, visit his website at www.dhillonkhosla.com.